Yale Historical Publications

Miscellany, 91

The Young Hegelians

by William J. Brazill

New Haven and London
Yale University Press
1970

Library of Congress catalog card number: 70–115366
International standard book number: 0–300–01275–6
Designed by Marvin Howard Simmons,
set in Baskerville type,
and printed in the United States of America by
The Colonial Press Inc., Clinton, Massachusetts.

Distributed in Great Britain, Europe, and Africa by
Yale University Press, Ltd., London; in Canada by
McGill-Queen's University Press, Montreal; in Mexico
by Centro Interamericano de Libros Academicos,
Mexico City; in Australasia by Australia and New
Zealand Book Co., Pty., Ltd., Artarmon, New South
Wales; in India by UBS Publishers' Distributors Pvt.,
Ltd., Delhi; in Japan by John Weatherhill, Inc., Tokyo.

to Elizabeth

Contents

Preface

In his *Civilization of the Renaissance in Italy,* Jacob Burckhardt confessed that "the same studies which have served for
this work might easily, in other hands, not only receive a
wholly different treatment . . . but lead also to essentially different conclusions." [1] Anyone writing intellectual history now-
adays is especially conscious of the wisdom in his confession.
By way of preface to the following pages I can only underscore
Burckhardt's words.

My work would not have been possible without the resources
of the libraries of Yale University, Harvard University, Am-
herst College, Williams College, the University of Minnesota,
and the Library of Congress. The President and Trustees of
Williams College made available grants from the Class of 1900
Fund to help meet the costs of research and also provided a
semester's leave of absence in which to complete the task of
writing. Miss Bessie Wright proved once more her excellence
as a typist.

1. Jacob Burckhardt, *The Civilization of the Renaissance in Italy,* tr.
S. G. C. Middlemore (New York, 1954), p. 3.

This study began as a doctoral dissertation at Yale University. I am happy to record my gratitude for the privilege of studying with Professors Leonard Krieger, Franklin L. Baumer, Lewis P. Curtis, and the late Professor Hajo Holborn. I do not mention these historians in an attempt to establish a line of apostolic succession, nor in an effort to evade my responsibility for the judgments expressed in this work. Anyone who studies Hegel's disciples must be mindful that no man can be responsible for the ways of his students. I mention them simply to express my thanks for their generosity and their example as teachers and scholars.

I am also delighted to thank Professors David J. Russo and Thomas E. Willey. Their friendship made the beginning stages of my work a happy occasion. Elizabeth's role is too important to be made public.

W. J. B.

East Lansing, Michigan
March, 1970

Introduction

This is the vocation of our own and of every age: to grasp the knowledge that already exists, to make it our own, and in so doing to develop it further and raise it to a higher level; in thus appropriating it to ourselves we make of it something different from what it was before.

—Hegel

"No philosophy," Hegel insisted, "transcends its age." [1] He meant, of course, that each philosophy elucidated in terms of its own time the stage to which the rational mind had developed, that no philosophy was absolutely true for all times. Yet he also maintained that no philosophy ever died, since all thought contributed to the development of the rational mind and thus became part of the living present. It was in the nature of his dialectical thought that every philosophy was time-bound in content and timeless in form. With this view he bequeathed to his disciples, by his unexpected death in 1831, the problem and the heritage of his ideas: what to do with Hegel's philosophy in a new age.

That it was a new age none of his disciples doubted. They had heard him claim recurringly that "a new epoch has arisen in the world," that "our age is a time of birth and of transition to a new period." [2] Hegel was, however, a philosopher, not a prophet: he urged that philosophy be used to comprehend the past and elucidate the present, but he knew it could not predict the future. While he apprehended a new age was at hand, he did not forecast its nature or the ways in which philosophy would comprehend it. For his students, though, the new age was a more immediate issue—they lived in it.

The year 1835 seemed to mark its beginning in Germany. Fittingly enough, it was the year of the publication of David Friedrich Strauss's *Life of Jesus,* a work signaling the dissolution of the Hegelian school. Twenty-five years later Strauss looked back on 1835 in a conversation with another Hegelian, Wilhelm Vatke, who had also made his reputation by publication in that year. "Do you know, Vatke," observed Strauss, "1835 was a good year for wine!" "It was also a good year for ideas," Vatke responded knowingly.[3]

1. Georg Wilhelm Friedrich Hegel, *Werke,* ed. P. Marheineke et al. (Berlin, 1832–45), vol. 15, *Vorlesungen über die Geschichte der Philosophie,* p. 618.

2. *Geschichte der Philosophie,* p. 622; *Werke,* vol. 2, *Phänomenologie des Geistes,* p. 10.

3. Cited in Heinrich Benecke, *Wilhelm Vatke in seinem Leben und seinen Schriften* (Bonn, 1883), p. 489.

But the significance of the year 1835 was not simply to be judged with hindsight; even to observers at the time there were clear indications that it was a year of moment. To those who believed in heavenly signs the appearance in that year of Halley's Comet might have seemed portentous, an astronomical augury of human change. Yet this, after all, was the nineteenth century, a time of science and learning, a time when such superstitions were mere vestiges of the benighted past. Who would make of the comet more than the natural phenomenon it was?

Much more moving to the general imagination in 1835—an even more dramatic forecast of the changes that would soon overtake Germany—was the introduction of its first railroad. Progress could now be seen in physical motion and measured in mechanical horsepower. The railroad became a robust symbol of change, a striking indication that the time of stagnation was over.[4] The older romantic poets were pessimistic: they saw in the advancement of industrialization the end of the poetic, rural, and spiritual life they cherished. The younger generation, however, was jubilant over the rush of change. One young poet, Emanuel Geibel, seemed to speak the voice of his generation as he celebrated the mood of change that came with the railroad:

> My breast swells proudly with racing throbs
> When I see the youthful age, its countenance
> Covered with perspiration as it struggles violently,
> As it accomplishes the colossal, a new Hercules
> With the hands of a child, its loins girded for work . . . .
> Good luck, good luck, you youthful age of metal! [5]

With the sense of change was associated the self-consciousness of youth, the confidence that change was overtaking the world

4. For a study of the cultural impact of the railroad in Germany, see Manfred Riedel, "Vom Biedermeier zum Maschinenzeitalter: zur Kulturgeschichte der ersten Eisenbahnen in Deutschland," *Archiv für Kulturgeschichte* 43 (1961): 100–23.

5. Emanuel Geibel, "Die junge Zeit," in *Heroldsrufe: aeltere und neuere Zeitgedichte* (Stuttgart, 1871), pp. 40, 42.

and that the old ideas and the old ways of previous generations were no longer adequate. Restoration Europe and the Holy Alliance became for the young generation the symbol of all the old ideas that no longer applied to such dramatically changing times; the new generation raised the cry of youth against the old. In Germany two groups, composed of members of the younger generation insisting upon change, adopted the self-conscious image of youth to distinguish themselves and dramatize their cause: Young Germany and the Young Hegelians. In the larger context of Europe, however, these were only two in a cluster that included Young Italy, Young Hungary, Young Ireland, Young Poland, and others—each rising to challenge the assumptions of the past, each believing a new epoch was dawning.

The year 1835 was decisive for Young Germany as well as for the Young Hegelians. It was the year in which Theodor Mundt published *Madonna,* a work that combined criticism of society and religion with a plea for humanism. Mundt's book reflected the influence of Saint-Simon particularly in its vision of the religion of humanity as the foundation for a new era in the history of mankind. In 1835 another member of Young Germany, Karl Gutzkow, published *Wally the Skeptic,* also reflecting the influence of Saint-Simon by way of George Sand. His novel dealt with religious skepticism and rejection of Christianity, but it was, at least in the eyes of its conservative critics, a glorification of the life of the flesh.

If 1835 was a year of achievement for Young Germany, it was also a year of disappointment. For in that year the Prussian government and the German Confederation condemned and banned the works of Young Germany. The public reason for the ban, as the Prussian government order declared, was that the Young German authors were "against the revealed religion" and their works were "bold assaults on Christianity." [6] The efforts of Metternich and Frederick William III were

6. Cited in H. H. Houben, *Jungdeutscher Stürm und Drang* (Leipzig, 1911), p. 41.

combined in this decision: they would defend the Vienna Settlement and the establishment of Christianity as the best as-
surances for preserving the kind of society they wanted. For
they concluded that an attack upon religion was as dangerous
to their regime as an attack upon the political order. If authority were questioned and denied in one area, the inevitable
next steps would lead to the rejection of authority in all areas.
The critique of religion, in their view, was only the first step
toward an assault on the Vienna Settlement and the assumptions of Restoration Europe. Moreover, an attack on religion
implied an attack on the state. The Christian religion was an
established religion, and in Prussia it was part of the state. To
attack the established state religion was to attack the state; to
criticize Christianity was to criticize the foundation and the
function of the state. One could not strike at the altar without
also striking at the throne.

Yet there were indications in 1835 that religious changes
were stirring not only within dissident groups but within the
ranks of theology itself. In that year, F. C. Baur, leader of the
Tübingen School, showed the results of his recent conversion
to Hegel's philosophy by applying to scripture Hegel's description of historical development. His *The Christian Gnosis*
was a new departure because it embodied objective criticism
based on a broad perspective of early Christian history. With
this work, Baur officially inaugurated the biblical scholarship
of the Tübingen School.

Another important theological study to appear in 1835 was
Wilhelm Vatke's *The Religion of the Old Testament*. Vatke's
book, based also on the Hegelian philosophy, was a study of
myth in the Old Testament and an attempt to view the development of Judaism in terms of philosophy rather than history.

A more famous theological work published in 1835 was
David Friedrich Strauss's *Life of Jesus,* a study of myth in the
New Testament and a critique of the historical origins of
Christianity. This work was the beginning of the public min-
istry of the Young Hegelians, that group of Hegel's disciples

who were especially conscious of their youth and aware of the profound sense of change that was overtaking their times. As one of the Young Hegelians wrote of Strauss's book, it "is not for the old men of our century, but rather for those who, themselves young, dare to recognize and publicly greet in this phenomenon youthfulness and robust freedom." [7]

Yet Strauss's work, unlike those of Young Germany, was intended for scholarly, not inflammatory, purposes. Therefore, the Prussian government accepted the judgment of the eminent theologian, J. A. W. Neander, the man who successfully urged the banning of the works of Young Germany, and did not censor Strauss's book. Perhaps the Prussian government was comforted by another event that occurred in 1835—the installation of Hegel's successor at Berlin. Though Hegel died in 1831, difficulty in selecting his proper successor led to protracted conflict within the government and within the academic world. When Georg Andreas Gabler was finally chosen and installed in 1835, the government believed he would dominate the Hegelian school and prevent it from moving in radical directions. In that expectation the government was proved wrong. Gabler had neither the intellectual strength nor the personal prestige even to stay the dissolution of the Hegelian school that was publicly inaugurated by Strauss's *Life of Jesus.*

The importance of the Young Hegelians in both representing and furthering the sense of change in Germany pointed to religion as the key to understanding that change. Indeed, one of the Young Hegelians, Bruno Bauer, frequently referred to his time as "the Reformation of the nineteenth century," by which he meant to convey not only the drama of a profound historical convulsion, but also the widespread defection of intellectuals from Christianity and the growth of humanism as the new faith.[8] The criticism of Christianity, as Bauer and Metternich both realized, had far-reaching implications.

7. Friedrich Theodor Vischer, *Kritische Gänge* (Tübingen, 1844), 1:3.
8. Cf. Alexander Dru, "The Reformation of the Nineteenth Century: Christianity in Germany, 1800–1848," *Dublin Review* 116 (1952):34–36.

One important German publisher, alarmed by those implications, wrote in the early 1840s that "there is great danger in this opposition to all things—even to Christianity and the state —that has increasingly taken possession of the spirit of our educated youth."[9] Criticism could not be confined to religion because religion was not an isolated compartment of thought and activity; it pervaded the whole structure of society and politics, the culture and thought, the institutions and morality of the time. The alliances that developed between liberalism and humanism, between conservatism and Christianity were, for that reason perhaps, natural and inevitable. Yet it would be wrong to conclude that the Young Hegelians' concern for religion masked some other motive, that they were actually social and political reformers who spoke in religious language through deviousness or convenience or ignorance of the real issues. Such reductionism would confuse implications with intentions. That the Young Hegelians expected all the forms of life and thought to change was certainly true, but they unvaryingly saw religion as the key to such change.

Hegel asserted that a philosophy must reflect all the features of the historical context in which it appeared. Germany in the years from 1835 on was marked by restlessness and change, a religious reformation, a growing uneasiness about institutions, a feeling that senescence was yielding to youth. The philosophy of the Young Hegelians epitomized all this. They saw their historical function not only in comprehending their time but also in guiding their generation in its mission.

Germany saw a dramatic representation of the change in generations: Hegel died in 1831, Goethe in 1832, and Schleiermacher in 1834. A great cultural hiatus was left, to be filled by the new generation. "Les dieux s'en vont," wrote Heine. "It is as if . . . Death had suddenly turned aristocratic, and sought to distinguish the notables of this earth by sweeping

9. Friedrich Perthes, *Leben*, ed. C. T. Perthes (Hamburg and Gotha, 1848–55), 3:520.

them into the grave at once." [10] A profound sense of change accompanied these deaths, a symbolic indication that the old generation had passed and the new generation was to assume its place on the stage.

If there was a sense that one generation was giving place to another, there was also a sense that there were no new discoveries left for the new generation to make, that the new generation's task was merely to understand and comment upon the answers and wisdom developed by the older generation. In a conversation a few years before his death, Goethe reported that he believed all questions were answered, all complexities unraveled, all knowledge complete. His generation had these accomplishments to its credit. The younger generation, he regretted, now had nothing to do but accept the truth that its parent generation presented to it. "I thank heaven," Goethe said, "that in this time in which all things have been accomplished, I am not now young." [11] The only task for the young generation was the unexciting one of providing exegesis for the systems already created.

The younger generation seemed to be condemned to the same role by the eulogist at Hegel's funeral who predicted that the Alexandrian kingdom would have to be shared among the satraps.[12] Clearly Hegel's philosophy was the final answer, and the younger generation—the disciples, the epigones—had only to be students of his philosophy in order to serve the demands of truth and knowledge.

The prediction seemed true enough. German intellectual life in the period from 1835 to 1848 was a time of discipleship when men accepted the weltanschauung of a human master and developed their own ideas and contributions within what

10. *The Poetry and Prose of Heinrich Heine,* ed. Frederic Ewen (New York, 1948), p. 720.

11. Goethe to Eckermann, 15 February 1824, *Gespräche mit Goethe in den letzten Jahren seines Lebens,* ed. Fritz Bergemann (Wiesbaden, 1955), p. 77.

12. See Johann Eduard Erdmann, *A History of Philosophy,* tr. W. S. Hough (London, 1892), 3:5.

they took to be its contours. It was in terms of the weltan-schauung a man accepted that he was defined. Some intellectuals felt resigned to their role as epigones, others were delighted by the opportunities. In his novel, *The Epigones*—published, appropriately enough, in 1835—Karl Immermann depicted the dolorous plight of a generation condemned to a discipleship against a background of cataclysmic historical change:

> We cannot deny that a dangerous epoch of world history has broken about our heads. Men have always had misfortune; but the curse of the present generation is to feel generally wretched without any particular grief. A desolate tottering and vacillation, an aimlessness and ridiculous pretension of seriousness, a sense of striving—to what goal, we do not know—a fear of terrors so ghastly that they have no form! It is as if mankind, buffeted about in its little ship by an overpowering sea, suffers from a moral seasickness whose end is scarcely in sight . . . . We are, to express our affliction in one word, epigones; and we bear the burden which is the heritage of those born too late.[13]

Immermann's cultural pessimism stemmed from his acute sense of loss and his apprehension about the future. His voice was, however, one in a small minority. To most German intellectuals, especially the younger ones, the prospects offered by discipleship were far more exhilarating. One Young Hegelian joyously recalled the spirit of liberation and mission involved in discipleship: "We were propelled by a fervent and proud trust that the Hegelian philosophy, which we brought to increasing dominance among the educated youth, gave us possession of the real truth."[14] Looking to the future the younger generation saw the opportunities of the new age, opportunities made even more fruitful by the wisdom inherited from the previous age.

13. Karl Immermann, *Werke*, ed. Robert Boxberger (Berlin, n. d.), vol. 5, *Die Epigonen*, p. 123.
14. Friedrich Theodor Vischer, "Mein Lebensgang," in *Altes und Neues* (Stuttgart, 1882), 3:289.

Thus the younger generation had to fulfill two roles. It was to receive from the previous generation ideas, values, systems, and answers as the assumptions and framework for its own historical performance. But it was to apply the legacy of the previous generation to the new circumstances, situations, and problems that emerged, in order to liberate its own creative genius. The younger generation was, then, conscious of its youth, of being a new generation, and, paradoxically, also conscious of using the developments of the previous generation to understand and guide the changes that characterized its own time. It was using the ideas of the older generation to liberate itself from the control of the older generation. The epigones would live in Alexander's kingdom, but they wanted also to wear Alexander's robes.

"We live," wrote a leading German intellectual in 1838, "in a time of great party divisions." [15] Young Germany, the Young Hegelians, the Hegelians of the right, the pietists, the party of the *Evangelische Kirchenzeitung*, the historical school of law, the south German liberals were only some of the party divisions to which he was referring. Men identified themselves and others by association with a party, by sharing the dogmatic positions of a party.

The historian Friedrich Meinecke, in writing of the same period, described it as a time of great individualism, a time when men, as individuals, sought personal answers and insights.[16] Both views are correct. For, though it was indeed a time of parties, these parties were at best only loose organizations of strong personalities who shared some of the same assumptions. There was a Young Germany, but Heine, Börne, Gutzkow, Laube, and the others were far too important as individuals not to be thought of apart from their association

15. Gotthart Oswald Marbach, *Der Zeitgeist und die moderne Literatur* (Leipzig, 1838), p. 12.
16. Friedrich Meinecke, "Drei Generationen deutscher Gelehrtenpolitik," *Historische Zeitschrift* 125 (1922): 253.

with a literary party. The same was true of Hegel's disciples, whether they belonged to the Hegelians of the right or the Young Hegelians. One of the leading intellectuals of the mid-nineteenth century, Karl Rosenkranz, wrote of Hegel's disciples that "no school, not even the Socratic, has produced such an abundance of original individuals." [17] That he was himself a member of the school, while it may have prompted his judgment, does not confute his conclusion. Indeed, his recognition that the term "Hegelian," although descriptive of the school, did not account for the individual contributions and creativity within the school was an appreciation of an important problem in intellectual history. That problem is to distinguish between the individual and the general, to recognize that a generic term like "Hegelian" is not fully explanatory, to perceive the individual variations within a legitimate collective party label. This study of the Young Hegelians is an attempt to address such a problem. It is the study of several individuals whose lives, for an historical moment, intersected, whose presuppositions, goals, interests, and destinies momentarily coincided. Their development to that point was independent, their subsequent histories divergent; but for that moment they formed a party. Like all the parties at the time, the Young Hegelians never formed a rigid phalanx of thought. Unity never meant unanimity; the party never transcended the individuals who composed it.

Some years ago Professor Jacques Barzun persuaded us that what gives an historical period its unity is not that all the individuals within it think alike but that their thought is directed to the same problem; it is the question that men feel needs answering, not the individual answers they give to it, that unites an age.[18] The same argument needs to be applied to the Young Hegelian school in order to distinguish its unity

17. Karl Rosenkranz, *Hegel als deutscher Nationalphilosoph* (Leipzig, 1870), p. xi.
18. Jacques Barzun, *Romanticism and the Modern Ego* (Boston, 1943), pp. 21–22.

and its internal diversity. For the Young Hegelians all agreed on the question that needed answering and disagreed in their individual answers. In that lay their unity as a school and their personal creativity as individuals.

There are two concerns for the study of the Young Hegelians as a school. The first is the intellectual history—the assumptions, the common agreements and philosophical interests, and the nature of their dependence on Hegel—that determined the unity of the school, the problem of the age that all the members recognized and sought to answer. The second is the external history of the school: its nature as an organization, the attempts to weld the group into a cohesive party, the personal friendships and conflicts involved, the joint publishing efforts in which they were engaged. These two concerns form the initial focus, the first two chapters, of this study. To emphasize the individuality of the members of the Young Hegelian party, each individual is discussed separately: his origins and life, his personal experiences, his divergence from the others, his life prior to and following his association with the Young Hegelian party.

The major figures of the Young Hegelian school were David Friedrich Strauss, Bruno Bauer, Ludwig Feuerbach, Max Stirner, Friedrich Theodor Vischer, and Arnold Ruge. Just to list them is to make apparent their historical significance as individuals even apart from their generic scholastic label. These men were the epigones, the men who felt an immediate responsibility to transmit the consequences of the Hegelian philosophy to their society and their generation. They fulfilled that memorable mission of their generation by being conscious of their youth and the rapidly changing times in which they lived, and by being conscious as well that their function was to apply the Hegelian philosophy, a product of the previous generation, to the new times. They used the Hegelian philosophy to free themselves from the rule of the previous generation, aptly aware of the responsibilities and the opportunities offered by discipleship.

Some would prefer to call this the first generation of Young Hegelians, suggesting that it served for the second generation —notably, Karl Marx, Friedrich Engels, Michael Bakunin, and Moses Hess—the same function as Hegel served for it. Perhaps such a distinction is useful. It can also be misleading, both in suggesting too persistent an historical continuity and in making the term "Young Hegelian" too broadly definitive. That a younger generation of intellectuals became adherents of the Young Hegelian views was clearly true; that Marx, Engels, Hess, and Bakunin were part of it was equally true. It also included Robert Prutz, Georg Herwegh, Rudolf Gottschall, Ludwig Buhl, Robert Mohl, Reinhold Köstlin, Rudolf Haym, Richard Wagner, and a host of others who learned their Hegel by way of the Young Hegelians. Yet it would be particularly hazardous to define this generation as "Young Hegelians" or to expect the term to maintain any meaning if used this way. Although all these men bore traces of the Young Hegelian influence throughout their lives and their work, that proves only that, historically at least, men add to their experience but cannot subtract from it. Many were influenced by the Young Hegelians, and some experienced a Young Hegelian phase in their intellectual development only to pass on to other concerns. To distinguish between the Young Hegelians and those they influenced, whether disciples, adherents, or hangers-on, is to recognize that the term "Young Hegelian," however tolerant of individual diversity, was quite specific.

An even more hazardous result of delineating generations has been the endeavor to judge the Young Hegelians in terms especially of Marx and Engels. In part the endeavor is the consequence of the writings of Marx and Engels on the Young Hegelians, the rather effective propaganda found in *The Holy Family, The German Ideology,* and *Ludwig Feuerbach and the Outcome of Classical German Philosophy.* In part it stems from the recognition of Marx's importance and the need to understand the origins of his thought. Whatever the reasons, the results have been clear: the study of the Young Hegelians has been dominated by the figure of Marx. Scholars have sought the answer to the problem of the origins of Marx's ideas or—what amounts to the same thing—have asked how Marx developed out of Hegel. While it is true that the Young Hegelians lie at the heart of the answers to these questions, it is also true that we get answers only to the questions we ask. There is no doubt that the essence and significance of the Young Hegelians have been obscured by questions formulated solely with reference to Marx.

Croce found it interesting that Hegel's better disciples in the late nineteenth century, "feeling themselves unable to go beyond Hegel," spent diligent effort in tracing the relationship of Hegel to Kant, "in making the necessity of the transition from Kant to Hegel the object of their continuous study." [19] Today it is equally interesting that Marx's better students—perhaps for similar reasons—spend their efforts in tracing the relationship of Marx to Hegel.[20] It is, of course, an important exercise, though frequently colored by that enduring genetic view which insists on making a system of ideas equivalent to its history or a philosophy explicable by its origins. Some of these students have the admirable aim of further elucidating Marx's ideas. Others have the more personal didactic purpose of striving to prove that Marx, long misunderstood, was actually a humanist.[21] Doubtless their studies have all contributed to a reinvigorated scholarly debate over Marxism; many have contributed to a better understanding of Marx. But in the process the Young Hegelians have remained in undeserved obscurity, seen only as an intellectual bridge, assigned

19. Benedetto Croce, *What Is Living and What Is Dead of the Philosophy of Hegel*, tr. Douglas Ainslie (London, 1915), pp. 208–09.

20. The more interesting of these efforts are Sidney Hook, *From Hegel to Marx* (New York, 1936); Herbert Marcuse, *Reason and Revolution: Hegel and the Rise of Social Theory* (New York, 1941); and Robert Tucker, *Philosophy and Myth in Karl Marx* (Cambridge, 1961).

21. The most obvious example is Erich Fromm. See his *Marx's Concept of Man* (New York, 1961) and *Beyond the Chains of Illusion* (New York, 1962).

the sole historical function of transmitting Hegel's ideas to Marx. Charity, if not scholarship, should react to such partiality.

Viewing the Young Hegelians as stepping-stones from Hegel to Marx has led to some serious misconceptions. In his important study of Marx's intellectual development, Professor Sidney Hook persists in viewing the Young Hegelians only in terms of Marx, continually slighting the importance of religion to the Young Hegelians. Indeed, he insists that they dealt with religion only because they had not "grasped the social and political implications of their respective positions," and that only Feuerbach and Marx later realized that their real aim was "radical social criticism." [22] His argument is misleading in two ways. The first is the implicit conviction that Marx was the necessary culmination of the Young Hegelians. The second is the reductive reasoning—worthy of Marx himself—that suggests that men do not mean what they say because what they say can be reduced to hard social reality, the real stuff of history. It is the suggestion that men, consciously or unconsciously, speak in code, and the task of the historian is to decipher their real meaning. It amounts to denying integrity to the Young Hegelians' concern over religion.

Sir Isaiah Berlin is equally misleading on the Young Hegelians in his study of Marx, again because he views them in light of Marx. He reduces their religious interest, however, to deviousness, suggesting they masked their revolutionary politics in religious language in order to pass censorship: "But since open political pamphleteering was forbidden, the opposition was driven into less direct means of attack: the first battles against orthodoxy were fought in the field of Christian theology . . . ." [23] His point is, of course, gratuitous, since religious censorship was as strict as political censorship—at times even stricter. What is more disturbing is again the as-

22. Hook, *From Hegel to Marx*, p. 79.
23. Isaiah Berlin, *Karl Marx, His Life and Environment* (Oxford, 1939), p. 65.

sumption that what the Young Hegelians said must be reduced to something else. This assumption occurs in all works whose authors view the Young Hegelians through the eyes of Marx.

It would be a dreary and unnecessary exercise to trace this reductive view of the Young Hegelians, broadcast through so many of the works that mention them. It originates, however, not only in judging the Young Hegelians in reference to Marx, but more particularly in relying on Friedrich Engels's inter- pretation of the school. In his *Ludwig Feuerbach and the Outcome of Classical German Philosophy*, Engels propounded the doctrine that the Young Hegelians were radical bourgeois reformers who used religious criticism merely as the language in which to express their real political and social interests and as a cover to avoid censorship. His judgment has become a part of accepted scholarly folklore despite the fact that he wrote for highly personal and highly polemical reasons. This particular work by Engels has also propagated other widely accepted misconceptions about the Young Hegelians. The first was his simplistic explanation that the split of Hegel's disciples into two schools, a right and a left, resulted from the master's ambiguity in his famous dictum, "Whatever is rational is real; whatever is real is rational." [24] Engels claimed that this dictum was open to two divergent interpretations. The first, made by the Hegelians of the right, saw it sanctifying all existing in- stitutions and ideas on the grounds that their existence proved their rationality and, hence, their necessity. This conservative interpretation was especially applauded by the Prussian gov- ernment. Another, a revolutionary interpretation, was made by the Young Hegelians. They held that rationality must be used as the test for all existence, and the irrational had to perish. They saw the dictum not encouraging a passive ac- quiescence to whatever existed but demanding a revolution to make reality rational. Engels's formula, like all such attractive explanations, is most misleading because of the hint of truth it contains. What is untrue, however, are the claims that such

24. Hegel, *Werke*, vol. 8, *Philosophie des Rechts*, p. 17.

an ambiguity was inherent in Hegel's thought, that his disciples split into neat categories of conservative and revolutionary, and that the issue of division was compounded in this phrase. Engels's special point of view in relation to Hegel itself constitutes a warning against unquestioning acceptance of his judgment.

A second misconception emerging from *Ludwig Feuerbach and the Outcome of Classical German Philosophy*—one that has also earned wide currency—was Engels's assertion that there was a distinction between the system and the method of Hegel's philosophy. The system was the dogmatic content, the acceptance of the finality and absolute truth of Hegel's positions in his own time. The method was the dialectic, the process of constant change in history whereby all positions were declared mutable in favor of the process itself. Engels argued that the Hegelians of the right stressed the system and were, thus, conservative in their acceptance of Hegel's positions and Prussia's institutions as absolute. The Young Hegelians accepted the dialectic and urged change against stability, adopting radical political and religious views. Again, Engels's explanation is misleading in suggesting that a paradox existed in Hegel's thought which had of necessity to lead to his disciples' accepting one or the other of its components. It is quite clear that the Hegelians of the right accepted and used the dialectic and that the Young Hegelians accepted and used the system. However useful Engels's interpretation is to understanding his own intellectual perspective, it is of less value in understanding Hegel's disciples. Indeed, Marx admitted that the impetus which directed Engels's and his critical excursions into the study of the Hegelian school was the need "to settle our accounts with our former philosophic conscience," and that the "main purpose" in depicting their ideas in relation to the school was "the clearing up of the question to ourselves." [25]

25. Karl Marx, "Preface," in *A Contribution to the Critique of Political Economy*, tr. N. I. Stone (Chicago, 1904), pp. 13–14.

Any document written in self-analysis or self-justification tells much about its author but considerably less about the materials he uses in his project.

The perils of an interpretation that dwells upon historical continuity are obvious: the implications of a necessary development, the intimation that a later phenomenon in the continuum explains an earlier one, the denial of discrete experience, the belief that a phenomenon can be understood only in the context of the continuity. To judge the Young Hegelians by way of Marx is not only to deny that these are perils, but also to accept them as truths. Historical judgment more surely requires that the Young Hegelians be understood on their own terms, that they be considered in light of the particular concerns of their own time, that they be assessed by what they said; only then will their historical significance be appreciated. The requirement is no more unlikely than asking that Hegel be understood on his own, regardless of how the Young Hegelians interpreted his ideas or their own relation to them.

If misconceptions have arisen because historians have stressed the relationship of Marx to the Young Hegelians, it is important to be wary of developing comparable misconceptions in emphasizing the connections between the Young Hegelians and Hegel. To be sure, they called themselves Hegelians, they studied Hegel's philosophy carefully and adopted it as their weltanschauung, and, though some of them finally undertook a critique of particular aspects of Hegel's thought, they all admitted themselves his disciples. But there were two major differences in the fact of discipleship that set the Young Hegelians off from Hegel. The first was that they inherited Hegel's philosophy without having to experience the personal travail that went into its composition. Croce always insisted it was important to recognize Hegel as an historical figure as well as a philosopher, and he concluded it was significant for the Hegelians that after the master's death "little or nothing was then remembered of the prehistory of the system, the history of the travailed formation of Hegel's thought." [26] Hegel's philosophy was for him the consequence of a personal need; for the Young Hegelians it was the means of fulfilling their personal needs. The difference was between a philosophy developed and one adopted, between a personal reflection and an ideology. The reasons that propelled Hegel's philosophical quest were different from those that moved his disciples to accept his results. The Young Hegelians, therefore, while always concerned with his work were indifferent to his private motives.

Hegel, born in 1770, lived through the great age of German philosophy and literature and through the French Revolution. Since he admitted that no philosophy transcends its age, it is clear that his philosophy, at least in its historic appearance, must be considered in relation to his context. The issues and questions in the years after 1835 were perforce different from those that dominated the great epoch through which Hegel lived. Indeed, Hegel had an intimation of the change. In a preface dated one week before his death, he wrote of "the unavoidable diversions resulting from the magnitude and changeability of the interests of the times," and he expressed his doubt whether in the midst of "the loud din and stunning garrulousness of the day, the imagination . . . can find room for participating in the passionless calm of the pure experience of thinking." [27] His intimation, though stated with impatience and perhaps a touch of weariness, had become the clearly recognizable reality by 1835. And it was in this new world, not the world of Hegel, that the Young Hegelians lived. The difference meant, of course, that the Young Hegelians were seeking to cope with what they felt to be a new age by using a philosophy that had been developed as a personal response

26. Benedetto Croce, "An Unknown Page from the Last Months of the Life of Hegel," in *Philosophy, Poetry, History,* tr. Cecil Sprigge (London, 1966), p. 190. Walter Kaufmann, *Hegel* (Garden City, New York, 1965) endeavors to develop the relationship between Hegel's life and thought.
27. Hegel, *Werke,* vol. 3, *Wissenschaft der Logik,* p. 23.

to the problems of the previous age. Hegel was more closely related to his contemporaries, to those who lived during the same epoch and struggled with the same problems—men like Hölderlin and Schelling, Goethe and Beethoven—than he was to those who later chose to call themselves his disciples. Both the element of personal passion and the difference of historical contexts were only reminders of the fact that the life experiences of the Young Hegelians were substantially different from Hegel's. Any historical interpretation that dwells upon the continuity between the two experiences will surely obscure the discrete existence of each.

If the Young Hegelians are to be considered apart from a continuum of thought from Hegel to Marx, if their unique historical experience made of them something more significant than mere shadows of Hegel or forerunners of Marx, then it is essential that historians recognize their intrinsic historical meaning. For Hegel's sober-minded though perceptive disciple, Karl Rosenkranz, did not doubt the monumental importance of the division of the Hegelian school from which the Young Hegelians issued. Indeed, he described the division as "the theological and political crisis of the Hegelian philosophy that in force, extent, and meaning has no equal in history." [28] If he exaggerated, the fault lay in his perspective rather than in his verdict. Nonetheless, he did recognize the preeminent importance to nineteenth-century intellectual life of the movement of which he was a part. Others also came to discern its importance. The historian Heinrich von Treitschke, writing in the late 1880s, concluded that "the school of Hegel exercised in German life an influence comparable only to the sophists in Athens." [29] Rudolf Eucken, some ten years later, admitted that "our age still stands under the influence of the problems" created by the division of the Hegelian school.[30] And Kuno

28. Rosenkranz, *Hegel als deutscher Nationalphilosoph*, p. 312.

29. Heinrich von Treitschke, *History of Germany in the Nineteenth Century*, tr. Eden and Cedar Paul (New York, 1919), 4:568.

30. Rudolf Eucken, *Die Lebensanschauungen der grossen Denker* (Leipzig, 1897), p. 465.

Fischer described the Young Hegelian contribution in particular as precipitating a "world-shaking crisis." [31] Similar admissions are legion in the literature of the nineteenth century, and not just in Germany, as such figures as George Eliot, Quinet, Chernyshevsky, and Renan, among many others, testified. There was no doubt in the minds of most contemporaries that of all Hegel's students the Young Hegelians made the greatest impact, propounded the most significant ideas, and directed the movement of nineteenth-century thought.

What was it that European intellectuals saw in the Young Hegelians beyond the thought of Hegel himself? In part, of course, it was the influence that the Young Hegelians exerted. Few thoughtful Europeans were not moved by the work of Strauss and Feuerbach; and though the work of the other Young Hegelians was more geographically limited, its emotional and intellectual impact was no less. Their contemporaries further recognized their contributions to the plethora of intellectual designs that marked nineteenth-century cultural life: idealism, higher criticism, historicism, anarchism, materialism, secularism, and humanism. In this sense, the Young Hegelians were central to the intellectual life of the century.

Their contemporaries doubtless apprehended in the Young Hegelians something even beyond their centrality to the specific religious and philosophical disputes of the day, some ways in which their contributions to the disputes defined and elucidated the higher questions that stirred the age. Why else did Kuno Fischer, like so many others, see their work as "world-shaking"? To answer the question is to suggest an interpretation of both nineteenth-century intellectual life and the place of the Young Hegelians within it.

In 1933, Thomas Mann, speaking from the perspective of a new century, remarked on the tendency of his fellow intellectuals to look down on the achievements of the nineteenth century. "We shrug our shoulders," he said, "alike over its belief

31. Kuno Fischer, *Geschichte der neuern Philosophie* (Heidelberg, 1889–1901), 8:1160.

—which was a belief in ideas—and over its unbelief—that is to say, its melancholy relativism." [32] These phrases could, in fact, be used to convey the essence and significance of the Young Hegelians: their relativism and their belief in ideas, their apostasy and their faith. Mann was undoubtedly right in ascribing these qualities generally to the thought of the nineteenth century, and it is remarkable how the Young Hegelians epitomized that thought, proving once again, perhaps, Hegel's judgment that no philosophy transcends its age. However uneasy a historian might be in using such time-worn and imprecise terms as "spirit of the age" and "climate of opinion," he will surely admit that there were in the intellectual life of the nineteenth century certain thought patterns, moods, assumptions, and priorities that distinguished it from the thought of another age. The Young Hegelians enjoyed a double relationship to the intellectual life of their century; they both partook of and formed its character, they were both products and creators of its patterns of thought. The two roles never conflicted, for they were always one and the same. Their contemporaries responded to the double relationship, seeing in the work of the Young Hegelians not only guidance, instruction, and elucidation, but also the reflection of their own minds and presuppositions. Much of the vision that the Young Hegelians provided already existed as a pre-vision, latent in the minds of a generation of intellectuals.

Perhaps even more important, the Young Hegelians both identified and helped create what Nietzsche, at least, saw as the central problem of the age. If we may believe Professor Erich Heller, Nietzsche's special insight—one that raised him in his own mind far above the level of his contemporaries who, at best, experienced what Nietzsche knew but did not comprehend or admit it—was that God was dead. "He never said that there was no God," Professor Heller reminds us, "but that the Eternal had been vanquished by Time and that the

32. Thomas Mann, "Sufferings and Greatness of Richard Wagner," in *Essays*, tr. H. T. Lowe-Porter (New York, 1957), p. 198.

Immortal suffered death at the hands of mortals . . . ."[33] Many historians would now agree that Nietzsche did indeed recognize the central cultural fact of his century along with the consequences and significance it bore for the men of that century and their descendants.[34] Nineteenth-century thought was marked by careful and critical work in science and history, the earnest reflection on a faith lost, the unbending insistence on intellectual honesty, the quest for some substitute, some secular ideology or intellectual posture, to replace what was lost; and Nietzsche, alone in his private agony, recognized the course of this thought as both cause and result of the death of God. Amid this range of thought—again, as both products and creators of it—stood the Young Hegelians, with their historicism, their historical criticism, their humanism. They provided for most intellectuals of their time the means by which the Immortal became mortal and the Eternal became temporal.

The Young Hegelians experienced none of Nietzsche's anguish over the course of nineteenth-century thought. They saw only the liberation, only the triumph, only the advance: their apostasy was followed by a new faith. For in attempting to transmit the Hegelian philosophy to a new age and a new generation, in choosing to play the role of epigones when they clearly rose above the role, in coping with the process of change as it occurred, they proceeded with élan and assurance, touching the minds of their age and exposing, if not defining, the central questions of the century. And to those questions they offered definite answers. It was this broad range of impact that their contemporaries and successors recognized.

For Nietzsche it was "the death of God"; for Bauer it was "the Reformation of the nineteenth century." The process of thought, in either case, was the same; only the perspective of

33. Erich Heller, "The Importance of Nietzsche," in *The Artist's Journey into the Interior and Other Essays* (New York, 1965), p. 176.

34. See, for example, Franklin L. Baumer, *Religion and the Rise of Scepticism* (New York, 1960), pp. 128–86; and Basil Willey, *More Nineteenth Century Studies* (New York, 1956).

judgment was different. Each is, however, a reminder of the central role of the Young Hegelians in nineteenth-century intellectual life and the central concern in Young Hegelian thought. It was not petulance that led Ernest Renan, himself a religious skeptic, to write in an essay on the Young Hegelians that "Germany is not capable of being irreligious; religion, that is to say, aspiration after the ideal world, is the very foundation of its nature." [35] It was the careful appraisal of a man who knew German thought and the Young Hegelian philosophy intimately enough to judge them with disinterest.

35. Ernest Renan, *Studies of Religious History and Criticism,* tr. O. B. Frothingham (New York, 1864), p. 339.

1 Hegel and the Young Hegelian Metaphysic

A party shows itself to be victorious when it splits into two parties. . . . What appears to be an unfortunate dissension within a party is really a proof of its success.

—Hegel

"Each man wills and believes himself better than the world in which he is," suggested Hegel; "but he who is better only expresses his world better than others express it." [1] For an entire age Hegel was himself the philosopher who expressed the world better than others. Few figures in modern history have exercised an influence as pervasive and as puzzlingly complex as Hegel's, few have exercised so profound an ascendancy over the minds of generations of intellectuals. Even those who opposed his ideas felt compelled to attack them, their incapacity for indifference itself a sign of his influence. One German intellectual recalled that in his student days in the 1840s "to be a Hegelian was considered a *sine qua non*, not only among philosophers, but quite as much among theologians, men of science, lawyers, artists, in fact, in every branch of human knowledge . . . ." [2] And the philosopher who introduced the British to Hegelian philosophy dramatically insisted that "what Aristotle was to ancient Greece, Hegel is to modern Europe." [3]

For those who chose to consider themselves his disciples in Germany in the 1830s and 1840s, Hegel's influence was a direct and specific experience. They accepted the master's views totally and were content to develop their own ideas within the framework provided by his philosophy. Rosenkranz, for one, admitted in 1836 that the members of the Hegelian school were epigones: "What a difference there is between reflecting on a philosophy handed down to us and having original ideas. As for the first we have some competence; as for the second, however, we are now mere dilettantes." [4] Yet there developed within the Hegelian school a split that, in the form of the Young Hegelians at least, elevated the disciples far above the

1. Hegel's Aphorisms, in Karl Rosenkranz, *Hegel's Leben* (Berlin, 1844), p. 550.
2. F. Max Müller, *My Autobiography: A Fragment* (New York, 1901), p. 130.
3. J. H. Stirling, *The Secret of Hegel* (London, 1865), 1:145.
4. Karl Rosenkranz, *Aus einem Tagebuch* (Leipzig, 1854), p. 43.

level of epigones, whatever their intentions. This split divided the disciples into discordant factions and diffused Hegel's influence into all scholarly fields and into the most diverse positions. Hegel's philosophy came to be invoked in defense of conservative monarchism and socialism, bureaucratic authoritarianism and anarchism, pious Christianity and secular humanism. Seldom has the interpretation of one man's philosophy been so vital an issue, so controversial a matter.

German intellectual life at the time was given over to the spirit of ideology. Truth was evident not in empirical and pragmatic existence but in the ideology, the values and philosophy with which men viewed the world and themselves. The important quality of Hegel's disciples was that the conflict lay in interpreting Hegel, in defending positions in terms of his philosophy. His philosophy formed their assumptions, the total framework of their thought; that framework, brooding over what was otherwise a vast spectacle of philosophical differences, was used to give justification to many apparently divergent views. But the most important arguments among the disciples concerned not the intrinsic virtue of their views so much as the insistence that their views, and no others, were the proper interpretation of Hegel. The Young Hegelian, Bruno Bauer, wrote *The Trumpet of the Last Judgment on Hegel, the Atheist and Antichrist* in 1841 and *Hegel's Teachings Concerning Religion and Art* in 1842 to prove that Hegel was an atheist and to show thereby that his own atheism was valid not necessarily because of its intrinsic virtue but because it could be traced to Hegel. Even those disciples, like Feuerbach, who became critical of Hegel criticized him on the basis of his own philosophy and with tools that he had provided. Hegel's position was accepted. It was the meaning of that position, the application of his philosophy to areas on which he never pronounced, the relevance of his views to new situations, that became the source of disagreement. The conflicts within the Hegelian philosophy were a family affair: they dissolved the family, they shattered the pedigree, but the family name remained as a reminder of the past and of the heritage. In their loyalty to the Hegelian philosophy, the Young Hegelians became more than epigones.

That there were sharp differences in interpreting Hegel's meaning has been clear enough. Engels argued that Hegel's philosophy could be used to justify both reactionary and revolutionary political stances, the result of an ambiguity in Hegel's own thought.[5] The Scottish Hegelian, Edward Caird, however, insisted that Hegel's philosophy "is as hostile to reaction as to revolution . . . ."[6] Caird further claimed that Hegel's philosophy was not only Christian in its intent and construction, but was itself "identical with the essential idea of Christianity."[7] Yet Bruno Bauer insisted Hegel's thought was anti-Christian and atheist. Heinrich Heine complained that Hegel designed his philosophy to justify the existence and activity of the Prussian state in whose employment he thrived.[8] Karl Rosenkranz, however, asserted that Hegel was never servile to the Prussian government and that, in fact, his idea of the state was an open criticism of Prussia.[9] And so it has gone. Antithetical understandings of Hegel's basic ideas are legion; for every interpretation there is its opposite. Such a condition has led most recently to two contrary conclusions: on the one hand, the suggestion that Hegel's philosophy cannot be known as a thing in itself, and, on the other, the demand that a reinterpretation of Hegel's philosophy be undertaken in an effort to understand it untainted by the ways in which it has been understood in the past.

To an historian concerned with the Young Hegelians, the problem of Hegel's philosophy is less acute than for a philoso-

5. Friedrich Engels, *Ludwig Feuerbach and the Outcome of Classical German Philosophy*, ed. C. P. Dutt (New York, 1941), pp. 10–14.

6. Edward Caird, "Philosophy," in Alfred Russel Wallace et al., *The Progress of the Century* (London, 1902), p. 157.

7. Edward Caird, *Hegel* (Edinburgh and London, 1909), p. 203.

8. Heinrich Heine, "Die romantische Schule," in *Werke und Briefe* (Berlin, 1961–64), 5:94–95.

9. Karl Rosenkranz, *Hegel als deutscher Nationalphilosoph*, p. 51.

pher specifically concerned with that philosophy. For, in the case of the first, what Hegel meant is of little significance compared with how the Young Hegelians interpreted what he meant. Such a statement is intended to be neither a shocking admission that Hegel cannot be understood nor a disturbing contention that trying to understand his philosophy in its own terms is without value. These are, indeed, the very efforts that philosophers must make. But it would be a mistake to confuse these efforts with a study of the Young Hegelians, for the issue of historical importance here was how they understood Hegel, not whether their understanding was correct. Hegel's immediate disciples themselves were deeply divided over the proper meaning of his ideas, but it is fair to conclude that the historical impact of any of them was not determined by the actual precision of his interpretation of Hegel, even though his claim to precision was for him an important intellectual demonstration. That each of the Young Hegelians, as well as each of the Hegelians of the right, believed he understood Hegel properly was the important fact. What is ultimately significant in understanding the Young Hegelians is comprehending their interpretation of Hegel, for their interpretation, not its accuracy, determined their stature.

However divergent specific readings of Hegel have been, a general pattern is observable in the literature. J. H. Stirling claimed that the secret of Hegel was that he "made explicit the concrete Universal that was implicit in Kant." [10] Jacques Barzun has suggested that Hegel is to be understood as a man busy with the intellectual mission of his generation to reconstruct thought after the critical philosophies of the eighteenth century and the French Revolution made the old forms of life impossible.[11] More recently, Walter Kaufmann, insisting that we need a re-interpretation of Hegel, has sought to demonstrate that such a re-interpretation must be based on the recognition that Hegel's "thought was intimately related to

10. Stirling, *The Secret of Hegel*, 1:xi.
11. Jacques Barzun, *Romanticism and the Modern Ego*, p. 22.

what happened during his life time." [12] This range of three opinions extending over a period of one hundred years, though not selected entirely at random, suggests one important perception needed to begin an understanding of Hegel's philosophy. That is, simply, that his thought must be comprehended in terms of meeting the specific needs of his historical and philosophical ambience as well as in terms of meeting his personal needs. It was this point that led Croce, in 1906, to distinguish between what was living and what was dead in Hegel's philosophy.

In dealing with the Young Hegelians, the same point must be made. Their thought developed within Hegel's influence, but specifically in response to the demands of their historical experience and to their personal need. And their age and their need were self-consciously different from Hegel's. Precisely because of the difference of their needs from Hegel's, it would be a mistake to assume that a study of the Young Hegelians' ideas tells us what Hegel really meant, just as it would be a mistake to conclude that a study of Marx tells us what the Young Hegelians really meant, or a study of Hegel leads to the comprehension of Kant. There are good studies of Hegel's philosophy available, and there is no need to summarize them.[13] What is important here is what Hegel meant to the Young Hegelians, and a brief treatment of their understanding of his philosophy is essential. It is offered with the caveat that how they understood Hegel tells much about the Young Hegelians and less about Hegel, more about the influence of his thought than about the thought itself. This difference is, historically at least, the important issue.

It is doubtless a testimonial to Hegel's greatness that every age has been able to find for itself significance in his philosophy. Comprehensiveness, totality of view, a mind straining to

12. Walter Kaufmann, *Hegel* (Garden City, New York, 1965), p. 31.

13. The best studies of Hegel currently available are J. N. Findlay, *Hegel: a Re-examination* (London, 1958), and Walter Kaufmann, *Hegel*. Needless to say, they are not in complete agreement.

grasp all reality are surely the hallmarks of his thought and the reason why so many thinkers have found in it the particular meanings they sought. The Young Hegelians developed their metaphysic within the comprehensiveness of Hegel's philosophy, but their emphasis on parts of this philosophy led them to neglect its comprehensiveness and to evolve its parts into a metaphysic distinctively their own. By continuing his influence they converted it to their own need, concentrating on and developing three areas of his thought in particular: his philosophy of history, his political philosophy, and his religious philosophy. These formed the specific base of the Young Hegelian metaphysic.

The most distinctive feature of Hegel's philosophy for the Young Hegelians was the insistence that history had a purpose and direction, an intrinsic meaning. The meaning of history was not to be found in reference to transhistorical judgment, to some transcendent force; its meaning lay entirely within itself.

Hegel's view of history resulted from his postulating ultimate reality as the absolute spirit. Absolute spirit not only permeated the world, it also was the world that it permeated, the totality of all existence. It was time and the events that occurred within time; it was history and the knowledge of history. History, then, was part of the totality of the absolute spirit and historical progress was the continual revelation to the absolute spirit of its own nature. Historical events were the externalized nature of the absolute spirit.

Hegel saw all reality as a manifestation of the spirit that had in some way alienated itself and was returning to its own unity through progressive moments of self-realization. The forms in which the spirit expressed itself in its journey through history to self-realization were society, the state, art, music, religion, literature, and so on. These were the ideas and institutions that Hegel used to demonstrate the movement of the spirit.

The realm in which the spirit developed its self-realization was history: Hegel's method began with belief in a single pattern of historical development, a pattern that was immediately recognizable through the proper arrangement of the data and facts of history. The pattern that emerged from the organization of the facts of history was inherent in the facts, not an interpretation of those facts by the historian. The historian had to understand the pattern of historical development in order to differentiate between the important and the incidental, the vital and irrelevant, and to distinguish the mainstream of historical continuity from the many backwashes and branches.

Hegel's position was that history had a purpose and goal; it was teleological. After its patterned development through the world, the spirit attained to complete self-realization and thus reached absolute truth. The self-fulfillment of the spirit was completed when it united within itself all forms of reality, when it had rendered all negation neutral, when all temporary, moving forms of truth combined in absolute truth. The end of history was monism:

> The truth is the whole. But the whole is only the essence attaining its completeness through the process of its own development. It must be said of the absolute that it is essentially a result, that it becomes what it is in truth only at the end. . . .[14]

Absolute truth was the goal of history, the end towards which all movement was directed. The goal was reached when all partial truth, when all negation, was united in one whole. Each step in the progressive movement to the whole was based on the step before it and replaced that preceding step; but the replacement was not a dismissal of the antecedent step, rather it was a preservation of it plus a forward movement, a progression. When the spirit proceeded through all steps—and all the steps were united in one—then the goal of history was attained.

14. *Werke*, vol. 2, *Phänomenologie des Geistes*, p. 15.

Hegel saw the very content, the very essence, of history as reason. The spirit unfolded itself, he explained, in a rational manner; history, therefore, could be nothing else but a rational development. By the content of history, however, he did not mean a potpourri of historical data, an accidental collection of facts, names, and dates. Rather, the content was that which made a rational whole out of historical development, the order and laws to which the proper arrangement of the data pointed and from which they obtained meaning. Thus, Hegel insisted, the only hypothesis that lay behind philosophy was that reason reigned supreme in history:

> The only thought that philosophy brings with it [to the study of history] is the quite simple thought of reason, namely that reason rules the world and that things have happened according to reason in world history . . . . This idea of reason alone is the true, the eternal, the absolutely powerful, . . . it reveals itself in the world and nothing else is revealed in the world except this idea, its honor and its grandeur . . . .[15]

Since the development of the spirit was a rational process, history was rational.

Hegel's famed statement that "what is rational is real and what is real is rational" [16] was a necessary conclusion. Each step in historical development was more rational than its antecedent, so that what did exist was the product of reason. History was a rational, logical, and orderly development, with no place for chance or luck to form the historical process. Where chance and human passion seemed to precipitate historical change, it was merely that men did not understand that the spirit used chance and passion to further its own ends, that it made them instruments in its rational development. It was the "cunning of reason," Hegel said, that it could use human passions and apparent chance as part of its plan of necessary development, that it could use apparent irrationality in the rational process of history.

15. *Werke*, vol. 9, *Philosophie der Geschichte*, pp. 12–13.
16. *Werke*, vol. 8, *Grundlinien der Philosophie des Rechts*, p. 17.

The term Hegel used to describe the rational development of history, the pattern in which the spirit moved through its temporal medium, was "dialectic." Much confusion exists over what Hegel's dialectic was.[17] It is necessary to point out that for Hegel the dialectic was not the monotonous triad of "thesis-antithesis-synthesis." Hegel did not use this formula in his philosophy, and, in all his writings, mentioned it but once, only to disclaim it as a senseless and monotonous formalism.[18] The formula was a later addition by those seeking to explain Hegel, a phrase that distorts in its effort to explain.

For Hegel the dialectic described the process by which the spirit was driven forward by the movement of its own analytical thought to a higher comprehension of truth. Every moment of truth in the development of the spirit had to be criticized by the logic of philosophy, but the criticism was carried on by the spirit itself. The spirit would criticize each of its momentary, historical forms by absorbing the opposite or negation of that form and evolving a higher form that comprised both the original position and its negation. The spirit, then, in reflecting on the stage of its own development, criticized each stage by considering the negation of that stage—no form could be thought of without its opposite—and then answered its own criticism by creating a new stage that encompassed the former position and its negation. Reality for Hegel was totality, which meant it comprised negation, denial, and evil, as well as affirmation, profession, and good. Criticism lay at the very heart of reality, for criticism was the motive force, the inner necessity, that propelled the spirit through time toward total unity. Hegel's teaching of this essential role of criticism in historical progress was most significant to the Young Hegelians.

Hegel's dialectic was more than a theory of logic, it was a theory of reality. The dialectic did not merely describe the

17. See Gustav E. Mueller, "The Hegel Legend of 'Thesis-Antithesis-Synthesis,'" *Journal of the History of Ideas* 19 (1958): 411–14.
18. See *Werke*, vol. 15, *Vorlesungen über die Geschichte der Philosophie*, p. 551.

path of the spirit, it *was* the path of the spirit. Thus, his idea of monism was in complete agreement with the idea of opposition. Reality was life—it was development, process, change, movement—and without opposition as an intrinsic part of reality there was no movement. Besides, opposites were opposed to one another, not to unity. Unity, the end of history, was the absorption of all opposites, the end of all conflict.

Any position short of final unity was but momentary, an historical form of the spirit destined to be overcome and absorbed in a higher form of truth. The inexorable progress of the spirit meant that absolute truth could not exist in history: absolute truth meant the end of history. Historical forms of the spirit meant just that—they were true for the time and place in which they appeared but they were not true for all time. Truth was developing historically, and all the stages of its development would be finally absorbed in the attainment of absolute truth. History was the process by which spirit attained self-realization; truth, in any historical moment, was merely becoming.

Hegel's philosophy of history was the basis of Young Hegelian thought, and that basis might be summarized in a few sentences. History was the story of the development of the spirit to ultimate unity. That development was rational, since spirit proceeded according to the laws of reason. The development also meant the use of criticism, since spirit had to negate each of its forms and absorb all opposites. Each position that the spirit took in history was true only for an historical moment; it had to be overcome and absorbed in the inexorable progress to monism. Behind the entire process were assumptions important for the Young Hegelians: that history had an intrinsic meaning, that spirit was immanent in history, that history could be judged only in terms of its own development.

Reliance on Hegel's philosophy of history carried important implications, especially significant in the Young Hegelians' intellectual descent from Hegel and the dissolution of the Hegelian school. For Hegel, it must be affirmed, the dialectic was not entirely embodied in history and not all reality was historical. Hegel asserted a broad interest in the full content of spiritual life in all its representations and all its forms. For him logic, the dialectic, was embodied in this full range of spiritual life, in nature as well as history. His system aimed at articulating the logic that explained and, at the same time, interconnected all aspects of reality. To emphasize history alone would have been, for Hegel, too confining, a narrowing of the system that was to encompass all reality. His philosophy of nature was an integral part of his system; it was the affirmation of an objective existence, the externalization of the spirit, the spirit's self-alienation in objective representation. The spirit explained nature as well as history. Hegel insisted, however, that the realms of nature and history were different, that nature was not historical. The Young Hegelians were essentially, perhaps solely, concerned with the dialectic in history —despite the occasional speculations of Feuerbach and the older Strauss in the realm of natural science—and that concern represented a break with Hegel's all-encompassing interests, a break, in truth, with Hegel's system. Hegel once wrote that "God has two revelations, as nature and as spirit. Both of these forms are temples of God that he fills with his presence. God as an abstraction is not the true God . . . ." [19] Hegel sought God in nature and as spirit in history; the Young Hegelians, judging all reality to be historical, sought God as spirit in history. Hegel's all-inclusive system subtly gave way to the historicism of the Young Hegelians.

Hegel wrote that "if it is difficult to comprehend nature, it is infinitely harder to understand the state." [20] To grasp Hegel's idea of the state, it is necessary to see it as the result of his

19. *Werke*, vol. 7, part 1, *Vorlesungen über die Naturphilosophie als der Encyklopädie der philosophischen Wissenschaften im Grundrisse*, p. 22. For a discussion of Hegel's distinction between nature and history, see Findlay, *Hegel*, pp. 267–87.

20. *Werke*, vol. 8, *Philosophie des Rechts*, p. 346.

view of the immanence of the spirit in history. Since history was the story of the development of the spirit, since the state was one of the historical forms that the spirit adopted, the state was a spiritual reality—it partook of the spiritual or divine life because it was a form of the spirit. That is the meaning of Hegel's statement that "man must therefore venerate the state as an earthly deity." [21] The state, for Hegel, was the externalization of the spirit.

As the myth that Hegel used the rigid dialectical formulation of "thesis-antithesis-synthesis" must be dismissed, so must the myth that Hegel developed his political philosophy in response to the needs of Prussia, that he was an intellectual servant of the Prussian state. There is no ground for arguing that, after he went to Berlin in 1818, he patterned his views of the state to please Frederick William III.[22] On the contrary, he developed his political philosophy prior to his call to Prussia, and, once in Prussia, he delayed the publication of his *Philosophy of Right* out of fear that the Prussian censor might strike it down. Moreover, as Hegel's disciple and biographer, Karl Rosenkranz, pointed out, Hegel insisted upon constitutional government, freedom of the press, equality before the law, public trial by jury, popular participation in the legislature.[23] And Prussia denied each of these.

Hegel's view of the state did not arise in response to the needs of Prussia; it responded to his own inner need and to the demands of modern society. His aim was to combine liberty with authority, to develop a political theory that saved men from the extremes of anarchy and authoritarianism. The extremes would be reconciled in his view of the state.

Freedom was, for Hegel, part of the goal towards which

21. Ibid. For a good discussion of Hegel's political ideas, see Leonard Krieger, *The German Idea of Freedom* (Boston, 1957), pp. 125–38; and Herbert Marcuse, *Reason and Revolution: Hegel and the Rise of Social Theory* (New York, 1941), pp. 169–223.

22. See T. M. Knox, "Hegel and Prussianism," *Philosophy* 15 (1940): 51–63.

23. Rosenkranz, *Hegel als deutscher Nationalphilosoph*, p. 51.

history was developing: freedom, reason, and totality were inseparable. To be free was to overcome the dualism between spirit and nature, ideal and real, reason and passion, ego and the objective world; freedom meant the achievement of the ultimate unity in which these antinomies were bridged. History, then, was the story of the development of freedom, since in the process the spirit became increasingly aware of itself and ended with the achievement of total unity, all antinomies united. The spirit became, in history, increasingly free because it was continually overcoming all inherent contradiction and dualism, because it was developing in accord with reason. The end of history meant the attainment of complete freedom, the victory of reason and the victory of monism.

What did the development of the freedom of the spirit mean for the individual who had to carry on the everyday tasks of civilization? For Hegel individual or human freedom meant that man had to recognize the historical forms that the spirit adopted; politically it meant that man had to recognize the spiritual nature of the state and live in accord with its nature. The state was the externalization of the spirit, the institutionalization of divine force in history. The spirit was immanent in history, and the state was the physical representation of that immanence. The state, then—because it was a part of the rational process in which the spirit was to attain freedom and monism—was, for man, the locus of freedom and reason. If a man ordered his life to conform to the state, he was living in accord with freedom and reason, allying himself with the development of the spirit. If, however, a man did not accept the dominion of the state, he was opposing the development of the spirit and was, thus, unfree and irrational. Only a life lived in accordance with the spirit—whereby a man consciously identified himself with the historical forms of the spirit—was free.

Once a man was aware that he could live freely and rationally only by consciously dissolving himself in the development of the spirit, he became a part of that process that had freedom, reason, and unity as its end. In obeying the laws of historical development, man was truly free:

> Only that will which obeys the law is free, for it obeys itself and is thereby independent and free. When the state, the country, constitutes a community of existence, when the subjective will of man submits to laws, the contradiction between freedom and necessity disappears. The rational is necessary as the substance of things, and we are free when we recognize it as law and follow it as the substance of our own being . . . .[24]

Freedom was not arbitrarily subjective and capricious action; it was acceptance of the forms of the free and rational spirit, absorption into the process that developed higher forms of freedom. It was the responsibility of the state to be a conscious part of the development of the spirit; it was the responsibility of the individual to live in accord with the demands of the state. Only then were the unhappy extremes of subjective anarchy and authoritarianism avoided.

For Hegel the history of the world was the history of the contributions of particular national states to the spiritual process that ended in freedom. States, not individuals, were the proper centers of historical investigation: "in the history of the world, the individuals we have to do with are peoples, totalities that are states." [25] Each totality, each *Volk*, had its proper purpose and mission to perform for the spirit. The Jewish nation, for example, provided monotheism; it was the German mission to be the guardian of philosophy. At the same time, however, a *Volk* had to be conscious of its mission. It had to be rationally committed to its historical role or it was not a state. Unless the *Volk* lived in accord with reason and the purposeful development of the spirit, it did not, for the real purposes of history, exist as a state. Thus, he wrote in 1802 that "Germany is no longer a state," for "what cannot be understood, does not exist." [26] Unless the state accepted its

24. *Werke,* vol. 9, *Philosophie der Geschichte,* p. 49.

25. *Philosophie der Geschichte,* p. 18.

26. "The Constitution of Germany," in *The Philosophy of Hegel,* ed. Carl J. Friedrich (New York, 1954), p. 527.

responsibility to serve in the historical process, it did not really exist.

The individual had to accept his responsibility to live in true freedom by immersing himself in the higher needs of the *Volk*. Man was capable of experiencing freedom only in the light of reason; without reason there could be no freedom. Since the state was the product of reason, the more the individual made his will coincide with that of the state the closer to true freedom he approached. The state was the precondition for genuine freedom. An individual, Hegel concluded, found freedom only within the framework of the state: "Since it [the state] is the spirit objectified, it is only as a member of it that the individual has objectivity, truth, and morality." [27] At the same time, individual freedom was protected only by the legal and moral institutions that the state provided. The important point was that the spirit found its objective historical life in *human* institutions.

The state was the true worldly embodiment of morality, reason, and freedom. To try to make the state compatible with human, abstract principles, as the Jacobins had done, was to oppose with the capricious and subjective conceit of individuals the movement of absolute reason. The government of the state was not to be founded on the consent of the governed, for it was the state, established by the spirit, that itself made a totality out of the chaotic anarchy of individuals. The state, developed rationally and divinely, was "spirit in its substantive rationality, . . . and therefore the absolute power on earth." [28] The individual had his freedom, his morality, his life of reason only by being a member of a state, only by consciously associating himself with the purposes of the state in contributing to the development of the spirit.

The third area in the brief discussion of what was important in Hegel's thought for the Young Hegelians is Hegel's

27. *Werke,* vol. 8, *Philosophie des Rechts,* p. 306.
28. *Philosophie des Rechts,* p. 417.

view of religion. Hegel saw religion, art, and philosophy as ideal spheres in which spirit objectified its values. Religion was especially important for his philosophy, and its meaning permeated his thought and his intentions. Religion also was the means by which a particular *Volk* understood and expressed its mission in history. "Religion," Hegel wrote, "is the sphere in which a nation gives itself the definition of that which it regards as true . . . . The representation of God, therefore, constitutes the general basis of a people's character." [29] Historically, human understanding of religion demonstrated the level of spiritual development, the stage of revelation.

Human understanding of religion, of course, progressed; man's comprehension of the spirit advanced through history. Religion began when man first had the consciousness to break the separation between himself and the "other," when he ceased to think of himself as alien from the universe and from spirit, when he integrated himself into the whole. Religion and philosophy had the same content—the basic truths with which each dealt were the same—but religion differed from philosophy in that it needed to view these truths in some representational form. Religion always remained connected with some artistic creation, some stories or myths that presented in external and finite form the truths that it sought to convey. The representations of religion—the stories, the myths, the artistic forms—varied from people to people and varied according to the particular stage of their spiritual development.

Hegel saw three stages in the development of religious consciousness: natural religion, artistic religion, and absolute religion. Natural religion was the awareness of an object, separate from the viewer, that was of a spiritual character: the ancient religions of Persia, India, and Egypt were examples of natural religion. In the stage of natural religion, the spirit, actually immanent in the world and in man, was seen as separate from man, personified in natural forces and disem-

29. *Werke*, vol. 9, *Philosophie der Geschichte*, pp. 62–63.

bodied spirits. Those forces and spirits found their representations in myths. "Myths," wrote Hegel, "as creations of the spirit, contain . . . general thoughts upon the divine nature . . . . Thus mythological fables contain a wholly rational basis and profound religious conceptions." [30]

The second stage of religious development, that of artistic religion, emerged because the spirit needed to be expressed in an external, concrete representation. The religions of Greece and Rome were examples of this second stage. Here artistic religious consciousness fashioned the representations of the spirit as statues of the gods. The distinction between art and religion was virtually non-existent. Artistic representations of the gods had the effect of externalizing the spirit and bringing it to earth in a concrete form; they were groping attempts at the union of self-consciousness and the material world. The Greeks created their gods artistically by abstracting the spirit inherent in themselves and externalizing it in the form of artistic representation. "The natural," wrote Hegel, "as explained by man—in its internal essence—is, as a general principle, the beginning of the divine." [31] When man objectified the spirit that lay within him as a representation of the divine, he was actually alienating immanent spirit and continuing the distortion of transcendence. Consequently, even among the Greeks, "the honor of the human is swallowed up in the worship of the divine." [32] Because spirit, out of inner necessity, had to overcome the separation between divine and human that was still present in artistic religion, it had to move on to a higher step in religious consciousness. "The divinity of the Greeks is not yet the absolute, free spirit, but the spirit in a particular stage, limited by humanity. . . ." [33]

The third stage of religious consciousness was that of absolute religion, in which the union of spirit with matter, the

30. *Werke,* vol. 10, part 1, *Vorlesungen über die Aesthetik,* pp. 390–92.
31. *Werke,* vol. 9, *Philosophie der Geschichte,* pp. 290–91.
32. *Philosophie der Geschichte,* p. 293.
33. *Philosophie der Geschichte,* p. 298.

achievement of divine self-consciousness in man, was the chief characteristic. For Hegel, absolute religion and Christianity were synonymous. Christianity was the union of the spirit with the world, and the incarnation was the recognition of the immanence of spirit. Since the union of God and man took place in the self-consciousness of Jesus, the philosophical truth of divine immanence was expressed in religion by means of the representation of the person of Jesus and the gospel stories associated with him. Religious consciousness, after all, had to have an external representation of the truth that philosophy could accept as pure conceptual thought—Jesus was that representation. The Christian religion used the symbol, Jesus, as its guide: it expanded Jesus's individual self-consciousness to a general self-consciousness with the aim of making all men one with God.

For Hegel, his philosophy and Christianity had the same content—the immanence of spirit in man, the denial of God as wholly other—but Christianity, as a religion, needed to express that content in a symbolic form while philosophy did not. That was why Hegel, despite a youthful sputter of interest in the subject, did not engage in the quest for the historical Jesus. Speculative philosophy showed him the truth of the union of God and man, and he did not need to look for the "soulless recollection of an ideally constructed individual figure and its existence in the past." [34] Philosophy needed no such external symbol. Herein, perhaps, lay the basis of Kierkegaard's criticism of Hegel for turning Christianity into an intricate web of philosophical abstraction in place of the simple imitation of Christ that, Kierkegaard was convinced, it was meant to be.

The development of religion through history, for Hegel, justified his own philosophy. Although the spirit or God was always inherent in man, man did not understand that immanence. He came to perceive it only because of the inexorable development of spirit in history. In primitive religions man

34. *Werke,* vol. 2, *Phänomenologie des Geistes,* p. 567.

recognized spirit only in forces external to himself. He saw divinity as totally other, entirely separate from humanity. History progressed and man began to create representations of that spirit in artistic endeavors. To do that, man externalized the spirit immanent in himself and set up that alienated spirit as his pantheon of gods. The representation of spirit in artistic forms was a step forward because it united the self-consciousness of the spirit with the material world. Then in the Christian revolution the great truth of divine immanence became manifest. The union of divine and human natures in the person of Jesus heralded the end of transcendence and marked the beginning of man's understanding that divine nature must achieve self-consciousness in humanity. The historical development of the spirit, then, to truth, reason, freedom, and monism justified Christianity. It also justified Hegel's philosophy: the aim of spiritual development was to end all antinomies and dualism, including that of God and man.

If Hegel's philosophy justified Christianity, as the Hegelians of the right believed, it also created some difficulties in terms of orthodox religion. For Christianity is essentially theism, and the end of the Hegelian philosophy would render theism only a distorted representation of the truth. A God, external to man, who saved man by loving grace was a distorted representation of the spirit immanent in man. If God were a force, and not a person, and if man became one with God not as an individual but as part of humanity, as part of the historical process, what happened to the Christian doctrines of redemption and personal immortality? There was, ultimately, no distinction between God and man; as the spirit progressed, it absorbed man in the necessary development of its higher purpose. It was no wonder that Kierkegaard condemned Hegelian theology for turning the mob into God.

There were further problems in Hegel's denial of transcendence and his insistence that history was the development of the immanent spirit. If God were present in all of history, if all of history were the story of his development to final unity, then how explain the moment of incarnation? Was it possible, in view of his teaching that God was immanent in all of history, to see the appearance of Jesus as a unique phenomenon, a unique appearance of God in history? How distinguish between God in history at one moment and God in history in general? If human history was a continuing incarnation, could there have been a unique incarnation?

Heinrich Heine contended that, because of these questions, the Hegelian philosophy led him and his generation to irreligion, to the renunciation of the Christian faith.[35] His admission only confirmed the fears of some of Hegel's conservative colleagues at Berlin. It was doubtless more than the petulance of an academic rival that led Savigny to express alarm over Hegel's "haughty and superficial criticism" that had the effect of making "his eager students renounce all religious connections . . . ."[36] He recognized implications that the Young Hegelians were to develop fully.

If Hegel's views on religion left troubling questions in the minds of his disciples, so did the problem of historical change. "Our age is a time of birth and of transition to a new period," Hegel wrote in 1807. "The spirit has broken with the world as it has hitherto existed, and with the old ways of thinking."[37] He had a profound sense of change as a result, or perhaps a cause, of his philosophical view that reality was always developing. But what did that change mean? What was happening? Where was the spirit leading next? Hegel had no answer. Indeed, he regarded these questions as unanswerable. Philosophy could only explain what had happened, it could never predict:

35. Heinrich Heine, *Religion and Philosophy in Germany*, tr. J. Snodgrass (London, 1882), pp. 12–13, 158–60. See also *Heine's Memoirs*, tr. G. Cannon (New York, 1910), 2:249–51.

36. Savigny to Creuzer, 6 April 1822, in Adolf Stoll, *Friedrich Karl von Savigny, ein Bild seines Lebens mit einer Sammlung seiner Briefe* (Berlin, 1927–39), 2:288.

37. *Werke*, vol. 2, *Phänomenologie des Geistes*, p. 10.

To say a word about teaching how the world ought to be, philosophy always comes too late for that. As the thought of the world, it appears at a time when reality has ended its process of development and has made itself ready . . . . When philosophy paints its gray on gray, a form of life has then become old, and it cannot be rejuvenated by this gray on gray. The owl of Minerva begins its flight at dusk.[38]

Though Hegel had a profound sense of historical change, he never fully explained the exact mechanism of change. The Young Hegelians believed that they were living in a time of total historical change, when the old Christian weltanschauung was being abandoned by the spirit for a new form, when the new form was struggling to be born. That sense of change haunted their minds and filled their hearts: they had to become involved in the new life of the spirit. Yet from the master they could get no statement on the exact mechanics of historical change.

If the Young Hegelians could get no specific direction of change from Hegel's thought, they could at least get guidelines. From his philosophy they knew that change was at the heart of reality and that the ultimate end of change was freedom, reason, and unity. They chose to ally themselves with change in order to ally themselves with the life of freedom and reason. For that life they had Hegel's views of history, the state, and religion to instruct them.

Like any philosophical division, the cleavage of Hegel's disciples into right and left transcended mere personal relationships. Personality was, of course, involved in the division. But where truth was at stake, more important issues dominated. Neither side considered itself a school created by petty partisanship, narrow interest, or factionalism. Philosophy did not allow for such a contracted vision; it aimed at a completeness of knowledge, a total view of reality.

Each side, then, had to defend its understanding of Hegel as the exclusive version of truth, bringing into the orbit of

38. *Werke*, vol. 8, *Philosophie des Rechts*, p. 20.

debate all areas of knowledge, all spheres of learning. The division was precipitated by religious issues, but philosophy, aesthetics, politics, history, all ultimately became involved in the cleavage. The struggle for truth and reality tolerated no limitations. It also tolerated no compromise: dogmatism, undoubted certainty, and doctrinaire assurance characterized both sides.

The Hegelians of the right affirmed the Christian faith and affirmed the existing institutions of society as the embodiment of the divine. Eduard Gans was the philosopher of law who based his views on the conservative interpretation of Hegel. Philipp Marheineke was the conservative Hegelian theologian. Karl Göschel, Johann Eduard Erdmann, Georg Andreas Gabler, Leopold von Henning, Hermann Hinrichs, Carl Michelet, and Heinrich Hotho were the chief philosophers of the Hegelian right. For them Christianity and the Hegelian philosophy were not only compatible but mutually justifying. In that they differed completely from the Young Hegelians.

There were other important areas of disagreement. The right held on to the traditional theistic notion of God as a transcendent personality and objected to any movement in the direction of pantheism; the left believed in God's immanence. The right insisted on the immortality of the individual soul; the left saw true immortality only in man's surrender of his finite personality to the life of the immanent spirit. The left sensed an impending apocalypse; the right did not.

Perhaps the most distinctive feature of the division of the Hegelian school was the nature of these issues over which the division developed. The split of the Hegelian school developed on the basis of such vital issues that the participants were willing to sacrifice their careers, their fortunes, and their honor for their views. Unswerving loyalty to its view of reality was the enviable property of each side. To understand the issues on which the Young Hegelians developed is to understand what men thought important in Germany in the 1830s and 1840s.

The division of the Hegelian school is not a phenomenon existing only in the minds of later historians—it was recognized and described by those who participated in it.[39] There was common agreement on all hands that the divisive issue was religion, specifically the person of Jesus. In 1837, Strauss described the division of the school into right, center, and left on the basis of each member's position on the christological question: those on the right accepted the evangelical history of Jesus as the union of divine and human, those on the left did not. The conservative Hegelian, Michelet, writing in the following year, agreed that the christological question was the point on which the school was divided.[40] The Hegelians of the right accepted an equation between Hegel's philosophy and the content of evangelical history and saw the master's philosophy as demonstrating the truth of Christianity. Christianity would reconcile man with God through salvation, and Hegel's presentation of the gradual reconciliation of spirit and man through history seemed to fulfill that function in a progressive revelation. Jesus offered the paradigm of the culmination of Hegel's philosophy and Christian theology—the fusion of God and man in an historical figure. Jesus was understood by the conservative Hegelians as the principle of antithesis in God, God's negation in human form, hence the necessity by which God returned to absolute unity with himself. Jesus was a necessity for God, and equally a necessity for man. Jesus's unique example demonstrated that individual human self-consciousness was capable of union with the fullness of divine

39. For perceptive discussions of the Hegelian right, see Jürgen Gebhardt, *Politik und Eschatologie: Studien zur Geschichte der Hegelschen Schule in den Jahren 1830–1840* (Munich, 1963), pp. 69–129; Hermann Lübbe, *Politische Philosophie in Deutschland, Studien zu ihrer Geschichte* (Basel and Stuttgart, 1963), pp. 27–84; and the anthology, *Die Hegelesche Rechte*, ed. Hermann Lübbe (Stuttgart, 1962).

40. D. F. Strauss, *Streitschriften zur Vertheidigung meiner Schrift über das Leben Jesu und zur Charakteristik der gegenwärtigen Theologie* (Tübingen, 1841), 3:95; Carl Michelet, *Geschichte der letzten Systeme der Philosophie in Deutschland* (Berlin, 1838), 2:637–59.

consciousness. As Hegel had said, Jesus was a philosophical necessity, his existence necessary for philosophy and religion.[41] For those on the right, then, Jesus provided the theological truth of Christianity and the philosophical truth of Hegel. This view was part of their larger insistence on maintaining the personality of God as an absolute or transcendent principle, on affirming the immortality of the individual soul, and on asserting the complete identity of philosophy with absolute religion.

The Young Hegelians, however, believed that Hegel's philosophy and Christian theology were not ultimately compatible. How, they asked, if God is immanent in the world and all history is the story of his development—as Hegel clearly taught—can Jesus be held to be the son of God, the unique divine embodiment in history? How can one unique moment in history—the incarnation—be chosen as the union of divine and human, when all history is the progressive union of divine and human? The Young Hegelians asserted divine immanence and denied a transcendent God; they repudiated individual immortality; they insisted that the entire process of history was the incarnation; and they contended that philosophy had advanced to a higher level of truth beyond religion.

The role of the Young Hegelians as religious critics is well known and will be considered in detail in subsequent chapters. That role was equally recognized by contemporaries: at the Prussian court a mocking phrase defined them as those who "Hegeled their Bible and Bibled their Hegel." [42] When the great enemy of the Hegelian school, the historian Heinrich Leo, listed the characteristics of the Young Hegelians in 1839, he too stressed their refusal to accept traditional religious views. He accused them of atheism, of viewing the gospels as

41. See, for example, Philipp Marheineke, *Vorlesungen über die Bedeutung der hegelschen Philosophie in der christliche Theologie* (Berlin, 1842); and Karl Daub, *Dogmatische Theologie jetziger Zeit* (Berlin, 1833).

42. Heinrich von Treitschke, *History of Germany in the Nineteenth Century*, 6:313.

mythology, of denying the divinity of Christ, of rejecting the immortality of the individual soul. All these articles, he argued, were the basic articles of Christianity. Thus, for Leo, the Young Hegelians had their definition and their unity as an anti-Christian group.[43]

In an important way, Leo's contemporary judgment was correct, though he defined the Young Hegelians negatively, stressing their anti-Christian rather than their positive tenets. Nevertheless, it was precisely the religious position alone that provided the unity of the Young Hegelians and divided them from the Hegelians of the right. For the Hegelians of the right the unity of God and man occurred in the unique form of Jesus; for the Hegelians of the left, the unity of God and man occurred in all humanity through a progressive historical development. The Young Hegelians were not Christians, they were humanists. And that humanism, the product solely of Hegel's influence, formed their essential unity and divided them from the Hegelians of the right.

Interestingly, the division of the Hegelian school in this way stemmed from one of what his disciples regarded as the two essential ambiguities in Hegel's philosophy. These two ambiguities—the question whether history was a secular or a sacred process and the question whether reality was objective or subjective—explain the division between Hegelians of the left and the right and also the division that appeared among the Young Hegelians themselves. To turn first to the division between the Old and Young Hegelians, it is important to see that division based upon a question in Hegel's view of the historical process, the question whether that process was secular or sacred.[44] In the ultimate consummation of Hegel's philosophy, of course, there was no such ambiguity. There could be no conflict between secular and sacred; all such antin-

43. Heinrich Leo, *Die Hegelingen* (Halle, 1839), pp. 2–3.
44. For a discussion of the importance of this issue for German cultural history in the nineteenth century, see Karl Löwith, *Von Hegel bis Nietzsche* (Zürich, 1940).

omies were overcome in the final end of the historical process. In the meantime, for those who had to live before the end of the historical process, the question whether that process was sacred or secular was, they felt, never clearly resolved by Hegel.

For those Hegelians who believed that the historical process was essentially sacred, there was sufficient evidence that Hegel thought the same. Indeed, the position could be impressively defended in terms of Hegel's philosophy. History was, after all, the domain of the developing spirit, the idiom in which the spirit overcame its self-alienation in progressive stages. All historical phenomena had their meaning in terms of this spiritual development, thus acquiring a higher meaning than that of their momentary existence. Equally significant, the historical process was teleological, its purpose and goal the overcoming of all antinomies in the total identification of God and nature. Its teleological nature only confirmed the basic religiosity of the historical process. Ultimately the process was understandable in terms of the christology of Christianity, the theological doctrine of the union of divine and human, or in terms of the Hegelian philosophy, the philosophical equation of the content of Christianity. Such was the view of the Hegelians of the right, the Old Hegelians.

Those Hegelians who believed that the historical process was essentially secular, had an equally impressive support from Hegel's philosophy. Hegel had described the representation of the historical process as passing upward through three stages of art, religion, and philosophy. In the process, then, religion must yield to philosophy as the idiom of truth; the historical process could not be understood in the last analysis by religion but only by philosophy. Moreover, history could not be the realm solely of the spirit since the process meant the progressive fusion of the spirit with matter, implying the necessity, perhaps even the equality, of matter. Since the spirit had no reality apart from the concrete historical forms it assumed, the historical process was truly these forms and not the spirit itself. Since the spirit could only be known by its works, those works made up the stuff of history. Thus, history was not a sacred process, but a secular process that involved the progressive development of human institutions. This progressive development was of singular interest—here was an important emphasis on the implicit historicism of Hegel—because the stress on the time-bound nature of all historical phenomena directed attention correctly to the content of history, the ultimate identification of man and spirit. Christianity in particular could not remain a constant guide to the historical process since it too was time-bound and a part of that process. Philosophy replaced Christianity as the means of understanding history as a secular process.[45] Such was the view of the Hegelians of the left, the Young Hegelians.

The implications of this cleavage over the secular or sacred nature of history divided the Hegelians completely over fundamental questions. The Hegelians of the right maintained their emphasis on absolute religion, on the essential place of Christianity as explanation and fulfillment of the historical process. The Young Hegelians maintained that Christianity was outmoded in the historical process, that philosophy was now exclusively the informer of reality. For the Hegelians of the right, religion—especially the most advanced form of religion, Christianity—was the foundation, the source, and the motive force of secular culture and knowledge. For the Young Hegelians religion and secular culture were now necessarily antagonistic; philosophy was the key to truth and religion but an outmoded encumbrance. Between these two views there could be no compromise; especially as the Young Hegelians undertook to enter the battle against religion in the name of philosophy and secular culture, in the name, ultimately, of the integrity of the historical process itself.

For the Young Hegelians, a great historical moment was at hand. The Hegelians of the right, they believed, were em-

45. Cf. Otto Pfleiderer, *The Development of Theology in Germany Since Kant, and Its Progress in Great Britain Since 1825*, tr. J. Frederick Smith (London, 1890), pp. 131–53.

bracing a metaphysic, Christianity, that was outmoded by the actions of the historical process. The world was experiencing a rare but essential moment in history, with the spirit divesting itself of its representation in the form of Christianity and beginning to seek its representation in a new, higher form. The reliance on Christianity, useful and correct at one time, was now a blind adherence to an anachronism. The proper function of the philosopher was to comprehend the direction and representation that the spirit would now take in order to facilitate the development of the spirit. Those who clung to Christianity failed to realize the great change the spirit was undertaking and actually impeded progress; those who moved beyond Christianity to the new form of spiritual development were aligned with the inexorable process of history. Those who clung to Christianity were enemies of freedom because they sought to restrain the spirit within a form that was no longer true; those who transcended Christianity were the true supporters of freedom because they rejoiced at the higher stage of spiritual development being accomplished before their eyes. The conflict between Christianity and the new form of secular culture was inevitable and necessary, and a higher form of spiritual freedom was the assured result. Such was the Young Hegelian vision of the apocalypse; for them Hegel's "owl of Minerva" had indeed taken flight.

"The catastrophe will be dreadful and must be a great one, and, I might almost say, it will be greater and more colossal than the one that introduced Christianity into the world." [46] Thus wrote Bruno Bauer almost in summary of the Young Hegelian vision. This apocalyptic tone, this sense of historical revolution, was the essential ingredient of the Young Hegelian metaphysic. Whereas the conservative Hegelians, the Hegelians of the right, were content to accept the finality of the identifi-

46. Bruno Bauer to Karl Marx, 5 April 1840, *Marx-Engels Gesamtausgabe*, ed. D. Rjazamov and V. Adoratski (Berlin, 1927–32), part I, vol. 1, section 2, p. 241 (hereafter referred to as *MEGA*).

cation of the Hegelian philosophy and the content of Christianity, the Young Hegelians argued that identification was temporary and had now ceased. They were, they felt, living in a rare time of historical change as significant as that which introduced Christianity into the world, when the spirit was moving upward to a newer form of historical representation, abandoning Christianity as a time-bound and momentary casing. Those who clung to the old form of Christianity were perverse and foolish. History would soon show them their error, the terrible error of the historicist position: clinging to the time-bound as if it were eternal.

Strauss seemed to define the tone of the anti-Christian sentiment that developed among the Young Hegelians in his book *The Romantic on the Throne of Ceasar, or Julian the Apostate.* In this work Strauss criticized the religious policies of Frederick William IV of Prussia, though his observations could have been applied to anyone who sought to preserve Christianity against the inexorable development of history. The original Julian sought in vain to maintain paganism against the necessary development of Christianity. Frederick William IV, the modern Julian, was also seeking to stay the historical process in favor of an outmoded religion. His efforts would also prove futile. The spirit could not be stayed, the historical process was inexorable. The spirit must cast aside its old confining representations in order to create higher forms of truth in its path to self-realization. Those who clung to the old representation sought truly to stop history, to prevent the necessary development of history. They were doomed, as Julian was, to failure.

What, then, were men to do? That they lived in a time of great change was clear to the Young Hegelians. That many did not recognize the change, that many sought to prevent the change, was equally obvious. Of course the historical development of the spirit could not be prevented by human action: the process would continue as an inexorable necessity. The Young Hegelians, however, did not preach a passivity, a quietism that might seem the logical result of their assurance that the spirit would develop in its necessity regardless of human action. They seemed to suggest that human action could either assist the translation of the spirit into its new and higher forms or it could hinder it. Each man had to choose either to try to facilitate the spirit's embodiment in new earthly forms or try to hamper it. In either case the spirit's development was inexorable, human actions affecting only the speed of its progress, not the progress itself.

Since the Young Hegelians saw history as a secular or human process, they knew it could take place only in human terms, using human action and human knowledge. That they were hostile to those who sought to impede the historical process, however unsuccessful such attempts must necessarily be, only indicated, presumably, that they had less faith than Hegel had in the "cunning of reason." Indeed, they stressed the value of being in accord with the process of history. The end of the historical process was absolute truth. To assist the process was to assist its end, to impede the process was to impede its end. This sense of historicism was essential to the Young Hegelian metaphysic. The content of history, not the form of history, was the point of emphasis. The content was the progressive overcoming of the distinction between nature and spirit, between divine and human; the form was the momentary representation of the stage that the spirit's progress took at any time within the process. Those who emphasized the forms of history above its content committed the error of exalting a moment within the historical process above the process itself. The Young Hegelians intended to preserve the integrity of the historical process, to point to the essential distinctions between the momentary truths of history and the absolute truth that was its end and goal.

Moreover, the Young Hegelians knew from Hegel's view of history that true freedom, true reason, true morality could only be enjoyed by an individual who lived in accord with the historical process, the development of the spirit. Apart from the spirit, reason, morality, and freedom could not exist because they would then be distinct from the process whose conclusion was their true definition. Reason, morality, and freedom required overcoming the dichotomy between nature and spirit, divine and human; they could not exist apart from the process whose end was precisely the overcoming of these dichotomies. Freedom, thus, meant living in accord with the development of the spirit and accepting the forms which it evolved. It meant, equally, abandoning the forms that the spirit abandoned.

With these views of the historical process adapted from Hegel, the Young Hegelians saw more clearly their own responsibility in the apocalypse. They must be in accord with the development of the spirit. They also knew from Hegel's reconstructions in religion and political theory what that accordance with spiritual development meant. They knew that the historical process was a *Bildungsroman* of the spirit, but at the same time a *Bildungsroman* of humanity because history took place only in terms of human institutions and human activity. In short, they asserted that history was a secular process in which the development of the spirit in human history was identical to the development of humanity itself. In a religious sense, man must recognize the spirit immanent in his own history as the correct god to worship. The Christian revolution had accomplished the most significant step in overcoming the distinction between the spirit immanent in history and the human institutions and actions that were the agency of history: it revealed the unity of spirit and man in the symbolic form of Jesus. The world had accepted that revolution and was freer because of it. The institutions of men, their ideas, their states were all predicated on the Christian religion.

Christianity was, thus, the highest form of religion. But the spirit was now straining within the fetters of the Christian metaphysic; the ideas and institutions of Christianity in the nineteenth century could no longer contain the progress of the spirit yearning for another step forward toward its final goal.

Religion was no longer sufficient to represent the spirit, and Hegel had shown that philosophy was the next stage above religion in which the spirit objectified itself. Religion in its highest form, Christianity, had shown the truth of the union of God and man; now the spirit was progressing to the higher stage of philosophy, not rejecting the truth of Christianity but subsuming it in a higher revelation. Philosophy, specifically Hegel's philosophy, had shown that the union of God and man was accomplished in all humanity, not merely in Jesus. As Strauss asked, "Is not the idea of the unity of divine and human natures a real one in a more lofty sense when I regard the entire human race as its realization than if I select one man as its realization?" [47] The spirit was immanent in all men, God was intrinsic to all humanity, man and God were one and the same. Philosophical humanism was thus the next progressive step of the spirit above Christianity.

The Young Hegelians were acutely aware of what Hegel had said about other religions in the past, and they began to apply these insights to Christianity, sensing the serious need to persuade other men of its demise.[48] Hegel, for example, had spoken of the burdensome daily life of the Hindus and of how their religion was designed as an escape from the hopeless weight of life, a withdrawal into a "dream world and a frenzied happiness by means of opium." [49] It was but a short step to the general principle that all religion was the opiate of the people. Hegel described the Roman religion as one employed by the ruling class to control the population, a tool in the hands of the patricians that they "used consciously for their own ends and to oppress the people." [50] Here again was a notion, when elevated to a general principle that suggested all religion was

47. D. F. Strauss, *Das Leben Jesu kritisch bearbeitet* (Tübingen, 1835–36), 2:734.

48. Cf. Ernst Benz, "Hegels Religionsphilosophie und die Linkshegelianer," *Zeitschrift für Religions- und Geistesgeschichte* 7 (1955):247–70.

49. *Werke,* vol. 9, *Philosophie der Geschichte,* p. 204.

50. *Philosophie der Geschichte,* p. 358.

the opiate of the people, a means of social control exercised by the ruling circles for selfish ends. Hegel also reminded his listeners frequently that Homer and Hesiod created the gods for the Greeks, and he noted that Greek religion was the product of human projection and poetic imagination.[51] The Young Hegelians saw this notion too as a general principle descriptive of all religion, all religion being a projection of the human spirit and a product of the human imagination where man created God in his own image and likeness. Hegel also taught that men originally represented their religious ideas in the form of myths, that they "created their myths as poetry and brought forth to consciousness their innermost and deepest experiences not as forms of thought, but as forms of imagination."[52] To see all religion, including Christianity, as myth was the general insight that the Young Hegelians developed. Thus, so many of the nineteenth-century criticisms of religion —religion as the opiate of the people, religion as a means of control over the masses, the gods as a human creation, religion as a myth—were general notions that the Young Hegelians developed from Hegel's specific observations. That they felt the need to develop them was an indication of the extent to which they judged criticism was a necessary philosophical weapon in their struggle to show that Christianity was outmoded and that humanism must be accepted as the new spiritual basis for civilization.

It is important to stress that Young Hegelian humanism was not a pious sentiment, a kindly attitude toward all men engendered by charity and a sense of love. That was the mistaken understanding of George Eliot and the other earnest Victorians who read the works of Strauss and Feuerbach. The Young Hegelian humanism was rather a philosophical necessity, the inexorable progress of the spirit. Their humanism comprised an impressive sense of religious awe precisely because the worship of humanity was, at the same time, the wor-

51. *Philosophie der Geschichte*, pp. 288–91.
52. *Werke*, vol. 10, part 1, *Aesthetik*, p. 392.

ship of God. History was the process in which God and man were progressively becoming united. The worship of God, for the Young Hegelians, was the worship of man, his ideas, his art, his state, his institutions—all the objective embodiments of the immanent spirit. It was only that Christianity had now to give way to the worship of humanity.

The development of the spirit to this new stage was intensely significant for the Young Hegelians. The spirit had progressed from Christianity to humanism, but the forms, the institutions, the ideas had not changed to accommodate this progress. Although the institutions of human life were objective reflections of the immanent spirit, as Hegel had taught, the state and other forms of human life did not change automatically to accommodate the progress of spirit. They had to be changed by human action to objectify the higher revelation of the spirit, philosophical humanism.

The Young Hegelians were impressed by the gap between the humanism of the spirit and the human institutions founded on the old form of Christianity. Since Christianity was clearly outmoded, the human ideas and institutions founded on Christianity were no longer purveyors of freedom but impediments to freedom. True freedom could only be had by accepting the higher form of spiritual development, humanism, and founding human institutions on it. The Young Hegelians found themselves in the position of knowing, from Hegel, that the state must embody and purvey freedom and recognizing in fact, that the states of Germany, founded on outmoded Christian principles, obstructed freedom. Anyone who supported Christianity or the traditional German states, the objectification of the Christian metaphysic, sought to exalt a moment in the historical process above the integrity of the process itself, a momentary truth above the absolute truth. Society was rent by a terrible tension between the new form of the spirit, humanism, and the institutions founded on the outmoded form of the spirit, Christianity. The Young Hegelian apocalypse meant fighting for freedom, fighting to change the ideas and institutions of the world to accord with humanism. Each of the Young Hegelians consulted his private conscience to uncover the best way he could help the process by which the ideas and institutions of society would objectify philosophical humanism. On the grounds that Hegel's dialectic proceeded by criticism, Strauss, Bauer, and Stirner exalted the principle of criticism in their works in order to show the reluctant world that its forms must be altered to accord with humanism. Feuerbach and Strauss both saw their method as one of education that would convince men to change their institutions. Ruge saw political action as the best means of changing institutions to meet the progress of the spirit.

All agreed on one point. The human institutions, the embodiment and objectification of freedom in Hegel's philosophy, were now the enemies of freedom because they were founded on an outmoded form of the spirit. They had to become the objectification of freedom and humanism once more. The methods of criticism, education, and political action were, variously, applied with the same intention in each case: human institutions must become the embodiment of freedom, the educators of men, the agencies of enlightenment, the instruments of freedom.

In the preceding portrayal of the Young Hegelian metaphysic an implicit distortion occurs. The portrayal is an abstraction, an "ideal type," a typical representation of a typical member of a philosophical group in which no one was typical. Consequently a careful study of each member of the Young Hegelians against this background is necessary.

Moreover, this abstraction of the Young Hegelian metaphysic would seem to suggest a uniformity to the group that simply did not exist. Wide divergence, even within this metaphysic, was characteristic of the Young Hegelians, a divergence often accompanied by personal bitterness. Some of the divergence can be explained simply enough in terms of personal chemistry and private interest. Each of the Young Hegelians applied the metaphysic to different areas of human knowledge and thereby departed from the others: Strauss was concerned with history, Feuerbach with religion, Stirner and Bauer with "pure criticism," Vischer with aesthetics, Ruge with politics. The metaphysic remained the core of assumptions for all of these men, but its application to varying fields led to considerable diversity.

Two major areas of divergence must be articulated specifically. The first was the question whether reality was objective or subjective, the second whether the final position was idealism or materialism. Each had its origins in Hegel's philosophy. Ironically, Hegel's philosophy provided the diversity as well as the unity for the Young Hegelians.

Two major questions remained in Hegel's philosophy for his disciples. The first, the question whether the historical process was sacred or secular, provided the decisive issue that divided the Hegelians of the right from the Young Hegelians. The second, the question whether reality was ultimately subjective or objective, provided the major division among the Young Hegelians. Both apparent ambiguities were, of course, subsumed in the end of history, the final unity, but in the process of history itself they bore great significance. Indeed, where any of the Young Hegelians departed significantly from the metaphysic portrayed above, he did so precisely on the basis of what he took to be the ambiguity between subject and object in Hegel's philosophy.

The Young Hegelians who saw Hegel's philosophy portraying reality as subjective were Stirner and Bauer. They saw reality ultimately as the product of thought, the thought of the spirit and, because the spirit was immanent in humanity, the thought of man. Since the institutions and forms of any historical moment were objective reflections of the immanent spirit, the reality was the thought of the spirit not the objectifications of it. Indeed, they regarded these objective forms as restraints upon human freedom for they were projections of the immanent spirit out of man. The realm of matter and history for Bauer and Stirner existed only in consciousness. The objective world was a creation of mind. They demanded the ending of the alienation of object from subjective mind as the necessary foundation for freedom.

The Young Hegelians who saw Hegel's philosophy portraying reality as objective were Strauss, Feuerbach, and Ruge. They saw reality ultimately as the concrete and objective forms in which spirit objectified itself historically. The spirit for them was not an abstract or ideal form, but something that had existence only in so far as it had objective representation. Nature and history were the concrete realities. Indeed, consciousness only had existence in so far as it was objectified; without an object consciousness could have no reality.

The distinction between the Young Hegelians on this point was enormously significant; it will occupy considerable attention in subsequent chapters. One side argued that reality existed only because it was a product of thought; the other side argued that thought existed only because it was objectified. More than a matter of emphasis, the disagreement carried to the very core of reality. But, more importantly, this distinction was argued within the framework of the Young Hegelian metaphysic, not against it.

A second major division among Young Hegelians—again, occurring within the metaphysic rather than against it—was over the question of idealism and materialism, a question intimately associated with the conflict over objective and subjective reality, perhaps stemming from it. Some of the Young Hegelians have traditionally been seen as betrayers of idealism, men who surrendered their idealistic origins in Hegel's philosophy for a crude materialism and vulgar worship of matter. Others have been seen as uncompromising supporters of idealism who continually disdained materialism.[53] Such a character-

53. See, for example, Koppel S. Pinson, *Modern Germany, Its History and Civilization* (New York, 1954), pp. 71–74, 255; and George L. Mosse, *The Culture of Western Europe: the Nineteenth and Twentieth Centuries* (Chicago, 1961), pp. 141–52.

ization is clearly false as it is based on the mistaken view that ideal and material are somehow separable in Hegel's philosophy. They are not separable, but, ultimately, one and the same; for the Young Hegelians the choice between idealism and materialism was inconceivable. It is true that Strauss and Feuerbach seemed to stress the material nature of reality while Bauer and Stirner seemed to stress the ideal. But Strauss and Feuerbach knew that the material could not exist without the ideal; and Bauer and Stirner knew that the ideal could not exist without the material. To affirm either materialism or idealism was to affirm a dualism intolerable to an Hegelian.

Hegel's philosophy was monistic, and the Young Hegelians pursued his monism relentlessly, seeing the process of history as the continual overcoming of all distinction between ideal and material. There was no choice, there was only monism; the material was infused with the ideal, the ideal was objectified in the material. Any other view was a denial of the freedom that could come only from monism. For the Young Hegelians idealism and materialism were fundamentally the same: they were both monistic; neither existed without the other. In his explanation of the identity of idealism and materialism, Strauss deserves to be quoted at length:

> If one finds that what I have said amounts to crass materialism, I shall not deny it. In fact, I have always considered the conflict, so loudly broadcast, between materialism and idealism . . . as a mere quarrel over words. They both have a common enemy in dualism, which has dominated the idea of the world throughout the entire Christian era, dividing man into body and soul, his existence into time and eternity, and opposing an eternal creator to a created and transitory universe. In comparison to this dualistic conception, both materialism and idealism may be considered monisms, *i.e.,* they aim to explain the totality of phenomena from a single principle, to form the world and life out of a single fragment. In this attempt, one theory starts from above, the other from below; the latter builds the universe out of atoms and atomic forces, the former out of ideas and idealistic forces. If they are to succeed in their mis-

sions, however, one must descend from its heights to the lowest realms of nature and, for this purpose, put itself under the control of exact observation; the other, in the meantime, must begin to consider the highest spiritual and moral issues . . . . We soon learn that each of these modes of understanding leads to the other . . . . We must not attribute one area of the attributes of our being to a physical and the other to a spiritual cause, but all of them to one and the same cause that may be viewed either way.[54]

The enemy was the old Christian dualism of body and soul. The Young Hegelian metaphysic sought, for freedom's sake, to end that dualism. That some of the Young Hegelians proceeded in terms of material and others in terms of ideal did not place them at cross purposes. Whatever the mode of approach, the end was monism. Thus, a Young Hegelian could be apparently a materialist or an idealist, yet still operate within the identical metaphysic.

These two divisions, the debates over the objectivity or subjectivity of reality and over the material or ideal nature of reality, only indicated that the unity of the Young Hegelians was never unanimity. Indeed, it would seem at times that the divisions, the personal animosities and the intellectual conflicts that developed, must deny any legitimacy to the generic title. The ultimate unity, however, stemmed from the Young Hegelians' complete agreement in defining the question that had to be answered for their age. The question, in its simplest form, was this: what were the consequences of the incompatability of Christianity and Hegel's philosophy? For those who were not Hegelians, the question made no sense. For the Hegelians of the right, the question was invalid because the premise was false. A man was a Young Hegelian when he conceded that this was the essential question of his time.

The Young Hegelians set about dealing with the question in two ways. First they sought to demonstrate the importance

54. D. F. Strauss, *Der alte und der neue Glaube* (Leipzig, 1872), pp. 207–09.

of the question and the truth of its premise and to convince all men of both. They had to devote themselves fully to criticism, analysis of Hegel's work, and propaganda of a scholarly or philosophical sort. As it turned out, these efforts consumed most of their intellectual activity. There was a second demand, more important than the first: answering the question. Each of the Young Hegelians had an answer and sought to persuade others of its exclusive truth. Where they agreed as to the question, they disagreed widely on the answer. Their unity stemmed from a common task. It was a unity that tolerated wide diversity precisely because all the diversity was directed at answering the same question.

Croce has insisted that the inevitable and logical conclusion of Hegel's philosophy had to be "the position of an absolute immanentism, an absolute humanism and historicism." [55] That Hegel never went to such a conclusion, Croce claimed, was because he was too strongly committed to "the patterns of ancient and especially of the neo-Platonic philosophy" and to the "religious and theological traditions" of Lutheranism and Protestantism.[56] There are several interesting points to Croce's contention. First is the implication that the Young Hegelians properly understood the direction and intent of Hegel's philosophy, while the Hegelians of the right were close to Hegel's personal intellectual stance. Such a view is in keeping with Croce's argument that there was a distinction between Hegel the man and Hegel the philosopher, and his suggestion that some disciples chose to follow the man and others chose to follow his philosophy.

An even more significant implication remains in the argument that Hegel himself would have developed his thought in the same directions as the Young Hegelians were he not personally committed to some principle of transcendence. This suggests that Hegel never gave himself over to historicism or

55. Benedetto Croce, "The Historicism of Hegel and the New Historicism," in *Philosophy, Poetry, History*, p. 610.
56. Ibid.

historical relativism because he kept faith in some absolute beyond change, a Platonic ideal and a notion of the transcendent Christian God. It is difficult to be certain whether Croce was right about Hegel in this regard, though this description fits the Hegelians of the right. What is most important, however, is that the suggestion raises a central issue in the comprehending of the Young Hegelians: the extent to which, in the face of their philosophy of historical relativism, they raised history itself into an absolute, into the source of abiding value for an age in which they judged traditional values to be bankrupt and obsolete. Were the Young Hegelians content to accept the full consequences of historical relativism, or were they seeking some substitute for a transcendent God slain by a philosophy of immanence? Since for them the old Christian faith was no longer possible, did they look to some new absolute or did they merely reflect on the relativity of all values?

To begin with, each of the Young Hegelians accepted the effect of historical relativism: each used it forcefully to argue that Christian civilization had ended and to convince contemporaries that the new age, the age of philosophy, was at hand. In answering the specific question about the consequences of the conflict between Hegel's philosophy and Christianity, each of the Young Hegelians did in fact forge a new principle beyond relativism, did grasp at a new absolute. The choices varied: for Strauss it was culture; for Feuerbach, humanism; for Vischer, aesthetics; for Ruge, politics; for Bauer and Stirner, an extravagant titanism in which the ego became, in effect, its own absolute. Divested of traditional notions of transcendence by their metaphysic of historicism, they found in history itself the source of a new absolute. Their individual positions varied radically, but they were all responses to the same question.

Ruge once succinctly described the Young Hegelian metaphysic as "the unquenchable criticism of all the old theological, the old Christian, and the old Hegelian views of the world, although it is only the simple consequence of the Hegelian view of the presence and immanence of the absolute." [57] Criticism was central to the metaphysic, criticism against transcendence and all the ideas and institutions founded on it. It was a group effort that led each individual along his own path and to his own contribution. To understand the metaphysic requires a study of how each Young Hegelian applied "the simple consequence of the Hegelian view" to reality and the discoveries and contributions he made in that application.

57. Arnold Ruge to Prutz, 21 April 1842, in *Ruges Briefwechsel und Tagebuchblätter,* ed. Paul Nerrlich (Berlin, 1886), 1:275.

2 The Hallische Jahrbücher and the Young Hegelian Party

Literature has now become the second power in the state.

—Georg Herwegh, 1839

They were Young Hegelians before they were a party: both the ideology and the name preceded the conscious attempt to form a philosophical party. Many of them, however, shared the sentiment that their mission could more readily be fulfilled if they united as a group. The poet Georg Herwegh, a frequent associate of the Young Hegelians, seemed to express their view when he answered Freiligrath's claim that a poet must stand above mere party interests:

> Party! Party! Who should not grasp
> That it has been the mother of all victories!
> How may the poet outlaw such a word,
> A word that has given birth to everything magnificent?
> Declare yourself openly like a man: for or against?
> And declare the password: slave or free?
> Even the gods descended from Olympus
> And fought on the battlements of a party.[1]

Despite an occasional dissenting voice, most young intellectuals saw their time, in contrast to that of Goethe and Hegel, as demanding the engagement of the disinterested intellect.

The Young Hegelian who best realized the need for forming a party was Arnold Ruge. Ruge recognized that there were many who held opinions similar to his own, but that these men were scattered through Germany, that the Young Hegelians were debilitated by lack of a focus. In Stuttgart there was Strauss, whose *Life of Jesus*, published in 1835, had caused such an intellectual stir. Feuerbach was living in isolation in Bruckberg, deprived of his teaching career because he denied personal immortality. Vischer, in Tübingen, had recently converted from Christianity to Young Hegelianism. In Berlin, meeting in the taverns and coffeehouses along Friedrich-Strasse and Dorotheen-Strasse near the university, were many young men who accepted the Young Hegelian views. And in Halle were Ruge himself and his friend Echtermeyer, both teachers and both avid Young Hegelians. It was Ruge's intention to

1. Georg Herwegh, "Die Partei," in *Werke*, ed. Hermann Tardel (Berlin and Leipzig, n. d.), 1:121

unite all these scattered individuals into an effective and active philosophical party, to publicize the Young Hegelian views, and to usher in the Young Hegelian apocalypse. Ruge's determination to unite the Young Hegelians into a party meant the union of men on the basis of a weltanschauung, a union intending to disseminate its ideas and transform society. As a party, rather than as individuals, their effectiveness would increase.

In early nineteenth-century Germany, the most effective way of forming a philosophical party was to found a journal. The journal would serve as a physical bond for all the members of the party, a center to which they could direct their energies. The journal would be the organ of the party, a propaganda sheet for the weltanschauung on which the party was founded. Disinterestedness was not desirable for any journal; it had, rather, to express the party's point of view and defend the party's position with scholarship and polemic, with reason and passion.

Ruge was painfully aware that the Young Hegelians had no journal. In 1837 he published an article criticizing German journalism for having no periodical to express "the principle of development," the essence of the Young Hegelian metaphysic. There was, he insisted, a need for a new journal, one that would be a vehicle for the Young Hegelian philosophy.[2]

Ruge's closest friend at Halle, Theodor Echtermeyer, literary critic, lecturer, aesthetician, and Young Hegelian, concurred so enthusiastically with Ruge's plea for a new journal that he suggested they found one. Ruge agreed, and they excitedly talked over their plans "to make development the principle of the journal," to criticize the romantics, to work for freedom in the world of thought, to prepare the way for the Young Hegelian apocalypse.[3] Hence the *Hallische Jahrbücher für deutsche Wissenschaft und Kunst* was born.

2. Arnold Ruge, "Unsere gelehrte kritische Journalistik," in *Blätter für literarische Unterhaltung*, 11–13 August 1837, pp. 905–07, 909–10.
3. Ruge, *Aus früherer Zeit* (Berlin, 1862–67), 4:444–46.

Ruge and Echtermeyer would serve as editors of the journal, but for success they needed a publisher and a company of contributors. The radical Leipzig publisher, Otto Wigand, agreed to publish the journal. To obtain contributors for the journal, Ruge undertook a lengthy trip in the autumn of 1837. He visited all the universities, from Königsberg to Zürich to Tübingen; when he returned he bore a list of the names of 150 scholars who were interested in writing articles for the journal. Needless to say, most of these never contributed. Many dropped out as soon as it was evident that the journal was the official organ for the Young Hegelian party. Nonetheless, the journal made its appearance on January 1, 1838, in an atmosphere of excitement and expectation.

Before long the *Hallische Jahrbücher* gained widespread popularity and notoriety. Vischer, one of the contributors to the journal, wrote to Ruge from Tübingen that "your journal is presently the most desired periodical in our literary society, each copy completely worn out from reading." [4] A leading German intellectual of the nineteenth century, only seventeen when the journal first appeared, summarized for his generation the meaning of Ruge's journal:

> The *Hallische Jahrbücher* . . . was the real source from which we drew our philosophy and our knowledge of the Hegelian teachings. It was the most eminent publication in German journalism and the most effective organ of that side of the Hegelian school that made the peaceful empire of absolute idealism into a fighting and conquering system. We tore into each new issue and gave to its brave editors our willing attention . . . so that it might fasten victory to its banner.[5]

The *Hallische Jahrbücher* served the important function of disseminating Hegel's philosophy among a generation of German intellectuals, transmitting the great philosophical system in the form of the Young Hegelian metaphysic.

4. Vischer to Ruge, 28 March 1838, in *Ruges Briefwechsel und Tagebuchblätter,* 1:118.
5. Rudolf Haym, *Aus meinem Leben* (Berlin, 1902), p. 104.

Ruge's journal attained a mounting popularity among university students, among young university teachers, and among those unemployed intellectuals who frequented the coffeehouses and taverns. "The *Hallische Jahrbücher* gains ground daily among our youth," wrote a worried opponent of the Young Hegelians in 1840. "Young men like to see decisiveness, boldness, self-reliance, the liberalism for which the times hunger, and what they are pleased to call 'intellect'—and they find all these in this journal." [6] The history of the *Hallische Jahrbücher*, then, is important in itself in the history of nineteenth-century Germany.

When Ruge wrote of his journal that "its history is a part of the history of our times," he meant more than its importance in the intellectual history of Germany in the 1830s and 1840s.[7] Since the *Hallische Jahrbücher* was the organ of the Young Hegelian party, whatever organizational unity that party had was provided by the journal. The foundation of the journal in 1838, its course of development, and its final suppression in 1843, formed the external history of the Young Hegelian party.

There were four geographical concentrations of Young Hegelians: the South German Young Hegelians, the Berlin Young Hegelians, those associated with the publication of the *Hallische Jahrbücher* in Halle, and those connected with the *Rheinische Zeitung* in Cologne.

Speaking of his trip in the autumn of 1837 on which he recruited contributors to the *Hallische Jahrbücher*, Ruge admitted that the South German Young Hegelians "were very important for the journal." [8] Among the South German Young Hegelians were three who must be counted as dominant figures in Germany's intellectual history: David Friedrich Strauss, Friedrich Theodor Vischer, and Ludwig Feuerbach.

6. Friedrich Perthes, *Leben,* 3:504.
7. *Zwei Jahre in Paris* (Leipzig, 1846), 2:75.
8. *Aus früherer Zeit,* 4:468.

Each was so important for the Young Hegelian party that he will be treated separately and in detail in later chapters, but a few comments can be made in general about the South German Young Hegelians. First, theology and religion were their dominant interests: Vischer and Strauss were ordained ministers, Feuerbach had been a theology student. They had undergone a conversion in reverse and abandoned Christianity. In place of Christianity, the old faith, they accepted the secular faith of Young Hegelian humanism. Yet theology continued to be their main concern. During the period of their connection with the *Hallische Jahrbücher*, Strauss wrote a critique of Christian dogma, Feuerbach wrote his famed *The Essence of Christianity* wherein he sought to discover the origins of religion, and Vischer wrote several essays criticizing Christianity in terms of the Hegelian philosophy.

The political and social views of the South German Young Hegelians cannot be described, except in highly individual and personal terms. Feuerbach was a-political. Strauss was a conservative who favored monarchical government. And Vischer, though he did vaguely support the idea of liberal democracy and later involved himself in the Revolution of 1848, generally regarded politics as a secondary activity.

Lesser known figures among the South German Young Hegelians were Friedrich Reiff, a philosopher at the University of Tübingen, and the poet and jurist, Reinhold Köstlin, both eager contributors to the *Hallische Jahrbücher*. Robert Mohl, Gottfried Keller, and Eduard Zeller were also associated with the Young Hegelians and, though they never published in the journal, were listed among the contributors.[9]

The Young Hegelians in Halle were of a different sort. Their concern was less scholarship than the conscious dissemination of the Young Hegelian philosophy. They were connected with the editing of the *Hallische Jahrbücher* and di-

9. Hermann Fischer, "Die Hallischen Jahrbücher und die Schwaben," *Württembergische Vierteljahrshefte für Landesgeschichte* 25 (1916): 558–71.

rectly associated with Ruge and his intentions of propaganda. Ruge was the leader of the group, as much from his boundless energy as from his conscious efforts to organize all the Young Hegelians into an effective party. Associated with Ruge as co-editor of the *Hallische Jahrbücher* was another Halle teacher, Theodor Echtermeyer. Although Echtermeyer's effectiveness was considerably lessened by a debilitating disease that robbed him first of his arm and then, in 1844, of his life, he was an important member of the first generation of Young Hegelians. He was born in 1805, fell under the influence of Hegel at the University of Berlin, became a publicist for the Young Hegelians, and made important contributions to literary criticism and aesthetics. It was he who first introduced Ruge to Hegel's thought and persuaded him to accept the Young Hegelian views. Yet he was always overshadowed by Ruge, a situation he increasingly resented.

Among the others in Halle associated with the Young Hegelians were several young intellectuals and university teachers. Hermann Hinrichs cooperated with Ruge and accepted the Young Hegelian views, though he began his career—and ended it—as a conservative Hegelian. The poet, Robert Prutz, then a student at the University of Halle, wrote essays on literary and aesthetic subjects for the journal and exulted in his Young Hegelian judgments.[10] In 1842, the Russian, Michael Bakunin, became associated with Ruge's journal and wrote several essays for it; like Stirner, he developed his Young Hegelian philosophy into anarchism. Karl Moritz Fleischer, a gymnasium teacher in Halle, also allied himself with Ruge's party, though he contributed only sparingly to the journal. Intermittent visitors to Ruge at Halle, like the poets Georg Herwegh and Hoffmann von Fallersleben, also showed an interest in the *Hallische Jahrbücher*.

Perhaps the most interesting group of Young Hegelians— if eccentricity, extremism, and excess form a basis for interest

10. Georg Büttner, *Robert Prutz, ein Beitrag zu seinem Leben und Schaffen von 1816 bis 1842* (Leipzig, 1913), pp. 42–53.

—were the Berlin Young Hegelians. Berlin was the center of the Hegelian philosophy, the place where Hegel himself taught during his strongest years and where his influence lingered long after his death. In the taverns and beer cellars along Friedrich-Strasse and Dorotheen-Strasse agitated young men— teachers at the university or students—discussed Hegel's philosophy and earnestly argued the conservative and Young Hegelian positions. The same people tended to gather at the same tavern and to consider themselves as a special group. One of these groups, meeting regularly in the 1830s, was the "Doktorklub." Among its members were Bruno Bauer, then a conservative Hegelian and teacher at the university; his brother, Edgar Bauer; Dr. Adolf Rutenberg, later editor of the *Rheinische Zeitung;* Friedrich Koeppen; Karl Nauwerk, a docent at the university; Heinrich Hotho; and Karl Marx, then a young student at Berlin. What interested this group most were the religious implications of Hegel's philosophy, and their endless debates rolled well into each night.[11]

The radical members of the "Doktorklub" formed the core of a new group, totally committed to the Young Hegelian views, that began meeting informally sometime in 1841 or early in 1842 at Hippel's Weinstube in Friedrich-Strasse. Nauwerk, Koeppen, Edgar Bauer, and Rutenberg formed the leadership of the original core. They engaged in debates and discussions from the afternoon late into the night and began to attract many rootless radicals, hapless intellectuals, and bored dilettantes to Hippel's. The group came to call itself the "Freien" and came under the scrutiny of the Prussian police, who, in an official report in March, 1842, described the group as "literati who make a vocation out of journalism and political reasoning." [12] Nothing important escaped the critical analysis of these tavern philosophers—politics, religion, phi-

11. See Marx to his father, 10 November 1837, *MEGA,* part I, vol. 1, section 2, pp. 213–21.

12. Cited in Gustav Meyer, "Die Anfänge des politischen Radicalismus im vormärzlichen Preussen," *Zeitschrift für Politik* 6 (1913):43.

losophy, social questions all fell within their purview. They had the vision of a new time about to emerge, and they were impatient for it to arrive.[13]

The views of the "Freien" were sanctified in the spring of 1842 when Bruno Bauer became the spiritual leader of the group. He had recently been converted to the Young Hegelian philosophy and returned to Berlin as a martyr for his views: he had lost his position on the Bonn faculty because of his religious criticisms. He and his brother Edgar became the guiding lights of the "Freien," leading them down the path to criticism and the subjection of all ideas and reality to the critical tests of absolute idealism.

Bauer's principle of criticism—the principle that quickly dominated the mental outlook of the "Freien"—was the method used by these philosophers who put their total faith in absolute idealism, who disdained empiricism and exalted theory as the highest truth. Their idealism was Hegelian, and they subjected all ideas and institutions to the critical method that Bauer extracted from the Hegelian philosophy. Whatever could not endure the test of theoretical criticism, whatever demonstrated a disparity or separation between nature and spirit, was wrong and had to be rejected. The Hegelian philosophy gave them, they felt, a vision of the future as a humanist and secular paradise, where all distinctions between spirit and nature would be overcome. Anything that stood in the way of the attainment of this paradise had to be dissolved by criticism. As Bauer himself described it, it was the "terrorism of pure theory." [14] Everything fell before the criticism of the "Freien"—Christianity, the church, religion, moral values, the state, social standards, and all the other values of the society, founded on an outmoded religion, that refused to accept the "Freien." The group never fashioned a positive

13. For a discussion of the "Freien," see John Henry Mackay, *Max Stirner: sein Leben und sein Werk* (Treptow bei Berlin, 1910), pp. 67–93.

14. Bauer to Marx, 28 March 1841, *MEGA*, part I, vol. 1, section 2, p. 247.

program; its criticism was completely negative, and intentionally so. Only a negative criticism that could demolish all the old remnants of dualism and Christianity could clear the field for the full emergence of the next stage of the developing spirit. What was needed, they thought, was the total expurgation of all the old forms of spirit so that the new form could appear, unhindered. Criticism was to perform the expurgation.

It was in the atmosphere of the "Freien" that another leader of the group—Max Stirner, who, next to Bauer, was its most important member—developed his theory of egoistic anarchism. Absolute individualism seemed to be the goal towards which each member of the "Freien" was moving; the ultimate extension of criticism meant the equation of the individual with the principle of absolute criticism. The "Freien," then, was not a party in any formal sense. It was but a group of dogmatic individuals who found companionship in the group without commitment to it.

Nearly all the "Freien" were young, between the ages of twenty and thirty. The membership, totalling nearly one hundred, included poets, students, authors, teachers, journalists, and a few emancipated women. Their conversations normally centered on censorship, the new era about to dawn, religious and philosophical subjects, and criticism of all authority. Hippel's was filled with their shouts and their cigar smoke, with their cries as they played the endless rounds of cynicism, vulgarity, and banter, commingled with the catchwords of Hegelian philosophy. They often roamed through the streets, begging and brawling, and those evenings they did not spend in Hippel's knocking over chairs in their heated debates they spent rioting in nearby brothels. The old ways and the old ideas were not for the "Freien"; they expected they would soon enter into the life of total freedom.

Aside from the left wing of the "Doktorklub," the brothers Bauer, and Max Stirner, the "Freien" included others who were well known and others who are lost in the obscurity of history. Ludwig Buhl, the forgotten author; Eduard Meyer, contributor to the *Hallische Jahrbücher*; Friedrich Sass; Rudolf Gottschall, the poet; Wilhelm Jordan; Walter Rogge; Karl Marx; Friedrich Engels; and many others formed the dissonant band.

The fourth locus for the Young Hegelians was the *Rheinische Zeitung*. The paper was founded in Cologne by a group of businessmen who wanted a liberal journal, but one that, unlike the Catholic *Kölnische Zeitung*, would be an exponent of Protestant and Prussian views. The sons of two of these businessmen, Georg Jung and Robert Oppenheim, were called upon to manage the paper. Both were Berlin Young Hegelians, both were members of the "Freien." Jung and Oppenheim asked another member of the "Freien," Adolf Rutenberg, to become political editor for the paper. From the very beginning the *Rheinische Zeitung* was in the hands of the Young Hegelians.[15]

The *Rheinische Zeitung* appeared for the first time on January 1, 1842. Ruge had only praise for it: "the new spirit found a political organ in the *Rheinische Zeitung*." [16] Many of the Young Hegelians and their younger friends contributed to it: Bruno Bauer, Moses Hess, Julius Fröbel, Max Stirner, Herwegh, Prutz, Hoffmann von Fallersleben, Koeppen, Feuerbach, and Marx.[17]

What Ruge sought to organize, then, when he founded the *Hallische Jahrbücher* in 1838, was a party consisting of the South German Young Hegelians, the Berlin, and the Halle Young Hegelians. All the groups were different in temperament and character, all were dogmatic and self-assured. At least the *Hallische Jahrbücher* might offer an external unity, might give an organization to the Young Hegelians. Ruge hoped so.

15. Cf. Ludwig Salomon, *Geschichte des deutschen Zeitungswesens* (Oldenburg and Leipzig, 1900–06), pp. 362–66.

16. *Zwei Jahre in Paris*, 2:88.

17. Cf. Georg Jung to Ruge, 18 October 1841, *MEGA*, part I, vol. 1, section 2, p. 261.

The Halle Young Hegelians, the Berlin Young Hegelians, and the *Rheinische Zeitung* were all located within the jurisdiction of the Prussian government. Because of this, and because the Young Hegelians centered their political hopes on the development of Prussia, it is important to observe the relations between the Prussian government and the Young Hegelians.

The Prussian government exerted two forms of pressure that were especially significant for the Young Hegelians: press censorship and the control over academic appointments. By use of both, the government was able to exercise a compelling influence on the careers and fortunes of intellectuals whose views it might consider dangerous to the fabric of society. The Carlsbad Decrees, promulgated in 1819, gave the German governments the right of prior censorship of journals or papers less than twenty pages in length. In addition, the governments had the authority to suppress any journal whose views they regarded as inimical; and the editor of a suppressed journal was not to be allowed for five years to edit another journal anywhere in Germany.[18]

Prussia, like the other German governments, was equally concerned with its universities. Academic posts were part of government service, and the candidates for academic posts were submitted to the choice of government. If views to which the government objected could be kept away from the university lecterns and kept out of the public press, their dissemination might be halted. No matter that such treatment usually made the intellectuals who were involved more intractable, their opposition more bitter and uncompromising.

There were two distinct periods in the relations between the Young Hegelians and the Prussian government: from 1835 to 1840, from 1840 to 1843. During the first period, 1835 to 1840, relations were friendly, and the government was not merely permissive but actually encouraged the Young Hegelians. The

18. Cf. Lucy M. Salmon, *The Newspaper and Authority* (New York, 1923), p. 59.

period began with Prussia's decision not to suppress Strauss' *Life of Jesus* and ended with the accession of Frederick William IV, obdurate opponent of Hegel's philosophy, to the Prussian throne.

In that five year period, the Young Hegelians prospered under the protection of an important member of the Prussian administration, Karl Freiherr von Stein zum Altenstein, minister of public worship. Altenstein was a remainder from the great period of Prussian reform, a protégé and friend of Hardenberg, a supporter of the rationalist Christian philosophy of the German Enlightenment. In 1817, the three-hundredth anniversary of the German Reformation, when Prussia celebrated the historical occasion by uniting all Protestant churches under government control, Altenstein was named minister of public worship, a post he held until his death in 1840. In this capacity Altenstein used his influence to obtain the appointment of Hegel to the chair of philosophy at the University of Berlin in 1818. It was Altenstein in 1835 who finally had Gabler, Hegel's first disciple and Hegel's own choice for his successor, appointed to succeed Hegel in Berlin. He won out over the objections of the Crown Prince, later Frederick William IV, who wanted Schelling, the opponent of the Hegelian philosophy. In 1839, Altenstein, in his efforts to disseminate the Hegelian philosophy, got Bruno Bauer an academic appointment at the University of Bonn. He was also interested in promoting Arnold Ruge on the faculty of the University of Halle.

What was most important for the Young Hegelians was Altenstein's protection of the *Hallische Jahrbücher*. In 1838, Altenstein summoned Ruge to Berlin to discuss the Young Hegelian journal, confiding to him that he shared the same interests in philosophy. He told Ruge that there was pressure on him to suppress the *Hallische Jahrbücher*, but, Ruge recalled, he firmly declared: "As long as I live, scholarly discussion will be free, and thought—the noblest endeavor—will not be prohibited." [19] The Young Hegelians had a champion in an influential position and benefitted considerably from his protection. At the same time, they paid their respects to Prussia, for it seemed, under the guidance of Altenstein, to be fulfilling its role as the rational, Hegelian state. But for the chances of history, the Young Hegelians might have continued under the protection of the Prussian government. In 1840, however, the relationship between the Prussian government and the Young Hegelians reversed completely, and the two faced each other with increasingly bitter and uncompromising hostility. The change in 1840 was precipitated by the deaths of Altenstein and Frederick William III.

Frederick William III had been content to allow the universities and theological faculties considerable freedom so long as no direct attacks were made on him or on the state. Not so Frederick William IV. He was passionately interested in the ecclesiastical policy of the state, governed on the lines of orthodox Christianity and romantic theology. His considerable intellectual abilities were directed toward pietism, romanticism, and orthodox Christianity, toward the full assumption of his responsibilities as king to serve as bishop of the church. His enemies were the teachers of theological rationalism and deism, the heirs of Enlightenment skepticism and rationalism, the thinkers who sought to make a tangled web of philosophical abstraction out of the simple faith of Christ. Frederick William IV knew what the Christian religion was meant to be, and he never doubted his responsibility to protect it from all attacks, from all dissent, from all the anemic rationalism that threatened it.

He was aware as well of the political nature of religion. Since Prussia, under him, was to be a Christian state, any attack on religion was, at the same time, an attack on the monarchy. If the monarch was head of the church as well as head

19. *Aus früherer Zeit,* 4:477.

of the state, there was, in the mind of Frederick William IV, no distinction between religious criticism and political criticism. The alliance between conservatism and religion and between liberalism and religious skepticism was, it seemed to him, only a natural result. Later Frederick William was to blame the Revolution of 1848 on the spread of that irreligion that he had tried so hard to halt. In a speech in 1849 to an assembly of theological and seminary faculties, he charged:

> All the misery that has beset Prussia in this past year is your fault, and yours alone. Yours is the guilt of disseminating vast quantities of irreligious pseudo-knowledge and calling it true wisdom. And with it you uprooted faith and belief from the hearts of my subjects and turned them away from me.[20]

Frederick William IV recognized the disciples of Hegel as enemies from the beginning. Hegel's philosophy was that rationalist scheme, that set of philosophical abstractions, that the new king hated. Hegel's philosophy, though pretending to defend Christianity, actually, in Frederick William's eyes, distorted and destroyed that faith with its subtleties and abstractions, with its logic and rationalism, with its apparent dismissal of simple faith and unsophisticated piety. What was more, Hegel's political ideas transferred loyalty to the state rather than the person of the monarch, exalted the abstraction of the state even over the divine right of the king. It was the divine right of monarchy, based on orthodox Christianity, not the state, that formed the heart of Frederick William's political ideology. As he opposed Hegel's religious views, so he opposed Hegel's political views.

Frederick William IV's attack on the Hegelian philosophy was aided by Johann Albrecht Friedrich Eichhorn, who became Prussian minister of public worship and education following Altenstein's death in 1840. Eichhorn, too, opposed ra-

20. Quoted in Friedrich Paulsen, *Das deutsche Bildungswesen in seiner geschichtlichen Entwicklung* (Leipzig, 1909), p. 155.

tionalism and naturalism in theology as well as the pantheism of which he believed Hegel most guilty. He purposefully allied himself with Frederick William's efforts to dispel the Hegelian influence from Prussia's universities, from the theological and philosophical areas which it dominated. In 1818, the Prussian government had bestowed its most precious academic honor on Hegel: it called him to the chair of philosophy at the University of Berlin. In the bitter words of Heine, Hegel "had himself crowned at Berlin" and exercised an absolute and unquestioned reign over philosophy.[21] But the policy of the Prussian government proved capable of striking reversals: by the early 1840s, the government that had once seen the Hegelian philosophy as one of its distinguished supports directed its power toward undermining and offsetting Hegel's influence. Hegel's crown had turned to thorns.

The reaction against Hegel and his disciples took many forms. In 1841, Schelling was called to assume the chair of philosophy at the University of Berlin to replace the Hegelian, Gabler. Hegel's very chair was, thus, given to a firm opponent of the Hegelian philosophy, a romantic, philosophical opponent of rationalism. Needless to say, Frederick William's opposition to the Young Hegelians was even more severe than his opposition to the conservative Hegelians. Bruno Bauer, recently converted to Young Hegelianism, was, under the judgment of Eichhorn, refused in 1841 the right to teach in a Prussian university. A similar ban was placed on all the Young Hegelians, a ban, interestingly enough, with which most university faculties were happy to concur.

Perhaps most important for the Young Hegelians was the decision of the Prussian government to move against the *Hallische Jahrbücher,* forbidding it in Prussia in 1841 and pressuring the Saxon government into suppressing it in 1843. One of the members of the "Freien" saw in the suppression of the *Hallische Jahrbücher* the occasion that "marked the fall of the Hegelian philosophy from the paradise of Prussian state

21. Heine, *Religion and Philosophy in Germany,* p. 156.

appointments." [22] The lines were clearly drawn: the Young Hegelians saw themselves, representing philosophy, pitted against the Prussian state, representing religion. Here was the conflict of the age, the conflict that Hegel seemed to forecast; here was the moment of historical change when the spirit would adopt a new form and appear in a higher stage of development. Victory was assured to the Young Hegelians. It was at this point that Strauss likened Frederick William IV to Julian the Apostate, the Roman Emperor who vainly sought to return the Empire from Christianity to the previous, outmoded religion of paganism.

If the Young Hegelians felt assured of the final victory, if they knew that the spirit necessarily decreed their triumph over the temporary reactionary policy of the Prussian government, they were also aware of the severity with which the Prussian government could treat them, perhaps even delaying the advent of the next stage of development, the progress from religion to philosophy. Indeed, the articles in the *Hallische Jahrbücher* that brought first censorship and then suppression of the journal were those that condemned the Prussian government for turning back from philosophy to religion, for abandoning its heritage as the vehicle of historical change. The articles defended Protestantism, defined as the spirit of freedom and the essence of the Hegelian philosophy, against the pietism and romantic philosophy the Young Hegelians saw gaining official ground in Prussia. Soon the journal began attacking the Prussian state because it was not Protestant enough.[23] The attacks grew in vehemence as the policies of Frederick William IV became more evident: the government was criticized for rejecting the enlightened tradition of Frederick the Great, for abandoning the mission to which its great philosophers called it, for refusing to become the model of the

22. Rudolf van Gottschall, *Die deutsche Nationalliteratur des neunzehnten Jahrhunderts* (Breslau, 1891), 2:281.

23. Cf. Arnold Ruge, *Aus früherer Zeit*, 4:445.

rational state that Hegel described. Indeed, Ruge claimed that the Prussian government was in "opposition to the spirit of the times," in opposition to the objective development of the spirit.[24] The journal's criticisms of the government became so outspoken that the hand of the censor was deemed insufficient to stay the threat of the Young Hegelians—in 1841 the government forbade the journal to circulate in Prussia.

Undaunted at having incurred the anger of the Prussian government, Ruge moved to Saxony, and in Dresden, in the same year, he began publishing the journal again under the new name of the *Deutsche Jahrbücher*. The editorial policy of the journal was now openly democratic, republican, and constitutional, expressing acid criticisms of the oppressive bureaucracies that dominated Germany. The main attacks were still centered on Prussia. The journal defined the Prussian state as the essence of the police state inspired by the Restoration and contended that Prussia failed the vision of its own philosophers—Kant, Fichte, Hegel—and the ideals of Frederick the Great. The Prussian state was failing the responsibility assigned to it by its own definers, it was attempting to stay historical progress rather than act as its vehicle. Hegel had seen the continuing development of the spirit from religion to philosophy, a rational progress embodied in rational state-forms; Prussia's policy under Frederick William IV was a denial of objective reality and a frightening anachronism.[25]

The Prussian government grew increasingly concerned by the attacks on it in the *Deutsche Jahrbücher* and finally, in 1843, pressured the Saxon government into suppressing the journal. On the grounds that "continuation in Germany would be nonsense so long as the fury of the police continues," Ruge announced that he and Marx, an unemployed exile from the

24. *Zwei Jahre in Paris*, 2:82.
25. Cf. Walter Neher, *Arnold Ruge als Politiker und politische Schriftsteller* (Heidelberg, 1933), pp. 32–88; and Willy Moog, *Hegel und die Hegelsche Schule* (Munich, 1930), pp. 438–41.

Rheinische Zeitung that had also been suppressed in the Prussian government's war on the Hegelian philosophy, had conceived of a new venture.[26]

The new project of Ruge and Marx was the *Deutsch-Französische Jahrbücher* which they began publishing in Paris following their emigration from Germany. It was a strange and predictably short-lived partnership, strained even from the first by conflicts of personality and ideas. They soon suspended publication of the journal and separated physically in a symbolic act that only underscored the fact that they were never united intellectually. For both men recognized what many have subsequently not seen clearly: that Marx, though influenced by the Young Hegelians, was not himself a Young Hegelian. Indeed, he showed a marked indifference to the very question that the Young Hegelians were bent upon articulating and answering, the question that provided unity to their intellectual stance. He was, after all, of another generation. The Young Hegelians, part of the generation of 1806, always maintained their emphasis on religion and the transition to the age of philosophy. Marx was part of a younger group that had absorbed the teachings and conclusions of the Young Hegelians and, ceasing to dwell exclusively upon them, used them as the foundation upon which to define and meet the needs of his age: an activist program of socialism, radical social transformation, and political agitation. His relation to them was the moral equivalent of their relation to Hegel.

Specifically, Ruge objected to Marx's view of the state, for Ruge believed that any Hegelian must see that freedom could only be realized within the framework of the state. Ruge saw all the ideas and institutions of history as reflections of the basic spiritual force. Marx insisted that social and economic forces were the basic reality of history, and he claimed that the spirit, Christianity, and philosophy that the Young Hege-

26. Ruge to Prutz, 25 January 1843, *Ruges Briefwechsel und Tagebüchblätter*, 1:296.

lians dwelt upon were themselves only reflections of these basic forces. He was doubtless not correct when he bragged that he had turned Hegel right side up; the Young Hegelians, however, all recognized and objected to the gymnastics that he performed with their ideas. When Marx concluded that the Young Hegelians merely expressed views that could be summarized in a range from bourgeois to petit-bourgeois, he declared both his own judgment of priorities and the autonomy of his own position.

The failure of the *Deutsch-Französische Jahrbücher* only underscored Ruge's fantastic ambition to bring together into a philosophic unity elements that turned out to be incompatible. It was only a more visionary effort than that which prompted—and doomed—the *Hallische Jahrbücher* and its Saxon successor.

The Young Hegelian, Vischer, had recognized that the external unity of the Young Hegelians was tenuous and that the *Hallische Jahrbücher* provided only an artificial unity to a philosophical party that was destined to burst asunder because of internal divisions. Ruge's journal, he argued, "strove for a living principle of movement, to be sure even a reckless principle, into which it finally hurried so fast that it would have gone under even if it were not slain by the authorities." [27] Vischer's argument was fully justified. The Prussian government's suppression of the Young Hegelian journal did not shatter the group; the group had little cohesion to begin with and the journal did not, in the end, provide unity but discord. In its early issues, the journal did provide a forum for the Young Hegelians, but continued publication created disunity instead of the hoped-for unity. The editorial emphasis passed quickly from the religious concerns of Strauss and Feuerbach and the aesthetic interests of Vischer to the more radical criticisms of Bauer and the democratic emphasis of Ruge. As early as November, 1838, Vischer wrote to Strauss that "the *Hallische*

27. Vischer, *Kritische Gänge: neue Folge* (Stuttgart, 1861–73), 1:xii.

Jahrbücher can no longer be regarded entirely as the organ of our views . . . ." [28] Strauss soon became openly hostile to the journal, and Vischer and Feuerbach soon expressed their disapproval of the course the journal was following. Strauss and Feuerbach ceased all connection with the journal long before it was suppressed by the Prussian government.

Ruge had wanted a journal that would be an organ for the "principle of development." That principle informed the journal itself, becoming an internal development that led finally to the shattering of whatever unity the party enjoyed from the journal. Despite the intentions of Ruge who wanted it to achieve cohesion for the party, the journal emphasized the divisions within the party and made cohesion, in the long run, impossible.

Ruge early defined the mission of the *Hallische Jahrbücher*: "to perceive the spirit, and also religion and the state, as they are and as they have become, *not how they will be or ought to be*." [29] It was both a concise summary of the Young Hegelian position and an indication of general agreement on editorial policy, accepting the consequences of the fact that philosophy and Christianity were no longer compatible, demonstrating to all the truth of that fact, employing criticism as a philosophical weapon to show the obsoleteness of ideas and institutions founded on Christianity. Whereas agreement on the question of the age was the source of intellectual unity for the Young Hegelians, the varied personal answers to that question were a source of disunity. So long as the journal concerned itself with articulating the question and demonstrating the validity of its proposition, it served as a focus of unity and mutual communication for the individual Young Hegelians. When it began to move on—as, seemingly, it had to—to con-

28. Vischer to Strauss, 4 November 1838, *Briefwechsel zwischen Strauss und Vischer*, ed. Adolf Rapp (Stuttgart, 1952–53), 1:71.

29. "Die Denunciation der hallischen Jahrbücher," *Hallische Jahrbücher für deutsche Wissenschaft und Kunst* (1838), p. 1433. Italics in the original.

sider an answer to the question, the initial unity it fostered quickly dissolved. For each of the Young Hegelians had his private answer to the question and deeply resented the journal's presenting any other. Ruge sought to avoid anticipating how the future ought to be, but he found both the external pressure of events and the internal pressure of philosophical necessity propelling the journal more and more into the role of prophet. Driven both by its quarrel with the Prussian government and the inclinations of its editor, it moved towards a political stance that Strauss, Feuerbach, and Vischer particularly resented, and that Bauer and Stirner saw as a futile gesture. Ruge sadly learned that it was impossible to combine a general metaphysic with individual applications into a single positive program. The hazards of dogmatism and applied philosophy predicated inevitable failure for such an attempt.

To understand the Young Hegelians it is necessary to recall the relationship of individual to party that characterized German intellectual life in the 1830s and 1840s. Parties were loosely defined metaphysical groupings of strongly distinguished individuals, men who did not abandon their personal stance in the name of party allegiance. The Young Hegelians all shared the same metaphysic, but as individuals they applied it differently, disagreeing bitterly with one another. Each supplied his own answer to the question they were all bent upon answering. If the *Hallische Jahrbücher* represented the unity of the Young Hegelians, it also represented their disunity; both are essential to the understanding of the Young Hegelians.

The external history of the Young Hegelians was, then, not only the history of the *Hallische Jahrbücher,* but also the private history of the individuals who were the Young Hegelians. What did the Young Hegelian metaphysic mean to those who adopted it? How did they apply it? What were the differences between them? What were their conclusions as they addressed the question of their age? The answers to these questions are essential to an understanding of the Young Hegelians. The private lives and careers of the dominant figures of the first generation of Young Hegelians—Strauss, Feuerbach and Vischer, Bauer and Stirner, Ruge—must be studied for a comprehension of the unity and diversity of the Young Hegelians. The lives of these men intersected for the five years of the existence of the *Hallische Jahrbücher* (1838–1843), and briefly again in 1848, yet the life of each man must be seen in its entirety for understanding the nature of Young Hegelianism. The historical contribution of the Young Hegelians came from the general metaphysic *and* the private application of that metaphysic by each of the individuals who composed the party.

3 Strauss and Historical Criticism

Those who regarded Strauss as a historian freed from all prejudice that was injurious to science, misunderstood his true character. Strauss—we must say it, surprising as this double assertion may sound—Strauss is at once a theologian . . . and a philosopher of the school of Hegel.

—Ernest Renan, 1857

Not since the time of the Council of Chalcedon in 451 was the personality of Jesus so important an intellectual issue as in the nineteenth century. Where that council produced the orthodox definition of the divine and human natures of Jesus that served for centuries as the basis of faith, the nineteenth-century interest in the historical Jesus produced doubt and apostasy. "My faith was destroyed by historical criticism," wrote Ernest Renan.[1] And many intellectuals could, and did, confess an identical experience.[2]

The best known, perhaps, of the historical studies of Jesus that inspired skepticism in place of faith was David Friedrich Strauss's *Life of Jesus*. Though it is a book now little read, at the time of its publication in 1835 it roused an intense intellectual controversy. A colleague of Strauss's on the Tübingen faculty, C. A. Eschenmayer, wrote a vibrant condemnation of the book in *The Iscariotism of Our Time* that sketched fearful images of Christian betrayal.[3] The Prussian government consulted the influential Berlin theologian Neander about the advisability of suppressing Strauss's book and, reluctantly, accepted his judgment against suppression.[4]

The defenders of Strauss's work were no less vigorous. Strauss's friend Vischer announced elatedly that the *Life of Jesus* contributed in a major way "to the mission of our century, which is the freeing of the spirit from the restraints of the written word." [5] To Strauss's contemporaries his work was,

1. Ernest Renan, *Souvenirs d'enfance et de jeunesse* (Paris, 1883), p. 258.

2. For a discussion of scholarship on Jesus in the nineteenth century, see Albert Schweitzer, *The Quest of the Historical Jesus*, tr. W. Montgomery (New York, 1961), and Heinrich Weinel, *Jesus im neunzehnten Jahrhundert* (Tübingen, 1914).

3. See C. A. Eschenmayer, *Der Ischariotismus unserer Zeit—eine Zugabe zu dem jüngst erschienen Werke: Das Leben Jesu, von Strauss* (Tübingen, 1835).

4. J. R. Beard, "Strauss, Hegel, and Their Opinions," in *Voices of the Church in Reply to Dr. D. F. Strauss*, ed. J. R. Beard (London, 1845), pp. 16–17.

5. Friedrich Theodor Vischer, *Kritische Gänge*, 1:3. This essay first appeared in the *Hallische Jahrbücher* in 1838.

and remained for some time, one of those rare books that could not be ignored, a scandal to the pious, a voice of liberation to the restless. Even Bruno Bauer, at the time an enemy of Strauss and his work, had to admit that "all theology is currently—one might even say exclusively—engaged in answering the questions that Strauss has raised . . . ." [6] Strauss, almost in spite of himself, became the center of a controversy from which he was never to recover.

Of all the reviews of Strauss's *Life of Jesus* that appeared in the midst of the controversy, none was more perceptive than that of Edgar Quinet. Quinet, a close student of German thought, observed that Strauss's work was neither original nor surprising, that the controversy surrounding its appearance was misleading since the work was the product of many minds, not one. Strauss, in Quinet's view, did not write as an original thinker inspired by a unique insight, but rather as a synthesizer who combined many disparate strands of German thought since Kant:

> If this work [*Life of Jesus*] had been the product of the thought of one man, so many minds would not have been alarmed by it at once. But, when it is seen as the mathematical consequence of almost all the work accomplished on the other side of the Rhine during the last half century, and that each had brought a stone to this sad sepulcher, learned Germany trembled and fled before its work . . . . If one thinks for a moment of the intelligence that has thrived there in philosophy, in criticism, and in history, one is only surprised that this result did not appear long before this.[7]

There was nothing unique in Strauss's book; there was only the union, perhaps long implicit, of separate developments in the study of philosophy, history and biblical criticism.

6. Bruno Bauer, in *Jahrbücher für wissenschaftliche Kritik* 14 (1840): 223.

7. Edgar Quinet, "De la Vie de Jésus par le Docteur Strauss," *Revue des deux Mondes* 15 (1838):587–88.

Quinet's judgment of Strauss's work was just. No one could claim that Strauss originated any aspect of biblical criticism or that he was the first to observe difficulties in the gospels as historical sources. There was a long tradition of biblical criticism from Pierre Bayle in the seventeenth century through Voltaire, Paine, Thomas Woolston, and Hume in the Enlightenment. In early nineteenth-century Germany—Strauss's immediate context—biblical exegesis and criticism had become a major element in academic and scholarly life owing to the work of Paulus, J. G. Eichhorn, De Wette, Bretschneider, and others. The Bible, treated as any historical document, was submitted to a close and critical scrutiny, miracles were rejected, contradictions and inconsistencies emphasized, mystery dispelled. Among Strauss's own teachers the critical approach to the gospels was further developed. Schleiermacher engaged in critical studies of parts of the New Testament; F. C. Baur, founder of the Tübingen School of biblical exegesis, developed criticism as a method of biblical analysis. These developments in the study of the gospels as an historical source paralleled the development of close textual and source criticism taking place in the historical profession under the influence of Niebuhr and Ranke.

Strauss's great achievement has traditionally been seen as his emphasis upon myth in the gospels, but even this emphasis did not originate with him. Following the inspiration of Herder, who insisted upon the intimate association of religion and primitive mythology and saw national poetic myths as representations of a community's attempts to explain its common experience, a whole field of scholarly investigation of mythology had developed. Otfried Müller sought in Greek mythology the original form of Greek reflection on and explanation of common experience. In 1825, he published his *Prolegomena to a Scientific Mythology* wherein he argued that myths arose not from the creative powers of one man but from the consciousness of the entire community. The Grimm brothers undertook a similar study of Teutonic mythology.

The study of myth in the Old Testament was developed by Semler, Gabler, De Wette, G. Bauer, and Schelling. In the same year that Strauss published his *Life of Jesus*, his friend Wilhelm Vatke published a study of the Old Testament that in part sought to discern the origin of Old Testament religion in earlier myths. In 1826, F. C. Baur—Strauss was a student of his at the time—argued, in *Symbolism and Mythology*, that in religious thought myth must play an important role.

Hegel too held that mythical representations were essential in the early development of spirit, that they were early forms of truth for societies too primitive to comprehend the higher truths of theology and philosophy.

> Myths, engendered by the spirit, . . . have a meaning as general thoughts about the nature of God . . . . If we penetrate to the inner truth of mythological representations, . . . we are able to justify the different mythologies. To justify man in his spiritual images and forms is a noble business, nobler than merely gathering external historical facts.[8]

Strauss, the disciple of Hegel, sought the nobler historical endeavor of discovering man as the creator of myth, of seeking the enduring ideas behind the time-bound myths of Christianity. Behind the symbols of Christianity, Strauss concluded, were philosophical truths to be made evident to the new age for whom the old symbols had lost their meaning.

In 1833, the Irish poet, Thomas Moore, published his interesting *Travels of an Irish Gentleman in Search of a Religion*. In this book he portrayed widespread apostasy and infidelity in the German academic world. He reported that few intellectuals accepted the Bible and most consigned its stories to the realm of myth and fantasy: even "the miraculous birth of Christ is to be ranked in the class of mythological fictions, along with the stories of the incarnations of the Indian

8. Hegel, *Werke*, vol. 10, part 1, *Vorlesungen über die Äesthetik*, pp. 390–91.

Gods." [9] It was in this context that Strauss's *Life of Jesus* appeared.

Strauss's work must then, as Quinet suggested, be seen as a synthesis of the fruits and methods of biblical criticism and historical scholarship within a framework strictly Hegelian. Strauss did not himself originate any of the elements of his synthesis; he did originate the idea of combining historical and scriptural criticism within the Hegelian philosophy of development in order to demonstrate the imminence of the Young Hegelian apocalypse. What was significant was that Strauss's philosophical principles did not emerge from the facts of biblical and historical criticism that he presented. Rather, those principles preceded the facts; indeed, the principles formed the framework on which Strauss organized the facts. His real contribution rested essentially in synthesizing the work in biblical criticism and historical research under a philosophical system developed independently of that research. Strauss first accepted the truth of the philosophical system and then sought to use the conclusions of biblical exegesis to demonstrate not only the truth of the system but also the passage from the age of religion to the age of philosophy. Biblical criticism for Strauss served the important function of showing not that Christianity was false but that it was no longer true for the new age into which the world was passing. Biblical criticism, then, would allow him to remove the myth, once necessary, from Christianity and to uncover the philosophical core; the new age would accept the philosophical truth at the core of Christianity, but it had no need of myth to represent that truth. The next stage of spiritual development beyond religion was philosophy.

Much misunderstanding of Strauss's work, when it appeared and subsequently, has occurred. Indeed, Strauss's two most famous books, *Life of Jesus* and *The Old Faith and the New* —marking, respectively, the beginning and the end of his lit-

9. Thomas Moore, *Travels of an Irish Gentleman in Search of a Religion* (London, 1833), 2:233.

erary career—were widely misunderstood and misapplied. The first has been seen as a critical presentation of the historical origins of Christianity with the intention of showing that Christianity was founded on falsehood and, thus, had to be rejected. Yet, Strauss's aim was to uncover the basic truth, not to demonstrate the falseness, of Christianity. He preferred not to lead men away from Christianity but to lead them up to the next stage of spiritual development from Christianity. The second book, *The Old and the New Faith,* was viewed as a worshipful address to materialism, a sign of Strauss's surrender of idealism for the materialism associated with *Machtpolitik,* steam engines, and the grinding gears of a mechanical universe. Yet in Strauss's own view, he had experienced no change: materialism was the fulfillment, not the denial, of the idealism of German philosophy. Materialism and idealism were, in fact, the same.

The misunderstandings of Strauss's work have stemmed essentially from the failure to view it within the Young Hegelian context. Strauss, like all the Young Hegelians, assumed as his sole responsibility the duty of ushering in the Young Hegelian apocalypse, of smoothing the passage from the age of religion to the age of philosophy. All of his work had this duty at its core; all of his effort was expended toward meeting his responsibility. To understand his work, then, it is necessary to comprehend his private vision of the Young Hegelian apocalypse and the method he hoped would achieve it. The private vision was a humanism presided over by a cultural elite; the method was historical criticism.

David Friedrich Strauss was born on January 27, 1808 in Ludwigsburg, Württemberg, the birthplace also of his friends Justinus Kerner, Eduard Mörike, and Friedrich Theodor Vischer. Strauss, like all of the Young Hegelians, came from a middle-class family: his father was a literate and successful merchant; his brother became a prosperous manufacturer. Young David early decided, with his family's prompting and blessing, on a career in the ministry. He entered the seminary at Blaubeuren—the seminary where a young teacher, F. C. Baur, was gaining his academic experience—and in 1825 he matriculated at the University of Tübingen. At the university he was subjected to the romantic influences that guided so many of his generation. He eagerly consumed the works of Schelling, Tieck, and Novalis; for a while he ranked the mystic, Jacob Boehme, above all other thinkers, and himself indulged in mystical aspirations. He came to frequent the salon of the romantic poet, Justinus Kerner, and exulted in the atmosphere of mystery, subjectivism, and occultism that wreathed the master. Strauss had become a romantic, and, regardless of the course of his scholarship for the next fifty years, romanticism remained an ingredient of his mind and of his heart. As late as 1849, Kerner could still write of Strauss's "inner longing that was the residue of his youth." [10]

Strauss's education did not end with romanticism, however. F. C. Baur, who was now lecturing at the university, interested him in religious symbolism and scriptural analysis. His interests became more and more philosophical, and, as the Tübingen faculty failed to satisfy this new desire, he turned to private study. He found Kant mystifying and unsatisfying; but in Schleiermacher he found the desired escape from mysticism, and he read widely in his theology and philosophy of religion. The real deliverance came with his discovery, by 1828, of Hegel, who had for him the answer to that perplexing and nagging problem of the relationship between the theology to which he was committed and the philosophy that more and

10. Justinus Kerner, *Briefwechsel mit seinen Freunden* (Leipzig and Stuttgart, 1897), 2:143. For studies of Strauss's early career, see Theobald Ziegler, *David Friedrich Strauss* (Strassburg, 1908), 1:1–106; Adolf Hausrath, *David Friedrich Strauss und die Theologie seiner Zeit* (Heidelberg, 1876–78), 1:3–76; Adolph Kohut, *David Friedrich Strauss als Denker und Erzieher* (Leipzig, 1908), pp. 11–24; and Albert Lévy, *David-Frédéric Strauss, la vie et l'oeuvre* (Paris, 1910), pp. 1–45. For Strauss's own discussion of his early growth, see his "Christian Märklin," in *Gesammelte Schriften* (Bonn, 1876–77), 10:205–26.

more inspired his interest. He and his friends formed a small private study group and spent their time devouring Hegel's *Phenomenology*. Significantly, this book that marked Hegel's own departure from romanticism also marked Strauss's departure from it. For the remainder of his life he regarded it as "the alpha and omega of Hegel's work" wherein "Hegel's genius stands at its height." [11] It was this book that had the greatest influence on Strauss, this book on which he based his entire acceptance of the Hegelian philosophy.

His studies at Tübingen ended in 1830, and Strauss made plans to go to Berlin to sit at the feet of Hegel. In preparation for that trip he read diligently in the works of Hegel and procured copies of the Hegelian journal, the *Jahrbücher für wissenschaftliche Kritik*. His abiding concern remained to draw together into one system the philosophy he accepted from Hegel and the theology he had accepted during his university studies. At Berlin the views of Hegel and Schleiermacher conflicted actively, and students and faculty at that university had to choose membership in one party or the other. Strauss, however, combined the views of the two men: having absorbed Schleiermacher and passed on to Hegel, he synthesized in his own mind the dominant Berlin philosophy and the dominant Berlin theology.

Strauss arrived in Berlin in November, 1831, excited at the prospect of meeting Hegel. Hegel died suddenly, however, just after his arrival. Dejected, Strauss decided to remain at Berlin for the year; at least he could study under Hegel's disciples— Marheineke, Hotho, Henning, Michelet—and attend some of Schleiermacher's lectures. His decision to remain in Berlin led to two important developments: his friendship with Vatke and his decision to write a life of Jesus.

Wilhelm Vatke was a young teacher at Berlin, a student of Hegelian thought. Many evenings Strauss spent listening to Vatke play the piano or engaging him in earnest philosophical conversation while strolling through the Tiergarten. They dis-

11. Strauss, *Gesammelte Schriften*, 10:224.

cussed their ideas openly and thought for a while of founding a journal: intellectually and personally they formed a close friendship.[12] Vatke was preparing a study of the Old Testament—it appeared in the same year as Strauss's *Life of Jesus* —in which he criticized the traditional accounts recorded there and consigned the early history to myths and legends of later origin, a study in which he devoted his attention, as an Hegelian, to the mental development and religious consciousness of the Jews.[13] Strauss watched with growing interest his friend's study of myth in the Old Testament and, before leaving Berlin in 1832, shared with him his own hope to write a "life of Jesus conformable to *my* idea." [14]

Strauss had recorded his intention of writing a life of Jesus as early as February, 1832, and had given suggestions of a developing interest in that direction as early as January, 1831.[15] At that time Strauss had not abandoned the Christianity he had dedicated his life to preaching. With hindsight later he believed that he reached his first step to the rejection of Christianity in 1828, when he became aware that he no longer believed in the resurrection of the dead.[16] But that was hindsight, not awareness. The actual course by which he renounced Christianity was gradual and imperceptible, a gentle process that, as Strauss himself recalled, "surprises and masters the individual without his being able to guard himself against it." [17] Like all the Young Hegelians, Strauss passed from belief to unbelief gradually, without a crisis, without agony. He

12. Heinrich Benecke, *Wilhelm Vatke in seinem Leben und seinen Schriften,* pp. 71–80.

13. See Wilhelm Vatke, *Die Religion des alten Testamentes* (Berlin, 1835).

14. Recorded in Benecke, 75. Italics in the original.

15. Strauss to Märklin, 6 February 1832, *Ausgewählte Briefe,* ed. Eduard Zeller (Bonn, 1895), pp. 12–15; and Strauss to Georgii, *Briefe von David Friedrich Strauss an L. Georgii,* 1 January 1831 (Tübingen, 1912), p. 4.

16. Strauss to Vischer, 8 February 1838, *Ausgewählte Briefe,* pp. 51–52. Cf. Vischer, *Kritische Gänge,* 1:98.

17. *Das Leben Jesu kritisch bearbeitet* (Tübingen, 1835–36), 2:744.

could give his tears to many things, but not to the passing of his faith.

In May, 1832, Strauss began lecturing in theology at the University of Tübingen and working on his study of Jesus. He could not, however, refrain from transcending the limits of theology in order to explain his new integration of philosophy, theology, and criticism. More and more his lectures became philosophical discourses until he brought down on his own podium the embittered fury of the philosophical faculty, which had him censured by the university senate and sent a protest against his views to the Württemberg government.[18] Strauss's answer to these attacks was his publication of his *Life of Jesus* in 1835, his synthesis of theology, biblical scholarship, and Hegelian philosophy.

The first volume of his *Life of Jesus* appeared in 1835, the second in 1836. In the publication—Strauss himself later described it, not without a touch of pride, as "epoch-making" [19] —he failed to accomplish his initial intentions. In his original plans he had intended to divide his study into three parts, a division that demonstrated his indebtedness to the Hegelian logic. The first part was to be a study of the naive or traditional view of Jesus as found in the evangelists, the second a negative or critical analysis that would reject the historical record of Jesus, the third a speculative or philosophical reconstruction of what had been destroyed. In the work he published in 1835–1836, he abandoned the first part altogether, reduced the third part to a mere supplement, and enlarged the second part—the critical and negative analysis—to the point where it was, in fact, the entire book.[20] Strauss hoped that the addition of the phrase *kritisch bearbeitet* ("critically

18. Ziegler, *David Friedrich Strauss*, 1:107–23.
19. "Literarische Denkwürdigkeiten," *Gesammelte Schriften*, 1:5.
20. Strauss, *Streitschriften zur Vertheidigung meiner Schrift über das Leben Jesu und zur Charakteristik der gegenwärtigen Theologie* 3:59–60. Cf. Karl Barth, *Die protestantische Theologie im 19. Jahrhundert* (Zürich, 1947), pp. 493–94. See also Strauss to Märklin, 6 February 1832, *Ausgewählte Briefe*, pp. 12–15, where he outlined his original intentions.

treated") to the title would indicate his intentions and save him from any charges of being too negative in his conclusions. His hope was summarily dashed. As he failed to write the positive reconstruction that he promised, as he offered to the world nothing beyond the critique, he had no effective response to the scholars who condemned him for his negative conclusions. His old teacher, F. C. Baur, spoke for a cluster of leading scholars, when he concluded that the book was "entirely too negative a criticism." [21]

In his *Life of Jesus,* Strauss sought to demonstrate two propositions. The first was the significant function that myth had in the gospels, in the stories of Jesus, in the origins of Christianity. The second was the confirmation of a christology that regarded all mankind—not just one figure, Jesus—as the union of divine and human natures.

Strauss intended to discover the degree to which the historical basis of the gospels could be accepted. He was dissatisfied with the explanations of the supernaturalists, who saw the divine hand in every event recorded in the gospels, and the rationalists, who sought to explain all events as the result of natural phenomena. He would consider the gospels from "the new point of view" which "is the mythical." [22] His work, then, was a criticism not of the gospels but of the events recorded in the gospels: he made no attempt to examine his sources, to determine the priority of the gospels or their mutual dependence, to establish the originality or authorship of each. His interest was to determine whether the recorded events could be accepted as real events in the light of the laws of nature and logic, whether parallel reports were compatible, whether an event could be accounted for as a later poetic discourse. [23]

21. Baur to Heyd, 10 February 1836, in Wilhelm Lang, "Ferdinand Baur und David Friedrich Strauss," *Preussische Jahrbücher* 160 (1915): 484.
22. *Leben Jesu,* 1:iv.
23. Cf. Barth, *Protestantische Theologie,* pp. 506–08.

He began his discussion of myth in the New Testament by setting up criteria to judge the reality of recorded events that would deny the possibility of miracles. If a reported event contradicted natural laws, it could not have taken place; if it was irreconcilable with what we know could have happened, it could not be an historical fact. But Strauss did not conclude, as did Thomas Woolston, the English deist of the previous century, that an impossible event was a conscious imposture. Rather, he said it was a myth.

Some scholars have charged that Strauss applied strict scientific method and a positivist spirit in his investigation, thus establishing scientific criteria that would disallow the possibility of miracle even before he looked at the supposed miraculous event. His positivist assumptions, they argue, obliged him to invoke the prestige of science and hence apply scientific procedure to a realm distinct from science. The result was a prejudiced case from the start.[24] Perhaps it is fair to assert that Strauss's criteria prevented him from allowing the possibility of a miracle, but it is wrong to see his assumptions as positivist, to see them as other than the results of his acceptance of the Hegelian philosophy and the theology of immanence. The significance of Hegel's philosophy for traditional Christianity has already been discussed, but a few points should be emphasized here. Strauss's accepting the doctrine of divine immanence meant rejecting the possibility of miracle in any traditional sense. Nature and supernature were not distinct, but one. How, then, could there be a supernatural imposition in the natural order? Whoever saw one, whoever accepted some isolated expression of divine intervention was, unhappily, deluded by the dualist error that saw God apart from creation. For Schleiermacher had explained that "every finite thing . . .

24. See R. G. Collingwood, *The Idea of History* (Oxford, 1951), pp. 135–36; and Christian Hartlich and Walter Sachs, *Der Ursprung des Mythosbegriffes in der modernen Bibelwissenschaft* (Tübingen, 1952), pp. 121–47.

is a sign of the Infinite." [25] There need be no miracles to show divine presence, for all was God: "miracle is only the religious name for the event." [26] It is in this context, not that of positivism, that Strauss's assumptions must be viewed. His philosophical view that all reality is the development of the immanent divine spirit allowed for no miraculous divine intervention in the traditional Christian sense. The rejection of miracles stemmed from his idealism, not from positivism. The gospel stories, then, that had traditionally been viewed as miracles were for Strauss myths. By myth he did not mean an intentional imposture, a conscious fabrication, or even a purposeful exaggeration of an historical occurrence. Myth, rather, was an imaginative representation, a symbol, not for an actual fact, but for a state of mind, an inner experience, a religious emotion. Myths were the poetry of an entire people inspired by philosophical experience or religious sentiment to express, unconsciously and spontaneously, in a concrete form the truth inherent in these experiences and sentiments. A myth was not the product of a single, artistic consciousness, but of "the spirit of a people or a community." [27] The form of the gospel narratives was that of myth, myth created in the consciousness of the early Christian community; not intentional fiction, but the folk lore of a community.

Myth contained truth, but as truth was vibrant and developing, no myth was to be preserved beyond the time for which it was composed. As a time-bound expression of a momentary truth, as a symbolic representation of truth in the process of development, a myth had meaning only for the time and place of its origin; it was, after all, "only a direct reference to circumstances of the time." [28] The mythical expression of mo-

25. Friedrich Schleiermacher, *On Religion: Speeches to its Cultured Despisers,* tr. John Oman (New York, 1958), p. 88.
26. Ibid.
27. *Leben Jesu,* 1:52.
28. *Leben Jesu,* 1:151.

mentary truth tells us about the stage of development, the mental condition of the time in which it originated. Strauss exulted that in modern times myth was no longer necessary because of the advanced stage of progress, because men had learned to distinguish history from poetry and fact from fable, because philosophy had contradicted the old recorded experiences. The new age was at hand.

In the light of the rejection of myth, Strauss analyzed the life of Jesus from his conception, birth, and early life to public ministry, death, and resurrection. He pointed out internal contradictions in the gospels, he rejected miraculous events as impossible. He concluded with the impossibility of accepting the gospel stories as historical records. Each of the recorded events was mythical.

Strauss saw two sources for the myths surrounding Jesus. The first was the messianic expectation in the mind of the Jews, independent of Jesus but applied to him after his death. The second was the penetrating impression left on his contemporaries by Jesus, an impression that inspired myths about him. The combination of these two, centered on the person of Jesus, accounted for the myths created in the mind of the early Christian community, the events and sayings attributed to Jesus. About Jesus as an historical person, however, we can know very little indeed, Strauss said, because we know him only through the myths created about him. In this way Strauss combined the scholarly interest in myth with the critical method of biblical exegesis.

Though the assignment of all the events associated with Jesus to the realm of myth might seem devastating to Christianity, Strauss insisted that "the inner core of Christian faith is independent of [my] criticism." [29] He was not attacking Christianity, he was attacking the perpetuation of the historical forms in which Christian truth was expressed centuries ago. The gospel stories were time-bound, symbols to convey truth to a primitive people; they were not to be kept as historical

29. *Leben Jesu,* 1:vii.

facts or eternal verities. By applying philosophical and historical criticism to the gospels, Strauss sought to reject the myths and portray the truth contained in those myths. For "the mythical interpretation," though it sacrifices "the historical body of such narratives, liberates and preserves the idea that resides in them, the idea that is alone their spirit and their heart." [30]

What was the idea, the truth encrusted and concealed by the myths of the Christian community? The answer for Strauss, as for all the Young Hegelians, was that the great truth of Christianity was the doctrine of the union of divine and human natures, the destruction of the dualism between man and spirit. The Christian revolution repudiated the Judaic idea of the total otherness of God: in the person of Jesus the divine and human spirits were combined, the alienation of spirit from man was ended. Since he had destroyed the historical basis of Christianity, Strauss turned to a positive reconstruction that would establish philosophically the truth of the union of divine and human natures. "At the conclusion of the criticism of the history of Jesus," he wrote, "the problem emerges to re-establish dogmatically what criticism has destroyed." [31] A christology in which the union of divine and human spirits took place in the entire human race was his dogmatic reconstruction.

Strauss argued that Jesus taught the revolutionary doctrine of the union of divine and human natures, but mankind failed to keep apace of the continuing revolution. Because of the myths associated with Jesus, mankind deified him, preserved the alienation of spirit by stressing and worshipping his uniqueness. The great error—and to the Young Hegelians this error was now clearly the chief heresy of religion—was the continued alienation of spirit from man. In worshipping Jesus, man alienated from himself his true spirit, objectified it in one person, and was then victimized by it: man, unknowingly,

30. *Leben Jesu*, 2:274.
31. *Leben Jesu*, 2:686.

was worshipping himself, his own spirit, his own image. For in the person of Jesus, "the consciousness of the human spirit is objectified as divine." [32] Since all mankind was the divine and human union, to accept a unique expression of the union was wrong. "If God is spirit," Strauss wrote, "it follows, since man is also spirit, that the two are not different . . . . The true and real existence of spirit is, then, neither God in himself, nor man in himself—it is the God-man." [33] Young Hegelian humanism meant that God and man were the same.

For Strauss the union of God and man took place in the total human race, not in one individual. The key to his christology was that "as the subject of the proposition that the church assigns to Christ, we place an idea rather than an individual." [34] The idea pervaded humanity:

> . . . it does not squander its fullness on one individual in order to be stingy to everybody else. Its desire, rather, is to distribute its wealth among the multiplicity of individuals . . . . Is not the idea of the unity of divine and human natures a real one in a more lofty sense when I regard the entire human race as its realization than if I select one man as its realization? Is not the incarnation of God from eternity more true than an incarnation limited to one point in time? [35]

As there could be no man without God, so there could be no God without man. Humanity was the Christ.

What was the individual then to do? Certainly not worship Jesus as the Christ. To do that would be to accept the alienation of man from himself. The individual had to have faith in the real Christ, humanity. To achieve salvation, each individual had consciously to participate in the life of humanity: by "nurturing within himself the idea of humanity, the . . . individual participates in the divine-human life of the race." [36]

32. Strauss to Märklin, 6 February 1832, *Ausgewählte Briefe*, p. 14.
33. *Leben Jesu*, 2:729–30.
34. *Leben Jesu*, 2:734.
35. Ibid.
36. *Leben Jesu*, 2:735.

By that participation and that sharing, the alienation of man from himself was ended and a great moment in the life of the spirit begun. It is important here to mention Strauss's own awareness of his debt to Hegel. "My critique of the life of Jesus," he wrote in angry response to an attack from the right-wing Hegelians, "stands in a close, inner relationship in its origins to the Hegelian philosophy."[37] True, he admitted, Hegel was no friend of historical criticism. Hegel did, however, distinguish between the absolute content of Christianity and the various representations of that content in different historical periods. Strauss concluded that the events recorded in the gospels were representations, not part of the absolute content of Christianity. To strike down these representations, then, was really to reveal the content, the truth of Christianity. "A critique, such as mine, that sorts out the untrue and the unhistorical" consequently served an important philosophical function.[38] His historical study served the cause of the Hegelian philosophy by pointing out Christianity as the absolute religion.

Strauss believed that his criticism demonstrated the impossibility of accepting any longer a unique and individual Christ. His positive reconstruction was to show the next stage in development—humanity as Christ, the Young Hegelian apocalypse. He believed his times demanded a new presentation of truth, and he determined to keep his theological post in order to preach the new presentation. Unlike the hero of Mrs. Ward's popular Victorian novel, *Robert Elsmere,* Strauss wanted to stay within the church where he would preach the truths, not the myths, of Christianity.[39]

The orthodox within the church had different ideas. The Prussian government might decide not to ban Strauss's *Life of Jesus,* but his academic colleagues were far less tolerant. Hengstenberg, leader of the orthodox party in Berlin and un-

37. *Streitschriften,* 3:57.
38. *Streitschriften,* 3:63.
39. Cf. *Leben Jesu,* 2:741–44.

compromising opponent of rationalism and the Hegelian philosophy, was jubilant over Strauss's book for to him it was a dramatic indictment of the consequences of scientific theology and the Hegelian philosophy.[40] Strauss's colleagues on the theological faculty of Tübingen, long unfriendly to him, publicly abused him. The Württemberg Council of Education inquired from him whether he could in sincerity hold a position as lecturer in theology when he rejected the historical grounds of the Christian religion. Dissatisfied with his answer and encouraged by the Tübingen faculty, the government removed him from his academic post and assigned him to the lyceum in his native Ludwigsburg. Strauss resigned from the new post, however, in 1836, and retired to Stuttgart to prepare a second edition of his *Life of Jesus* and to compose an answer to his critics.[41]

Seeing the opposition to his work, especially the criticisms by such eminent scholars as De Wette, Neander, and his old teacher, Baur, Strauss decided to make concessions in his new edition of his *Life of Jesus.* He published this new edition in 1837 and, in the same year, brought forth his answer to some of the attacks made upon his work in his *Polemical Treatises in Defense of my Book on the Life of Jesus.*

The third edition of his *Life of Jesus,* published in 1838, made even greater concessions.[42] In this, as in the second edition, Strauss sought to accommodate the suggestions of Baur, the one man whose criticism seemed to trouble him.[43] His chief concession in the third edition was to question his own rejection of the gospel of John as unauthentic. He apparently did not realize the seriousness of this concession: if the report of John was authentic, it was the report of an eye-

40. Theobald Ziegler, *Die geistigen und socialen Strömungen des neunzehnten Jahrhunderts* (Berlin, 1879), p. 198.

41. Ziegler, *David Friedrich Strauss,* 1:231–34.

42. See Strauss's *Gesammelte Schriften,* 1:4–8, for his own discussion of his concessions.

43. Lang, "Ferdinand Baur und David Friedrich Strauss," pp. 487–88.

witness and, hence, a record of historical facts. Strauss was later to recognize and regret the damaging effect of this concession.

In the meantime, Strauss, owing to the influence of his friend Vischer and his own seeming willingness to retreat from the strong criticisms he had made of the historical origins of Christianity, was offered a chair of theology at the University of Zürich. Immediately upon his acceptance of the offer, wild agitation broke out in Zürich against his appointment. The people, stirred by their ministers, were joined by academics and theologians. The government was unable to effect any compromise and it had to retire Strauss with a pension before he ever occupied the chair.[44] His dreams of a teaching career were once more frustrated.

Strauss was sorely disappoinnted at the events in Zürich,[45] and, in his disappointment, he turned his mind, sharpened and embittered by the recent controversy, to three things: the fourth edition of his *Life of Jesus,* a new study of Christian dogma, and formal alliance with the other Young Hegelians.

In the fourth edition of his *Life of Jesus,* Strauss withdrew all of his previous concessions, returning nearly to "the reading of the first edition." He had, he felt, made too many retreats, shown too much compliance.[46] Some of his critics have argued that throughout his career he was willing to shear his opinions, to temporize if he could be assured of academic appointment.[47] He retreated from extremism while being considered for the Zürich position. Once rejected, he lashed out indignantly at Christianity with his old fervor. Throughout his career Strauss strove above all for respectability; he was a radical in spite of himself, in spite of his personality. His re-

44. For a description of events in Zürich, with documents, see Friedrich Vogel, *Memorabilia Tigurina oder Chronik der Stadt und Landschaft Zürich* (Zürich, 1841), pp. 443 ff.

45. Strauss to Vischer, 16 March 1839, *Ausgewählte Briefe,* pp. 82–83.

46. *Gesammelte Schriften,* 1:8.

47. See, for example, Barth, *Protestantische Theologie,* pp. 494–95.

spectability was exactly what frightened the orthodox theologians who were less fearful of bohemian apostates. One of his opponents wrote that Strauss "is perhaps the most dangerous of all living enemies of Christianity because he . . . has a charming personality and leads a faultless middle-class life." [48] Strauss's great strength, however—his respectability—was also a great weakness: it led often to a desire to conform, to strike at religion only at the easiest moments, to justify again and again his abandonment of theology, to bewail his treatment at the hands of the orthodox. He seemed haunted by the need of proclaiming his own sincerity.

If the fourth edition of his *Life of Jesus* was not enough to show his return to his original opposition to Christianity, his *The Christian Doctrine in its Historical Development and in its Conflict with Modern Knowledge,* published in 1840–1841, presented more dramatic evidence. This work was a critical study of Christian dogma. In it he followed the same pattern as he did in his *Life of Jesus:* a study of the traditional church teaching, an analysis of the critical dissolution of this teaching by philosophy, and a positive reconstruction of dogma based on modern philosophy. Here, as in his *Life of Jesus,* the weakness was in the proposed reconstruction, which never fulfilled its promise and left the work with a negative tone and result.

The Christian Doctrine was an historical study that attempted to show how faith was destroyed in the progress of thought, how faith was replaced by knowledge and religion by philosophy. The historical study of dogma, then, was the study of its decline, its dissolution ending in its bankruptcy. "The true criticism of dogma," Strauss wrote, "is its history." [49] If the historical circumstances that determined the form of a particular dogma could be explained, then dogma could be freed from its historical casing and its basic truth revealed. Dogma

48. Friedrich Perthes, *Leben,* 3:446.

49. *Die christliche Glaubenslehre in ihre geschichtlichen Entwicklung und im Kampfe mit der modernen Wissenschaft* (Tübingen and Stuttgart, 1840–41), 1:71.

must be ruthlessly tested by modern philosophy in order to destroy what was no longer fit for the modern world. Times had changed; thought had progressed beyond the old historical formulation of dogma. The old formulation, true for the time and place in which it appeared, was no longer true and had to be effaced. The task for contemporary theology, then, was to analyze dogma historically and reject what was no longer true, for theology's "calling in the present time consists of pulling down a structure that no longer fits the blueprints of a new world." [50] "Theology," he concluded, "is only productive in so far as it is destructive." [51] Here, as in his *Life of Jesus,* Strauss was proclaiming the time-bound nature of truth, historicism. It was not history, but what history could teach in a critical sense that interested him. "The method I use," he wrote to Baur, "employs history only as a means to a dogmatic, *i. e.,* anti-dogmatic end." [52]

If Christian dogma could be explained away as the historical representation of some truth, what truth could be discovered at its core? The essential truth, Strauss argued, that lay behind Christian dogma was that the union of divine and human spirits took place in all of humanity throughout all of time. The union was wrongly viewed as having occurred in one person at one moment in history. It was really a continuous historical process in which humanity became more and more the incarnate God, the Christ, the union of the two natures.[53] Strauss's philosophical humanism was the result of seeing hu-

50. *Die christliche Glaubenslehre,* 2:624.

51. *Ibid.* It is interesting to compare Strauss's view of the history of dogma with that of F. C. Baur, who argued that dogma developed continually toward greater truth and that, hence, the historical study of dogma was the study of its progress and truth, not its decline. See Lang, "Ferdinand Baur und David Friedrich Strauss," pp. 503–04.

52. Strauss to Baur, 17 November 1846, in Lang, p. 126. Cf. Strauss to Märklin, 22 July 1846, *Ausgewählte Briefe,* p. 183; "I am not an historian; with me everything has proceeded from dogmatic (or, rather, anti-dogmatic) concerns . . . ."

53. *Die christliche Glaubenslehre,* 2:22–240.

manity as divine, of his seeing the divine spirit finding its
personality only in human history:

> So this earth is no longer a vale of tears through which man
> wanders towards a goal that exists in a future heaven. But the
> riches of divine life are to be realized right here and now, for
> every moment of earthly life pulsates within the womb of the
> divine.[54]

Strauss was able to write this book because he had broken
with theology, in its traditional sense, and with a tenet of Hegel's.[55] Hegel identified the agreement between the content of
religion and the content of philosophy, but Strauss now separated them and wrote of their opposition. Any possible reconciliation of religion and philosophy was a baleful illusion.
Strauss broke with theology because to him the Hegelian philosophy taught the impossibility of personal immortality and
explained the evangelical stories as myths.[56] He believed he
was now in disagreement with Hegel over one point—whether
religion and philosophy could be equated.

Strauss's rejection of the identification of religion and philosophy indicated his third important activity following publication of the *Life of Jesus:* his formal union with the Young
Hegelians. By his own admission, he rejected the identification
of the contents of religion and philosophy under the influence
of "the left wing of the young generation of philosophers
stimulated by Hegel." [57] The most important influence in that
direction came from Feuerbach. Strauss was always willing to
admit Feuerbach's influence on him, an influence that tem-
pered his view of Hegel:

> Feuerbach, I will now say, has broken the double yoke in which,
> according to Hegel's philosophy, philosophy and theology pro-

54. *Die christliche Glaubenslehre,* 1:68.
55. Cf., Ziegler, *David Friedrich Strauss,* 2:335–38.
56. *Die christliche Glaubenslehre,* 1:3.
57. *Die christliche Glaubenslehre,* 1:16.

ceed. He has shown that religion and philosophy do not have the same content and even have distinct forms.[58]

Feuerbach rescued him from the tyranny of theology, and he now understandingly regarded religion as "only a necessary frailty in human nature." [59]

Early in 1837 Arnold Ruge corresponded with Strauss about contributing to the *Hallische Jahrbücher;* Strauss agreed that Ruge's publication was "important in the interests of free investigation" and expressed his interest.[60] Ruge visited him in Württemberg in 1838 and induced him to write an article on Schleiermacher for the journal. From then on he published frequent articles in it on theology, anthropology, criticism, and aesthetics, generally restating the result of his previous work. He brought most of his essays together in book form as *Characteristics and Critiques,* published in 1839.[61] For a while he was happy writing for the Young Hegelian journal: it encouraged "free, scientific investigation," it was "free not only from authority and cant, but even more from philosophical formalism." [62] His happiness, however, was momentary. He soon became disillusioned with the journal and its editors, especially as the journal became politically more radical and philosophically the mouthpiece for the views of Feuerbach and Bauer. As these tendencies accelerated, Strauss decided to sever his connections with the journal and dissolve his formal connections with the Young Hegelians. By early December, 1841, he had done both.

Strauss terminated his connections with the Young Hegelians for several reasons. The chemistry of personality pre-

58. *Gesammelte Schriften,* 5:181.
59. *Gesammelte Schriften,* 1:14.
60. Strauss to Binder, 8–10 February 1837, in Theobald Ziegler, "Zur Biographie von D. F. Strauss," *Deutsche Revue* 30 (1905):100.
61. *Gesammelte Schriften,* 1:14. Cf. Kohut, *Strauss als Denker und Erzieher,* p. 31.
62. Strauss to Georgii, 24 December 1838, *Briefe von Strauss an Georgii,* p. 25.

vented him from being close, in any truly human sense, to any of the Young Hegelians except his old friend, Vischer. He bore a tenacious personal hatred for Bruno Bauer, and, as Bauer's views seemed to grow more important within the party and on the journal, Strauss turned from both. "I will explain to Ruge at the most favorable moment that I can no longer cooperate in the *Jahrbücher*," he confided to Vischer in 1841; "the relationship I have had with Bruno Bauer and others prohibits my remaining connected with it any longer." [63] In addition to the personal element, Strauss could not abide the radical tendencies that began to dominate the journal. He had a lofty disdain for the democracy that Ruge favored. Moreover, the journal began preaching a radical philosophical position that went far beyond Strauss: it "surrendered passionately to the tendencies of Feuerbach and Bruno Bauer, and its swift pace made me look like a laggard." [64] Strauss would become no more radical, he would abandon the Young Hegelians as they moved farther to extremes. He never wanted the title of a radical, he only wanted to be respectable and have an academic post. Even in 1835 he was furious at being called a radical, and he blamed his treatment on "that confounded Young Germany, with whose novels and miscellany my book is thrown into the same category." [65] In the rapid intellectual thaw in Germany in the 1830s and 1840s, the early radical was soon the late conservative.

During the troubled years of his brief marriage to an opera star, the years prior to the Revolution of 1848, Strauss's literary output was almost nothing. When news of the revolution in France reached him, he expressed an honest, though fleeting, joy, for "after all, these events are only the fulfillment of our most youthful wishes, of our inmost thoughts." [66] Perhaps the

63. Strauss to Vischer, 13 November 1841, *Ausgewählte Briefe*, p. 112.
64. *Gesammelte Schriften*, 1:14.
65. Strauss to Georgii, 12 December 1835, *Briefe von Strauss an Georgii*, p. 13.
66. Strauss to Rapp, 29 February 1848, *Ausgewählte Briefe*, p. 204.

revolution was the first sign of the coming Young Hegelian apocalypse. Once the revolution broke out in Germany, however, Strauss lost that fleeting enthusiasm and began to assume the habit of an Olympian Goethe who, in artistic loftiness, could gaze down in reserved disdain on mass movements. "The revolutionary principle is hostile to intellectual excellence," he wrote,[67] and to his old friend Vischer he revealed his soul:

> A nature such as mine was happier under the old police state, when at least order reigned in the streets . . . . In society one could speak of literature and art . . . , but this is no longer possible. . . . Towards this outpouring of the spirit on every lad and maid, towards this wisdom from the gutter, I can only adopt an attitude of bitter irony and scorn. "Odi profanum vulgus et arceo" is and will remain my motto.[68]

Strauss had the posture of a cultural aristocrat: he hated mob agitation and popular movements, he feared that democracy meant the end of culture.

For all his protests that he wished to stay aloof from the revolution, Strauss could not escape it. The people turned naturally to the cultural and intellectual community of Germany for leadership, and Strauss was part of that community. Some of his friends in his native Ludwigsburg persuaded him to be a candidate for the National Assembly from the district, overcoming his reluctance.[69] As soon as Strauss appeared as a candidate, the old religious issues were brought up again: the issues that kept him from an academic post were thrown up in an effort to keep him from a political one. Pietism and orthodoxy were strong in the district, and wide-

67. Strauss to Rapp, 3 April 1848, *Ausgewählte Briefe*, p. 206.

68. Strauss to Vischer, 13 April 1848, *Briefwechsel zwischen Strauss und Vischer*, 1:213.

69. For the story of the election and subsequent events, see R. Krauss, "D. Fr. Strauss im Jahre 1848," *Württembergische Vierteljahrshefte für Landesgeschichte* 18 (1909):161–72.

spread opposition to his candidacy appeared among the electorate. Interestingly enough, the conservative religious opposition to Strauss brought to his support all the liberals and radicals, with whose political views Strauss disagreed completely. He made six important speeches to the electorate on his political views, announcing that he stood for a constitutional monarchy, not a republic; for national unity, even above civil liberties; for the unification of Germany as a confederation of states led by Prussia. Here was his political program for the Young Hegelians apocalypse. Over and over he argued that, as he was seeking a political office, his religious views should not be considered. The protest did not help him; he could not separate himself from his reputation. The election was a decisive defeat for Strauss.[70] His native town, however, did not forget him—it elected him to serve in the Württemberg Landtag, to him "a role that even at the time seemed an odious one." [71]

Strauss was not a successful politician. He attended the sessions of the Landtag, but parties and majority rule meant little to him; his aristocratic temperament scorned the proceedings. He moved farther to the right as the assembly's mood moved farther to the left. The denouement of his political career came on November 16, 1848, when he refused to harmonize with the lament that rose from liberal throats over the execution in Vienna of Robert Blum, a liberal leader in the National Assembly. He had no sympathy for Blum, and asked whether Germany had to accept Blum's liberal ideas merely because he had become a martyr.[72] Recalling how a marauding mob had put to death two conservative leaders, he cried: "If the shot into the heart of Robert Blum was a shot into the heart of German freedom, was it not this very same German

70. Krauss, pp. 162–65.

71. Strauss to Vischer, 24 February 1849, *Briefwechsel zwischen Strauss und Vischer*, 1:223.

72. Strauss's speech is reprinted in Hausrath, *Strauss und Theologie*, vol. 2, appendix 2, pp. 4–6.

freedom that has torn Auerswald and Lichnowsky to pieces?" [73]
Strauss's friends were perplexed by his attitude, his electorate
angered. They should not have been surprised. Strauss defended his independence as a delegate and shortly thereafter
resigned from the Landtag. He deserted the revolution physically as he had, from the beginning, deserted it spiritually. He
only paused to turn and shake his fist at the entire episode:

> Present-day politics arouse my absolute repugnance to every-
> thing suggestive of revolution and the liberated mob . . . . Un-
> der Russian despotism I could still exist, though with clipped
> wings; but mob rule would destroy me. And I hate everything
> that leads to mob rule, hate as I have never hated before . . . .[74]

What Strauss claimed to have learned was that a man of letters
and culture could not be a politician. Politics, mob rule, democracy meant the end of culture.

Strauss had few dreams left now. His academic career was
long dead, his marriage dissolved, his colleagues drifted away
from him. "If he were only not so bitter and blasé about
everything," Vischer wrote at the time, "about the human
race . . . , and about history; and if he would only write
something." [75] Strauss soon fulfilled Vischer's wish and turned
to publication. Publication had made his reputation, perhaps
it could restore it.

Strauss became interested in biography and published several works—biographies of Schubart, Märklin, Ulrich von
Hutten, Reimarus, Voltaire, Frischlin.[76] The focus of attention here, however, is Strauss the Young Hegelian, and within

73. Hausrath, p. 6.
74. Strauss to Vischer, 14 February 1849, *Briefwechsel zwischen Strauss
und Vischer*, 1:224.
75. Vischer to Rapp, Autumn, 1852, *Briefwechsel zwischen Strauss und
Vischer*, 2:43.
76. For Strauss's scholarship during these years, see Ziegler, *David
Friedrich Strauss*, 2:488–570.

this focus there were three important episodes in his later life: his publication of a new study of Jesus's life, his support of Bismarck's Prussia, and the positive statement of his philosophy that he had promised long before.

There were many reasons why Strauss, after twenty years, turned to writing theology once more. The most important, however, was that the Christianity whose obsoleteness he had demonstrated to his own satisfaction years before was still thriving. He had to strike out at Christianity once again, to knock over the lifeless idol: like Renan, he would write a popular study of the life of Jesus directed to the people. His earlier works had been written for theologians, now he would bring the truth directly to the people he had scorned during the revolution. "We must address the people," he proclaimed, "since the theologians will not listen." [77] The result of his determination was *The Life of Jesus Adapted for the German People,* published in 1864.

His popular study of Jesus contained nothing new; it restated his original views. He argued that there was an historical Jesus; but Jesus was not God, he was only a man who envisaged an ideal humanity and urged others to achieve it, a human personality who sought to improve mankind. Strauss insisted upon viewing the life of Jesus "exclusively from a human point of view." [78] The gospels did not portray the historical Jesus, for they were rife with miracles everyone knew could not happen. The accounts were written long after Jesus's death, and during the interval many unhistorical elements entered; they were myths born from the supposition that Jesus was the messiah, myths that represented the level of religious understanding of the time in which the gospels were written. These myths have made the real Jesus inaccessible to us, and it has been the function of criticism to remove these symbols in an effort to approach the historical reality, to separate the

77. *Das Leben Jesu für das deutsche Volk bearbeitet* (Leipzig, 1864), p. xii.
78. *Leben Jesu für das Volk,* p. 202.

myth "from the object of study and make an historical view of the life of Jesus possible." [79]

The Jesus Strauss portrayed was a man about whom little was known except that he had an ideal vision of improving mankind. Strauss urged that Jesus not be accepted as God but as a reformer upon whose ideas and insights subsequent generations must build and improve, one of many human reformers who have sought to better mankind.[80] The ultimate message of Jesus—and this was the great truth of Christianity once the mythical accretions were pried loose—was the religion of humanism, the acceptance of mankind as divine. Strauss summoned everyone to the task of "carrying forward the religion of Christ to the religion of humanity, a process to which all the noble efforts of our time are directed." [81] Since Christianity had become obsolete, humanism must replace it.

Strauss settled back to await popular acclaim for his new book. It never came. This book never achieved the popularity of Renan's work, or even the notoriety of Strauss's first *Life of Jesus*. Besides, most people, including Strauss, were more animated by the policies of Bismarck and the politics of German unification than by theological debate.

Strauss, long silent on politics, spoke out, as he did in 1848, for Prussia in the period of unification. In 1863 he wrote to Vischer insisting that Prussia had to lead German unification, for Austria excluded itself from that role because of its Catholicism.[82] He was pleased that Frederick William IV, the modern Julian the Apostate, was replaced on the Prussian throne by William. This change, he felt, inaugurated a new era in which Prussia would recognize and fulfill its obligations. The war with Austria in 1866 and the policies of Bismarck Strauss applauded with great vigor. "I hate Austria," he as-

79. *Leben Jesu für das Volk*, p. 146.
80. *Leben Jesu für das Volk*, pp. 625–27.
81. *Leben Jesu für das Volk*, p. 625.
82. Strauss to Vischer, 17 June 1863, *Briefwechsel zwischen Strauss und Vischer*, 2:180–81.

serted. "My hope for Germany rests on Prussia; Germany will be saved by Prussia, or not at all." [83] Germany was in such a hazardous condition that its despair could only be cured by force. The events of 1848 showed that the force could not come from below; it had to come from above. Prussia had begun the cure, but by 1866 it was only half done. Strauss urged Prussia to complete the job. In an essay in the *Preussische Jahrbücher,* he defended Prussia's historical calling in German unification and wrote admiringly of Bismarck's policies.[84] Once again he stressed the need for Prussia to complete its historical mission, to unite the non-Austrian German states under its leadership, to form "the nucleus around which the rest of Germany can cluster to form a vigorous state." [85]

When the Franco-Prussian War came in 1870, Strauss jubilantly joined the side of the Prussian legions. Was it not the moment in which Prussia was to achieve its mission of uniting Germany? Was not the Hegelian state about to be created? In a public correspondence with Renan, Strauss defended German patriotism and exalted the great idea of German unity.[86] Renan took the position that, as Strauss and he were members of the European intellectual community, they were world citizens, above the petty conflicts of national states. Strauss would have none of it; he condemned France and insisted upon its defeat as a necessity for German unification. Prussian victory, German unity were "the call of history." [87]

Strauss's defense of Prussia was predictable. Always a political conservative, he stood on the side of order and established political authority. In the Revolution of 1848, he defined the alternatives as mob rule and royal authority; not for a moment did he hesitate to champion the traditional rulers and scorn

83. Strauss to Rapp, 12 July 1866, *Ausgewählte Briefe,* p. 484.

84. "Preussen und Schwaben," *Preussische Jahrbücher* 19 (1867):186–99.

85. Strauss to Vischer, 20 September 1870, *Briefwechsel zwischen Strauss und Vischer,* 2:278.

86. See "Krieg und Friede: zwei Briefe an Ernst Renan," *Gesammelte Schriften,* 1:299–341.

87. *Gesammelte Schriften,* 1:341.

the alternative. Social order, political stability, public quiet—these were the qualities, all favorable to the cultural life he cherished, that he demanded. Prussia, more than any other state, was able to ensure stability, and Prussia had even more to offer. Germany had to be united, for without a national state the German people had no locus for the life of morality, the life of freedom, the life of reason: a state was necessary for freedom, philosophical necessity demanded it. The movement to unify Germany had to be led by one of the powerful states —certainly not Austria, for it was devoted to Catholicism, a long outmoded form of an outmoded religion. Prussia was the only candidate: it alone had the proper qualifications. During the Wars of Liberation it began the process of unification and moved, in its own organization, towards becoming a rational state and, hence, the locus of both freedom and progress. During the period of Prussian reform and in the years thereafter, Prussia progressed towards becoming a true state in the moral and rational sense, away from the old Christian domination—despite a momentary apostasy during the reign of Frederick William IV—and it was destined to continue progressing to become the true Hegelian state. Prussia, therefore, had to be the missionary of German unification. Strauss's nationalism, like his humanism, had philosophical rather than empirical origins.

With Germany unified, Strauss had one major project left—the preparation of a positive statement of his philosophical position, the positive statement he had promised, and never made, in 1836 and in 1841. He finally published his affirmative position in 1872, *The Old and the New Faith*. Fortunately the world had not waited breathlessly for his statement. Ernst Haeckel described it as "a magnificent expression of the honorable convictions of all educated people of the present time," an outstanding work by "the greatest theologian of the nineteenth century." [88] But to be called a superlative theologian by Haeckel was hardly a compliment to Strauss's theology. A

88. Ernst Haeckel, *Die Welträthsel* (Bonn, 1900), pp. 357–58.

much more critical, yet perhaps more accurate, appreciation was given by Nietzsche, who savagely attacked Strauss as a philistine, a bourgeois moralist, a worshipper of national power, a man who deceived himself into accepting a new religion, a man who had abdicated all right to be called a philosopher.[89] Perhaps justice had come full circle: the new critic attacked the old.

Shortly after the appearance of his second life of Jesus, Strauss had found his brother urging that he write a popular study that would present the modern, scientific, naturalist weltanschauung as contrasted with the old Christian world view. Strauss agreed, excited by the task of writing "a testamentary creed of the thought of our day." [90] For some time he had been concerned that the Hegelian philosophy in which he had been trained, in which lay all his assumptions, included little of the empirical science that was becoming more and more the measure and criterion of modern knowledge. To overcome this deficit, to reconcile modern science with his philosophical position, he undertook an extensive study of science and a closer look at the philosophy of Kant. Two of his closest friends, Kuno Fischer and Eduard Zeller, had already sounded the call of a return to Kant. Strauss joined them, hoping to discover, through Kant's philosophy, a reconciliation between science and philosophy. Equally important, he began to read some of the more popular works in natural science, the works of Lotze, F. A. Lange, Darwin, and Haeckel.[91] He incorporated his scientific reading into his philosophical view.

Strauss divided his *The Old and the New Faith* into four essays, each based upon a single question. The first question

89. See Nietzsche's "David Strauss, the Confessor and the Writer," in *Thoughts Out of Season, Complete Works,* vol. 4, ed. Oscar Levy, tr. Anthony Ludovici (New York, 1924):3–95.

90. *Gesammelte Schriften,* 1:61–62.

91. Heinrich Maier, *An der Grenze der Philosophie: Melancthon, Lavater, David Friedrich Strauss* (Tübingen, 1909), pp. 334–47.

was, "Are we still Christians?" His answer to the question was "no," for we have gone beyond Christianity. We can no longer believe in a personal God or a life after death; we "have long since ceased to accept the founder of Christianity as a divine being." [92] For the first time Strauss gave a public statement that he was not a Christian. After nearly forty years he had summoned up the courage to announce his position unhesitatingly, but after all that time, few really cared.

Following from his first question, Strauss's second question was, "Do we still have a religion?" His answer to this question was "yes," if religion were defined as an external force on which the individual depended. Strauss saw this force as the world, the cosmos, the great universe—the fusion of matter and spirit—towards which man had to experience a feeling of piety.

Strauss's third question followed from his answer to the second: "How do we conceive of the world?" His answer was a conglomeration of the views of Kant, Laplace, Lamarck, Darwin, and Haeckel. He portrayed a universe permeated with spirit that gave man his life—a monistic view of the cosmos. In this universe the evolutionary process worked, animating matter and evolving higher forms constantly. His view of the universe indicated his new alliance with the Kantian revival, for much of his view was influenced by the thought of the early Kant, whose *General History and Theory of the Universe* in 1775, proposed a similar cosmogony.[93] Strauss, his critics claimed, though he had begun his career as an idealist, so often followed the trend of fads that he now succumbed to popular philosophical materialism.

His final question was, "How do we order our lives?" The answer he gave—it was the answer of all the Young Hegelians —was that man was to live in accordance with the philosophy of humanism, that man was to recognize that "the present

92. *Der alte und der neue Glaube, ein Bekenntniss* (Leipzig, 1872), p. 48.

93. Ziegler, *David Friedrich Strauss*, 2:700–02.

world is . . . the true vineyard of labor for men, the sum total of all the goals towards which they strive." [94] For the first time, Strauss described what the philosophy of humanism involved. It amounted to accepting the leadership of a few gifted individuals, accepting conservative values in politics, bourgeois morality, the need for an occasional war, the nation as "divinely ordained, *i. e.,* the natural form in which humanity manifests itself." [95] Arguing that "property is an indispensable basis for morality as well as culture," he exalted the middle class, its values and achievements, its propagation of humanism.[96] The actual philosophy of humanism would be celebrated, not in any formal sense as Comte hoped, but by spending Sundays in discussing politics and art, in reading history and literature, in listening to concerts and viewing artistic creations. It was no wonder that Nietzsche attacked Strauss's work as the epitome of philistinism. Karl Barth has given a calmer, if equally critical, judgment in describing *The Old and the New Faith* as an "incoherent, journalistic conglomeration of a little Darwin, a little Goethe, a little Lessing, a little artistic criticism, and a good deal of anonymous, flatly bourgeois morality." [97] Barth's judgment seems just.

In his attack on Strauss's *The Old and the New Faith,* Nietzsche made the profound observation that Strauss was still an Hegelian.[98] Despite Strauss's apparent approach to materialism, he remained an Hegelian. Much of his interest in materialism was an attempt to synthesize science with his Hegelian philosophy. Moreover, his major emphasis in this last work, as in all his works, was his fight against dualism, against the separation of spirit and matter. The thrust of his work—and this was his essential debt to Hegel—was his monism. To him, idealism and materialism were fundamentally the same: they

94. *Der alte und der neue Glaube,* p. 75.
95. *Der alte und der neue Glaube,* p. 259.
96. *Der alte und der neue Glaube,* p. 278.
97. Barth, *Protestantische Theologie,* p. 493.
98. Nietzsche, "David Strauss," in *Complete Works,* 4:46.

were both monistic, both counter to dualism. Strauss engaged in no betrayal of idealism, experienced no passage from idealism to materialism. Throughout his career he had always maintained that there was no distinction between the spiritual and natural realms. Indeed, his scholarly efforts were nearly all directed toward showing that any acceptance of dualism was an error. A materialism that denied spirit was as unthinkable for Strauss as an idealism that denied matter. The disciple of Hegel accepted the fusion of nature and spirit in a progressive development. If, in *The Old and the New Faith*, Strauss seemed to be stressing the material universe, it was a universe, like that of Feuerbach and Marx, informed by immanent spirit, a universe that was the fusion of spirit and matter.[99] Strauss did not become a materialist, but only, as in his rejection of miracles, accepted the full implications of his Hegelian philosophy.

The Old and the New Faith proved to be Strauss's last book. Suffering from a debilitating disease, he retired to his native village and died there on February 8, 1874. As his last wish he desired to be buried without religious ceremony or benefit of clergy. There had been little of the consciously symbolic in Strauss's life, and perhaps his final gesture symbolized his defiance. If so, it was a forlorn gesture. Strauss did not falter in the face of death, but to the Europe of 1874, that steadfastness meant little indeed.

Strauss often appeared to equivocate when his respectability, his reputation, or his academic appointment was in balance. He never equivocated in facing the full responsibility of the Young Hegelian metaphysic. He knew that he must face the question of his age: the meaning of the conflict between Christianity and Hegel's philosophy. He knew also that he must employ philosophical criticism in answering the question and in demonstrating to all its meaning and significance. Most of his energy was consumed in these two efforts, delaying his necessary answer to the question that determined the future.

99. *Der alte und der neue Glaube,* pp. 207–09. Cf. Maier, *An Grenze der Philosophie,* pp. 356 ff.

That was why he earned so often the charge of engaging in mere negative criticism, a charge that was just in the light of the bulk of his efforts but unjust in the light of his ultimate concern. For Strauss saw his efforts of criticism all directed toward showing men the truth in Christianity shorn of its myth, the necessary advance to the age of philosophy, and the potential for freedom only in accepting institutions and ideas founded on the new stage of the spirit. Criticism was all directed to a positive end: defining the category of humanism and easing its necessary emergence into the world of man.

In defining humanism Strauss was answering the question that all the Young Hegelians agreed needed answering, but his answer was a private vision, different from the answers of the others. For out of his historicism he derived a new transcendent principle that gave him a calm sense of order and dignity in the face of what might otherwise be a terrifying flux of ceaseless change and relativity. It was culture—scholarship, music, literature, art, and the other creations of the elite representatives of the human spirit.

"We shall retain the beneficial achievements of Christianity, as we have retained those of Greece and Rome, without the religious form in which that kernel ripened as in its husk." [100] So Strauss once wrote in summary of his historical metaphysic. His basic concern was that humanism develop into reality, freed from the restraints of obsolete Christianity, and produce a new age of cultural creativity. Humanism for him was always philosophical, never political and social. He was always the cultural aristrocrat. He saw a humanism that would be invariably confined to the study and the drawing room, the art gallery and the lecture hall. Such, for him, would be the comforts of the new age, the age of philosophy.

100. *Der alte und der neue Glaube* (19th ed.), p. 24.

4 Feuerbach, Vischer, and the Divinity of Humanity

And the God-man is each person who rises into the idea and into whom the idea rises.

—Arnold Ruge, 1840

"The characteristic of the present century," wrote Auguste Comte in 1853, "will be the overwhelming importance it assigns to history, by the light of which philosophy, politics, and even poetry will be pursued." [1] For the Young Hegelians, Comte's description was indeed accurate. Their metaphysic, based upon Hegel's philosophy, sought the historical dimension of reality as the understanding of the past and the direction of the future.

Yet as Strauss's work on the historicity of Jesus demonstrated, it was not the specific facts, the accuracy of details, the careful and patient uncovery of the events of the past that the Young Hegelians sought. Their aim, rather, was to interpret the meaning and direction, the purpose, of history. Hegel had seen history as the dimension in which spirit progressively attained to fuller self-realization through overcoming its alienation. History had, for him, an objective and inherent meaning, the goal of freedom and reason. As his disciples, the Young Hegelians accepted the same purpose and goal of history and sought in historical events the revelation of that purpose and goal. If the meaning of history was the progressive development to freedom and reason, the overcoming of alienation, their duty as philosophers was to understand that development and put themselves in time with it.

The Old Testament prophets had seen history as the progressive revelation of God to man. The Young Hegelians, in a way, shared that view of the nature of history. For them, history was not a divine process, it was not the city of God operating separately from the worldly city of man with an occasional intersection of the two. From what they took to be Hegel's ambiguity over whether history was a sacred or a secular process, they began to develop the view that history was secular, to emphasize that the divine was fulfilled only in terms of the world of men, of human history. In human history, then, lay the way of understanding the divine, of comprehending the relationship between God and man, spirit and

1. Auguste Comte, *Système de politique positive* (Paris, 1853), 3:1.

humanity. For the Young Hegelians, the essential feature of the historical age in which they were living was that it marked the spirit's progress from religion to philosophy. Men must accept that progress in order to be free—that was the meaning of history.

Among the South German Young Hegelians, Strauss, Feuerbach, and Vischer, the meaning of divine revelation in history was manifest. History for them was the progressive union of God and man, in religion and then in philosophy, ending with the total union of divine and human natures in reason and freedom. Men must place themselves in accord with this movement of history or they could never be free—such was the necessary relationship between objective revelation and subjective response.

Even among these three thinkers there were subtle differences in the interpretation of the meaning of history that were of considerable significance to the history of the Young Hegelians. All three saw history as the progressive union of God and man, with the final goal being the total union of a divine humanity. For Strauss, in that historical process the spirit knew itself increasingly in men, and progressively overcame its alienation in terms of human history and human institutions. For Feuerbach and Vischer, however, in the historical process men knew themselves increasingly in God and achieved the progressive self-consciousness of spirit by creating representations of the divine. For Strauss history was the revelation of God through men; for Feuerbach and Vischer history was the revelation of men through God. The distinction, though subtle in its expression, was significant in governing the direction in which the Young Hegelian movement developed. From Strauss to Feuerbach and Vischer there was a subtle shift of emphasis from God to man, a shift in the nature of humanism that symbolized the direction taken by the Young Hegelians.

Of all the Young Hegelians, Feuerbach had the greatest popular reputation, yet he was personally the most retiring.

Content to remain in his study aloof from the world of passion and tumult, he happily found that his influence nonetheless permeated that world. Among those who openly declared their indebtedness to his influence were Ruge, Herwegh, Stirner, Marx, Gottfried Keller, Strauss, Engels, Richard Wagner, George Eliot. Wagner announced that he "always regarded Feuerbach as the ideal exponent of the radical release of the individual from the thralldom of accepted notions" and, in his thanks for that release, dedicated his *Artwork of the Future* to him.[2] And the poet Herwegh put his admiration for Feuerbach into verse:

> Through heaven and through hell have you
> Made your way, like the great Dante.
> Man had always spoken of the divine comedy,
> Until your understanding recognized it as human.[3]

The comparison with Dante was apt, given Feuerbach's own predilections and the influence he exerted.

Feuerbach's devotion to scholarship was almost hereditary. Born on July 28, 1804, in Landshut, Bavaria, he was the son of the famed jurist, Anselm Feuerbach. The elder Feuerbach was a teacher and writer as well as a legal philosopher. His legal philosophy, based on Kant, and his developments in the science of criminal law brought him great renown.

Young Ludwig early found his interests leading him to theology and in 1823 he entered the University of Heidelberg to begin his training as a theologian. He was impressed by the lectures of the notable theologian Karl Daub, who later became a significant figure among the Hegelians of the right; but somehow the university seemed to lack the infectious spirit that he needed. Berlin was a far more exciting place for the study of theology—Schleiermacher, Neander, Marheineke, and a host of other theologians there were an irresistible attraction for a whole generation of German students—and Feuerbach

2. Richard Wagner, *My Life* (New York, 1911), p. 522.
3. Georg Herwegh, "Seinem Ludwig Feuerbach," *Werke*, 3:155.

decided to ask his father's permission to transfer there. The elder Feuerbach agreed, though unenthusiastically, for he was uneasy about his son's studying in Prussia.

Feuerbach went to the University of Berlin in 1824 and at once became a devoted attendant at Hegel's lectures. He wrote to his father telling how he was "boundlessly happy with Hegel's lectures," but, knowing his father's complete devotion to the Kantian philosophy, he carefully promised that he would not become a disciple of Hegel.[4] The promise, however, proved worthless. As he attended more of Hegel's lectures and mingled more with students who surrendered their total loyalty to Hegel's views, he found that the Hegelian influence on him increased daily. He wrote to his father about his growing acceptance of Hegel and confessed that he could not understand how anyone could escape "the powerful influence of his profound thought."[5] Finally the inevitable moment of confession came. Feuerbach had succumbed completely to the Hegelian influence and turned from theology to philosophy. He dutifully and carefully wrote a long letter to his father in which he announced that "I can no longer study theology."[6] He realized that he was rebelling against the wishes of his father, but the demands of truth would allow him to make no compromise. "Palestine is too narrow for me," he wrote. "I must, I must go into the wide world, and only philosophy allows this latitude."[7] The elder Feuerbach was enraged and distressed by his son's decision; he felt a personal repudiation in Ludwig's rejection of his own beloved Kantian philosophy. Painfully aware that his son's "head was full of Hegelian metaphysics," he reluctantly accepted his decision.[8]

4. Feuerbach to his father, 21 April 1824, *Briefwechsel und Nachlass,* ed. Karl Grün (Leipzig and Heidelberg, 1874), 1:180.

5. Feuerbach to his father, 24 May 1824, *Briefwechsel und Nachlass,* 1:181.

6. Feuerbach to his father, 22 March 1825, *Briefwechsel und Nachlass,* 1:190.

7. *Briefwechsel und Nachlass,* 1:191.

8. Anselm Feuerbach to Feuerbach, 20 April 1825, *Briefwechsel und Nachlass,* 1:198.

In abandoning theology for philosophy under the influence of Hegel, Feuerbach followed the same road taken by all the Young Hegelians. Hegel suggested that religion and philosophy had the same subject matter, that they were both directed to an understanding of the same process. Yet when the Young Hegelians turned from theology to philosophy for insight into truth, they were admitting that philosophy was more exciting, more penetrating. By implication they were admitting that philosophy was superior to theology, that it was a higher comprehension of truth. That implication they all, sooner or later, explicitly affirmed.

One concession Feuerbach did make to his father's feelings: he agreed to leave Berlin and present himself for his degree at a Bavarian university. In 1828 he presented his dissertation to the University of Erlangen, and the dissertation showed his total acceptance of the Hegelian philosophy. So strong was that acceptance that he sent a copy of his dissertation to Hegel himself, explaining that it owed its inspiration to Hegel's philosophy.[9]

Feuerbach's dissertation, *De Ratione, una, universali, infinita,* affirmed the unity of reason and its essence as the only universal and eternal reality. Reason in his view was both one and divine, and it alone created consciousness. Like Hegel, Feuerbach saw thought as spirit, immanent spirit. Each individual was significant as an individual only insofar as he participated in the spiritual life of thought. Indeed, it was only by such participation that an individual could attain immortality, by dissolving himself in the unity of eternal reason. Spiritual life was eternal, and each individual contributing to that life—in art, science, literature, and the other expressions of human creativity—could partake of the general immortality. Even this early Feuerbach scoffed at the subjective philosophies, like Christianity, that taught a personal and individual life after death. Basing his position on Hegel's philosophy, he allowed only a general immortality of reason and saw each individual

9. Feuerbach to Hegel, 22 November 1828, *Briefwechsel und Nachlass,* 1:214–19.

as having life eternal, not as an individual, but only as he contributed to the general activity of reason. Like Strauss, Feuerbach began to move away from Christianity with the rejection of individual life after death.[10] Feuerbach stayed on at Erlangen as a teacher. He began to develop ideas inherent in his dissertation, publishing his expanded views in 1830 in *Thoughts about Death and Immortality*, where he denied personal immortality. His public renunciation of an important Christian doctrine was more than the conservative faculties could tolerate. Though he published the work anonymously, his authorship was soon discovered. He lost his teaching position and never again held an academic post.

Feuerbach's *Thoughts about Death and Immortality* publicly declared war on theology. His assault on the belief in personal immortality was, at the same time, an assault upon theology for its refusal to learn from Hegelian philosophy the impossibility of personal immortality. Limitation, the implication of all existence, in individual human terms meant that each man's life was confined to this world and to the time and place in which he lived. Feuerbach argued that the idea of personal immortality was the theological product of Protestantism and modern individualism since both, basing their entire views on the individual, had to posit a life for the individual after death. Philosophy had rendered these two positions obsolete and theology had to recognize that fact.[11]

If Feuerbach denied personal immortality, he did not deny the possibility of immortality itself. Developing what he had said in his dissertation two years before, he argued that reason, consciousness, and spirit—the spiritual life of humanity—were

10. The best studies of Feuerbach's thought are S. Rawidowicz, *Ludwig Feuerbachs Philosophie, Ursprung und Schicksal* (Berlin, 1931), and Albert Lévy, *La philosophie de Feuerbach et son influence sur la littérature allemande* (Paris, 1904). A good brief sketch of his life and thought is Friedrich Jodl, *Ludwig Feuerbach* (Stuttgart, 1904).

11. *Sämmtliche Werke*, ed. Wilhelm Bolin and Friedrich Jodl (Stuttgart, 1903–11), vol. 1, *Gedanken über Tod und Unsterblichkeit*, pp. 6–14.

immortal. The death of each individual meant entry into immortality, not as an individual but as part of these universals. Death, then, liberated the immanent spirit to burst the ephemeral limitations of finitude and join eternal reason. There was a general immortality, but not a particular one; the general was eternal, the individual relative. "Spirit, consciousness, and reason," he declared, "are your true being and essence—these are the highest, the ultimate and eternal affirmations of your existence." [12] Each individual had existence only for a particular historical moment, and his life had meaning only as it contributed to these universals.

Since each individual was "only one successive moment in the process of the spirit," each individual became immortal only by contributing to the spiritual life of humanity.[13] Contributions to art, science, and literature measured each man's contributions to immortality. Further, art, science, and literature did not share the limitations that characterized all life, for they were immortal. His message was to all men to forget the nonsense of a personal existence after death in the Christian heaven and to turn their attention to this world where they could contribute to the progress of humanity. A specific articulation of the philosophy of humanism, the fundamental position of the Young Hegelians, was already Feuerbach's concern.[14]

In this work, as in his dissertation, Feuerbach's indebtedness to Hegel was apparent. Even though Hegel's position on personal immortality may not have been explicit, his philosophy formed the assumptions on which the Young Hegelians denied an individual life after death. Hegel had taught that reason and spirit were alone eternal, that each individual was transitory and ephemeral in relation to the development of the spirit. These positions were the presuppositions for Feuer-

12. *Tod und Unsterblichkeit*, p. 64. Cf., Lévy, *La philosophie de Feuerbach*, pp. 59–65.
13. *Tod und Unsterblichkeit*, p. 77.
14. Cf. *Tod und Unsterblichkeit*, pp. 44, 69–73, 80–83.

bach's views on immortality. Hegel had affirmed an immanent spirit whose highest expression was the spiritual life of religion, art, literature; he had expounded on the *Volksgeist,* the expression of the immanent spirit in which each individual was to participate. Here was as important foundation for Feuerbach's cultural humanism. A further indication that Feuerbach's views on immortality owed their origin to Hegelian philosophy came three years later when another Hegelian, Friedrich Richter, working independently, arrived, in his *Teaching of the Last Things,* at the same conclusions that Feuerbach did.

Deprived of his academic position, Feuerbach nonetheless kept active through publication. He began a history of philosophy from Bacon to Spinoza; in 1837 he published a work on Leibniz; and in 1838 he wrote his *Pierre Bayle.* His choices reflected a deep interest in earlier philosophies of immanence and in earlier forms of religious criticism. In each of these studies he drew sharp contrasts between philosophy and theology, between immanent spirit and transcendent God. He defended pantheism and denied the possibility of God's existence apart from humanity.

One source of inspiration Feuerbach did have during these years—his happy marriage in 1837 to Bertha Löw, who was part-owner of a porcelain factory in Bruckberg. This private income assured Feuerbach of a living without the need to compromise his views for the academic world. Relieved from all financial worries, he began the period of his most important literary work: his contributions to the *Hallische Jahrbücher,* his critique of the Hegelian philosophy, and his famed *Essence of Christianity.*

Feuerbach was a frequent and important contributor to the *Hallische Jahrbücher.* Ruge tried again and again to persuade him to move to Halle to help with the editing of the journal, but Feuerbach just as persistently refused.[15] He had found his happiness living with his wife in Bruckberg apart from the

15. Jodl, *Feuerbach,* p. 125.

world and its passionate unreason. He would not leave his seclusion. He would publish in the Young Hegelian journal—indeed, his intellectual development quickened during these six years, and his contributions to the journal's success were important—but he would have no formal or personal contacts with the Young Hegelian groups. He would not join the editorial staff of the *Hallische Jahrbücher,* he would not associate with the "Freien" in Berlin; he wanted only his happy and deliberate isolation in an unused wing of his wife's porcelain factory.

In 1839 Feuerbach published a work of particular significance to his own development and to the development of all the Young Hegelians—his criticism of Hegel's philosophy. He once declared that "the Hegelian philosophy is the last sanctuary, the last rational support of theology." [16] In a sense he admitted validity to the claim of the Hegelians of the right that they could use Hegel's philosophy to justify Christianity as the absolute religion. His critique of Hegel, thus, was intended not as an attack on the progenitor of his own philosophical premises but as a rejection of those aspects of Hegel's thought that appeared to be too amenable to the interpretations of Christian theology. He used the historicism that he acquired from Hegel's thought to criticize that thought, with the clear aim of demonstrating both the separation of philosophy from theology and the superiority of philosophy to Christianity. This work was part of his enduring effort directed against theology.

Feuerbach criticized Hegel on two grounds. First, he accused Hegel of disdain for empirical reality and sense-perception. Feuerbach was proceeding toward a criticism of idealism and the adoption of that apparent materialism that has been associated with his name. He demanded that philosophy rely on empirical observation, that it not dismiss the external world as illusory. Hegel, he argued, was too much of an idealist,

16. *Werke,* vol. 2, *Vorläufige Thesen zur Reform der Philosophie* (1842), p. 239.

concentrated too much on the life of the spirit to the neglect of the real world.

The second criticism that Feuerbach made of Hegel's philosophy was to dismiss any suggestion that it had claim to absolute truth. By using the historicism of the Hegelian philosophy itself, he argued that it did not possess absolute truth since all philosophies were time-bound, confined by the time and place in which they appeared. It was Hegel's own historicism that denied his teaching any absolute finality. "If the Hegelian philosophy were the absolute reality of the idea of philosophy," he wrote, "it would have been necessary that reason stop in the Hegelian philosophy and time itself come to an end." [17] This, of course, did not happen: the philosophy of Hegel was a product of its time, a phenomenon of its milieu. The task for Feuerbach and his generation, then, lay in re-interpreting Hegel's thought to apply it to the conditions and problems, the circumstances, of their own time.

Here was the basic philosophical justification of the Young Hegelians—the re-interpretation of Hegel and the separation of philosophy from theology. Strauss was profoundly impressed by Feuerbach's argument, as were Ruge and the young Marx. Ruge wrote ecstatically of Feuerbach's great work in destroying the claims to absolute truth made for the Hegelian philosophy. Feuerbach, he claimed, "exalted subjectivity . . . over the systematic objectivity of Hegel, asserted becoming over being, development over the stagnation of the absolute . . . ." [18] The Young Hegelians were now freed from the limitations of the philosophy that gave them their basic assumptions.

One thing, however, should be noted. Though Feuerbach subjected the Hegelian philosophy to criticism, he did not break with the master. Indeed, he declared that "Hegel is the

17. *Werke*, vol. 2, *Zur Kritik der Hegelschen Philosophie*, p. 164. Cf. Hermann Henne, *Die religionsphilosophische Methode Feuerbachs* (Borna-Leipzig, 1918), pp. 1–3.
18. Ruge to Rosenkranz, 25 February 1841, *Ruges Briefwechsel und Tagebuchblätter*, 1:224.

most perfect philosophical artist" and the "Hegelian philosophy is the culmination of speculative, systematic philosophy." [19] He would no longer accept the idealism of speculative philosophy, nor would he accept the Hegelian philosophy as absolute truth and final definition; yet he did not abandon the assumptions and understanding that he received from that philosophy. In 1840 he publicly declared his debt to Hegel's influence:

> Indeed, I stand in an intimate and influential relationship to Hegel, . . . for I knew him personally . . . . [He taught me the truth] Not theology, but philosophy! Not drivel and enthusiasm, but learning! Not faith, but thought. It was under his influence that I came to self-consciousness and world-consciousness. It was he who was my second father, as Berlin became my spiritual birthplace . . . . Hegel was my teacher, I his student: I do not lie when I say that I acknowledge this fact today with thanks and joy.[20]

Hegel's influence remained with Feuerbach however much he might analyze and criticize the master's philosophy. His most popular work, *The Essence of Christianity,* published in 1841, showed that his assumptions and background were still Hegelian.

Feuerbach's *Essence of Christianity* was one of those books that could be truly called seminal. Its popularity was universal, it was translated into all the major languages. "One must himself have experienced the liberating effect of this book to get an idea of it," Engels recalled. "Enthusiasm was general; we all became at once Feuerbachians." [21] In the changing world of the 1830s and 1840s, many young intellectuals quickly moved forward from the views of Strauss to this new piece of radicalism that was concerned not with the content of dogma but with the origin of dogma in human aspirations and fears.

19. *Werke,* vol. 2, *Zur Kritik der Hegelschen Philosophie,* pp. 174–75.
20. *Aus dem Nachlass, 1840, in Briefwechsel und Nachlass* 1:387.
21. Friedrich Engels, *Ludwig Feuerbach and the Outcome of Classical German Philosophy,* tr. C. P. Dutt (New York, 1941), p. 18.

Enthusiastically even Strauss wrote—and in his praise Young Hegelian historicism was implicit—that Feuerbach's "theory is the truth for our age." [22]

Feuerbach began his *Essence of Christianity* by restating his rejection of idealism and a purely speculative philosophy. "I reject completely all absolute, idealistic, self-sufficient speculation—speculation that reflects only on itself," he wrote.[23] He would understand Christianity not by speculation but by looking at the real world, by observing the wants and fears of man, by studying the city of man, not the city of God.

The universal feature of human life was the belief in some form of divinity. While theologians traditionally argued that this fact, a *consensus universalis,* was an indication of God's existence, Feuerbach saw it, rather, as an indication of man's universal urge to create God. He set forth the argument that religion was the product of man; that man incorporated the outstanding human qualities into his deity; that, reversing the normal theological formula, man has created God in his own image and likeness. "Man—this is the secret of religion—projects his essence into objectivity," he argued, "and then makes himself an object to this projected image of himself that is thus converted into a subject . . . ." [24] Man differed from lower forms of life because he had self-consciousness, the ability to think about his own nature. In thinking of his nature, man isolated certain ideals—ideals that were, in reality, the essence of his own being—made these ideals into objects definable apart from himself, and projected them into God. In all periods of human history, human attributes have defined God, have determined the character of the divine, for "religion is the alienation of man from himself." [25]

For Feuerbach Christianity dramatically represented the alienation of man from himself. "The essence of Christianity,"

22. Strauss to Märklin, 22 July 1846, *Ausgewählte Briefe*, p. 184.
23. *Das Wesen des Christentums,* 2nd ed. (Leipzig, 1843), p. ix.
24. *Wesen des Christentums,* p. 44.
25. *Wesen des Christentums,* p. 48.

he wrote, "is the essence of human feeling." [26] Since it was easier to be redeemed than to act for oneself, Christianity provided a supernatural redeemer. The instinct for self-preservation was characteristically human, so Christianity provided a life after death for each individual. A feminine principle was needed to balance a masculine God, so Christianity supplied the Virgin Mary. Every Christian doctrine fulfilled a human wish.

After the self-projection in which man created God and all the Christian doctrines, theology emerged to explain the nature of God and rationalize the illusory. Once the existence of a transcendent God was established by formal proof, theology began its reign: God and man were consciously separated, God was divorced from his human origins. The great offense of theology, Feuerbach argued, was that it exteriorized in God what was really the essence of humanity; it sacrificed man to God, to his own creation.

This sacrifice was wrong, and the great tragedy of history was that man was sacrificed to his own spirit.

> I show that the true meaning of theology is anthropology, that there is no distinction between the predicates of divine and human natures, and, consequently . . . that there is no distinction between the divine and human subjects—they are identical.[27]

God had no meaning apart from humanity, divine spirit did not exist except as immanent. Feuerbach, like all the Young Hegelians, insisted that humanity was God.

Theology, then, was best studied as anthropology, since "religion, in the qualities it assigns to God, . . . only defines or represents the true human nature of the word." [28] He wanted to turn men's interests away from a supernatural, illusory world to the real world of human existence. Christianity, he admitted, had reached a moment of truth when it proclaimed

26. *Wesen des Christentums,* p. 208.
27. *Wesen de Christentums,* p. xiii.
28. *Wesen des Christentums,* p. xv.

a religion of love; but it negated this truth when it set up a religion of faith that separated man from man. To return man to his true nature both as an individual and as a member of the human species, religious illusions had to be dissolved, theology had to be turned into anthropology, the love of God had to give way to the love of humanity. Essentially Feuerbach's message was a call for humanism, a call for man to love his fellow-man since "a loving heart is the heart of humanity beating in the individual." [29] His humanism was that of the Young Hegelians—the divine was inherent in man, man was God.

Feuerbach was one of the first to approach religion as an unconscious, but necessary, gratification of human emotional life, as rooted in the desires of man. He regarded himself as a profoundly religious man, recognizing the necessity of fulfilling man's emotional needs, but he objected to theology because it transferred these religious impulses to an object outside of man. The lofty human feelings—love, justice, truth, charity, and all the others—that man had abstracted from himself and set in God Feuerbach wanted returned to humanity. He wanted the spirit returned to man. His great quest was to discover the human in the supernatural and reveal the true nature of man in his emotional needs and failings: to turn theology into anthropology, to transform theists into humanists, to shift men's eyes from the supernatural to real life, to end the dualism of nature and spirit, to show that the God transcendent was actually immanent.

The Young Hegelian use of historicism was also evident in Feuerbach's *Essence of Christianity*. Like Strauss, he argued that Christianity was obsolete. It had become obsolete because philosophy had shown that the union of divine and human natures, not their separation, took place in all of humanity. Moreover, Christianity, only a momentary stage in the development of truth, no longer had relevance in the modern world of the nineteenth century:

29. *Wesen des Christentums*, 400.

> I have shown that Christianity has disappeared not only from reason but from the life of mankind, that it is nothing more than a fixed idea that stands in sharp contradiction to our fire and life insurance companies, our railroads and steam locomotives, our picture and art galleries, our military and business schools, our theaters and scientific museums.[30]

In the new world of change and progress, Christianity no longer had any place. In a world where man was to worship himself and his own works, Christianity was, indeed, obsolete.

The spirit of Hegel still brooded over Feuerbach's work. Hegel had taught that the motive force for the development of history was the self-alienation of the idea. Feuerbach spoke of the creative force of the self-alienation of man. But even this latter idea had Hegelian origins. Hegel had insisted that man's original comprehension of the divine occurred in human terms, that the divine was really man's production, his creation. "The natural," he claimed, "as it is explained by man—*i. e.*, in its inner and essential nature—is, in general, the beginning of the divine." [31] As for the representation of the divine in the form of gods, Hegel said,

> . . . the human being is the womb that conceived them, the breast that suckled them, and the spiritual that gave them grandeur and purity . . . . Thus the honor of the human is swallowed up in the honor of the divine. Men honor the divine in and for itself, but, at the same time, they honor it as *their* deed, their product, and their existence . . . .[32]

Feuerbach owed much to Hegel in affirming that man created God from his own spirit.

Perhaps there was even a more fundamental debt to Hegel in the humanism that Feuerbach loved to exalt. Hegel's teaching was that spirit was immanent in human history, that human institutions and human culture embodied it. Spirit,

30. *Wesen des Christentums*, pp. xxii–xxiii.
31. *Werke*, vol. 9, *Philosophie der Geschichte*, pp. 290–91.
32. *Philosophie der Geschichte*, p. 295. Italics in the original.

then, had its life within human history, not outside of it or beyond it. Feuerbach, thinking in purely Hegelian terms, condemned the alienation of spirit from humanity and the embodiment of it in a transcendent deity as a grave offense to man. The enemy was dualism: there should be no distinction between God and man. This Hegelian legacy carried through the work of all the Young Hegelians.

Reflecting on his *Essence of Christianity*, Feuerbach concluded that its great neglect was in not recognizing the importance of nature in the origins of religion.[33] His entire emphasis had been on man, on the human foundations of religion, his entire consideration homocentric. Now he wanted to consider the role of nature in religion and turned from anthropology to naturalism. His *Essence of Religion*, published in 1845, was the result of this turn.

"Nature," he wrote, "is the first, the original object of religion, as the history of all religions and peoples testifies." [34] In his *Essence of Christianity*, he had argued that man was the sole originator of religion, and religion was the alienation and objectification of the spiritual that lay within him. Now he was considering the idea of nature as forming the impulse for religion and religion itself as the objectification of the spiritual that lay within nature. He was still working away from what he regarded to be Hegel's dismissal of the natural world as illusory.

Though he was impressed with the force of nature in inspiring religion, especially among primitive and pagan peoples, Feuerbach still maintained his humanist orientation. Nature was the original object of religion; consequently it always formed the background for all religion. For him this fact meant only that religion could not be understood apart from natural science as well as anthropology. After all, it was man's relationship to nature that was expressed religiously and man's need for the natural world—"man's feeling of dependence is

33. *Werke*, vol. 8, *Vorlesungen über das Wesen der Religion*, p. viii.
34. *Werke*, vol. 7, *Das Wesen der Religion*, p. 434.

the foundation of all religion." [35] It was men's desires and fears that fashioned the gods, for "men's wishes are their gods." [36]

Feuerbach's devotion to the city of man was tested in the Revolution of 1848. A humanist might seem drawn to political action, but he was not the kind of man who enjoyed public attention or public life. Since political action demanded that he leave his scholarly seclusion, he was uneasy about the revolution. He had, six years earlier, written that "politics must become our religion" and that the aim of politics must be to establish the humanist state.[37] Even so, political action was secondary because "the Christian religion has to be destroyed" before the humanist state could be instituted, "for in the Christian religion you have your republic in heaven and do not need one here." [38] Atheism had to be the foundation of the state; atheism was for him, as for all the Young Hegelians, the union of divine and human natures in humanity, the rejection of spiritual transcendence, the recognition of the spiritual character of the state. "Practical atheism is thus the hinge of the state," he wrote; and with the establishment of the spiritual state, the true humanist state, "the state becomes God for man." [39] Here indeed was the Young Hegelian political philosophy: the acceptance of the Hegelian definition of the state as divine, the creation of the state on the basis of humanism, the progression forward from Christianity. It was, for Feuerbach, a philosophy that saw politics secondary to and derivative from the basic development of philosophical humanism, that saw political action secondary to sound scholarship.

Ruge, nonetheless, believed in the political importance of Feuerbach, who had given political action the theoretical basis of humanism. Ruge urged him to enter the discussion of po-

35. *Ibid.*

36. *Das Wesen der Religion,* p. 503. Cf. Rawidowicz, *Ludwig Feuerbachs Philosophie,* pp. 163–68.

37. "Grundsätze der Philosophie (1842–43)," *Briefwechsel und Nachlass,* 1:409.

38. "Grundsätze der Philosophie," p. 412.

39. "Grundsätze der Philosophie," pp. 410–11.

litical questions, but Feuerbach refused to submit to such promptings. His humanism was philosophical, strong in conviction and determination, but completely lacking in insight into the specific social and political problems that troubled his society. His concern was for questions of philosophy and theology, the life of scholarship.[40]

He could not avoid the consequences of his reputation. When the people of Germany looked to their national figures to sit in the National Assembly, Feuerbach was an obvious choice. Reluctantly, he accepted the call and left his cherished Bruckberg for Frankfurt. He was unhappy in the parliament, skeptical of his own qualifications and uneasy about political life. Belonging to no party, he was cautiously friendly to the leaders of all the diverse factions and wrote to his wife of his carefully noncommittal intentions: "I will first listen, first converse, first get to know the world and men, before I come forward actively." [41] He never did "come forward actively." As one member of the Assembly recalled, next to Freiligrath, Feuerbach was the most silent man there.[42] His presence made no difference.

What did make a difference, at least in Feuerbach's own mind, was the freedom he had to give a series of lectures on religion. From December, 1848, to March, 1849, he lectured regularly in Heidelberg, presenting his ideas on Christianity and religion. In these lectures he restated his position that man created God and that religion enshrined the alienation of man. His whole purpose was to re-unite man with his spirit, to change "the friends of God into friends of man, believers into thinkers, worshippers into laborers, candidates for the next world into scholars of this world, Christians—who admit to being 'half-animal and half-angel'—into men, complete

40. Cf. Rawidowicz, *Ludwig Feuerbachs Philosophie*, pp. 312–16.
41. Feuerbach to his wife, 30 June 1848, *Briefwechsel und Nachlass*, 1: 374.
42. Ludwig Bamberger, *Erinnerungen* (Berlin, 1899), pp. 107–10.

men." [43] If any one sentence summarized Feuerbach's idea of his mission, it was surely this one.

With the National Assembly dismissed and the revolution ended, Feuerbach watched the reaction from the seclusion of his retreat at Bruckberg. He had had no hopes for his own participation in politics, but he had hoped, like many of the Young Hegelians, that the revolution might open a march to the humanist state. In that hope he was sadly disappointed. Dejectedly he observed that "in harmony with the history of the German 'revolution' I begin the old life once more, . . . I hobble back again into the past, deeply afflicted." [44] Again, his dejection was caught in a letter to a friend in America when he wrote: "Europe is a prison." [45] Feuerbach's reaction was to turn more and more into himself.

What made the prison of Europe intolerable for him in his last years was that he was forced to leave his beloved retreat at Bruckberg. After its financial collapse, his wife's porcelain factory had to be sold; he and his wife were compelled to leave their residence in the factory and move to a small village, Rechenberg, near Nürnberg. Feuerbach was never happy there. He maintained his scholarly interests and an active correspondence, yet he seemed strangely remote from the new turns that intellectual life in Germany was taking. He realized that the younger generations were excited by exactly the questions of politics and social reform for which he had no answers. He lived through the Prussian wars for German unification and the proclamation of the German Empire in 1871, but in his mind the most pressing political issues of those years were female emancipation and the relationship of labor to capital. He had once declared that "my writings all have but one purpose, one intention and thought, one theme. This theme is just religion and theology and whatever is connected with

43. *Werke*, vol. 8, *Vorlesungen über das Wesen der Religion*, p. 360.
44. Feuerbach to Kapp, 3 March 1850, *Briefwechsel und Nachlass* 2:7.
45. Feuerbach to Kapp, 14 March 1851, *Briefwechsel und Nachlass*, 2:10.

them." [46] It was just this one theme that no longer interested the radicals to whom he had once appealed. His death, on September 13, 1872, seemed almost an anticlimax.

After 1848, Feuerbach wrote one important book, *Theogony According to the Sources of Classical, Hebrew, and Christian Antiquity,* published in 1857. This work expanded on his earlier thesis that all religion was founded on human wish and desire, and it summarized a good deal of his earlier work. He regarded this as his greatest book, but almost no one shared his opinion. It never had, either at the time or subsequently, the popularity and impact of his *Essence of Christianity.*

Feuerbach has commonly been described as a materialist. This charge—and it nearly always is a charge—is based on his criticism of speculative idealism. He insisted that philosophy deal with the real world, the external world, and not dismiss it as an illusion. His whole philosophical thrust was toward seeing the origin of gods in human beings and in nature. In a review he wrote in 1850, he composed the unfortunate pun, "der Mensch ist was er isst" (man is what he eats).[47] On the basis of this quotable phrase, Feuerbach has been classed by many as a materialist.

Yet Feuerbach regarded materialism as an inadequate term to describe his position.[48] He refused to see thought as a mere material activity or man as a mere product of matter. For him, as for all the Young Hegelians, man was both nature and spirit, and the aim of his philosophy was to end the alienation of spirit from man. From Hegel, he and the other Young Hegelians had received the impulse to unite matter and spirit, God and man. Some of them, like Bauer, wanted that union to come from the idea down to man; others, like Feuerbach, wanted the union to proceed from man to spirit. They were not in real conflict; they all supported Hegel's monism. Their

46. *Werke,* vol. 8, *Vorlesungen über das Wesen der Religion,* p. 6.
47. Review of Moleschott's *Lehre der Nahrungsmittel,* in *Briefwechsel und Nachlass,* 2:90.
48. "Nachgelassene Aphorismen," *Briefwechsel und Nachlass,* 307–08.

materialism and their idealism were the same in that they had the same goal. They were not opposites: the opposite of each was dualism. The best term to describe Feuerbach's position is monistic humanism, a Young Hegelian humanism that actually equated God with humanity.

If Feuerbach's materialism required a special definition, so did his atheism. For him atheism meant the rejection of a personal God, the rejection of the notion that there was a distinction between God and man. It did not mean a denial of divine spirit. It meant that that spirit could not exist apart from man. "I deny God," he wrote. "But that means for me that I deny the negation of man." [49] The divine spirit inherent in man found its expression in human history—it was, in fact, humanity itself. Here was Feuerbach's ultimate debt to Hegel.

Above all, Feuerbach insisted that his views not be used to justify an atheism that was merely a negative rejection of theology, that was a denial of faith and purpose. He did not want his views construed to suggest that there was no God. "Aimlessness," he wrote, "is the greatest unhappiness . . . . Each man must set before himself a God, that is, a goal, a purpose." [50] Unlike those in the twentieth century who denied a personal God, Feuerbach was not led to despair. His philosophy insisted that there was a purpose and meaning to life, that by contributing to the spiritual life of humanity—to art, science, literature, and the other creations of the human spirit—each man had significance and meaning, true immortality. Perhaps it was a restricted view, but it surely registered Feuerbach's own sense of priorities.

Those priorities stemmed from his total acceptance of a philosophy of divine immanence, which meant that any knowledge of God as a being in and of himself was impossible, since God could only be known in terms of his specific embodiments in human history. Feuerbach saw farther than the

49. *Werke*, vol. 1, *Erläuterung und Ergangzüngen zum Wesen des Christentums*, p. xiv.
50. *Wesen des Christentums*, p. 63.

mere opposite of divine transcendence, as his indifference to the doctrinal and biblical criticisms that occupied Strauss showed. He judged that since there could be no reference to a divine existence beyond human experience, there was no such divine existence. His interest thus turned to psychology, to understanding the mechanism and motive that propelled man into creating God. And his interest led him to the discovery of an alternative absolute that he held up for all to admire and serve: the creations of the human spirit. Thus, in his *Thoughts about Death and Immortality* he sought to reintegrate the idea of heaven into the present life of the world; in his *Essence of Christianity* he sought to reintegrate God into humanity; in his *Essence of Religion* he sought to reintegrate all gods into nature. The aim of each was to restore man's alienated spirit to him and to arouse reverence for man's creations, creations clearly recognized as human in origin. Feuerbach once wrote, "God was my first thought; reason my second; man my third and final thought." [51] It was, when all was said and done, a religious creed.

The life of Friedrich Theodor Vischer differed in one significant respect from those of the other Young Hegelians: he had an important career after 1848. The others of his generation acquired their fame, or their notoriety, as young men, and they spent their older years in relative obscurity. Strauss made his most important contribution at the age of twenty-seven, Bauer at thirty-two, Feuerbach at thirty-seven; Stirner died before his fiftieth birthday; after 1848, Ruge, then forty-six, lived in exile and retirement. In each case, these men were youthful radicals with a popular reputation, but the times seemed to race by them. Their reputations waned, and their later lives and deaths passed mostly unnoticed. In each case, "the name died before the man."

Not so with Vischer. Though he was certainly a part of the

51. "Fragmente zur Charakteristik meines philosophischen Entwicklungsganges," *Werke*, 2:388.

flowering of the 1830s that produced the Young Hegelians, much of his major work appeared after 1848. Four volumes of his *Aesthetics* appeared after 1848; his *Critical Passages: New Series,* from 1861 to 1873; *Even One,* in 1879; *Old and New,* in 1881 and 1882. In the same period, he held a chair in aesthetics at the University of Zürich and the University of Tübingen, a striking contrast to the ban that prevented Strauss, Bauer, Feuerbach, and Stirner from teaching.

When Vischer was called to a professorship of aesthetics at the University of Tübingen in 1866, he believed that "there was a symbolic meaning in this welcome, . . . the reparation of an old injustice." [52] For this was the university that, some twenty years earlier, had admonished him for his activities as a Young Hegelian publicist and, with a stern warning, suspended him from his teaching duties for two years. Now it called him back to occupy one of its important chairs: perhaps the event was symbolic of Vischer's new career.

Vischer's later career was spent, in large part, in an attempt to redefine and reinterpret the Hegelian philosophy he had accepted as a youth in order that it might respond to the new circumstances in which he found himself and the world. As a young man he, like all the Young Hegelians, undertook to write a great and definitive work that would not only establish his own reputation but also enlighten the world. If there was a touch of arrogance in the way these young men set out to systematize knowledge and provide all the answers, such was the heritage of the Hegelian philosophy. Vischer's great work was to be his *Aesthetics, or the Knowledge of the Beautiful,* the first volume of which appeared in 1847. It was frankly a restatement of Hegelian aesthetics, numbed by pedantry, burdened with countless divisions, subdivisions, notes, addenda, and the other paraphernalia of a systematizer.

Much of his later work on aesthetics can be seen as attempts to explain, alter, and moderate his *Aesthetics,* to bring within his view the new interests of the later part of the century. He

52. "Mein Lebensgang," *Altes und Neues* (Stuttgart, 1882), 3:337.

even undertook to write a *Critique of My Aesthetics*. The chief reservation that he expressed about his youthful work, in the strongly Hegelian period of his life, was that his view of aesthetics was too idealistic, too metaphysical. He wanted now, he observed of his work after 1860, to discover the "empirical beginning" of aesthetics, "the anthropological foundations" that lay "outside of metaphysics." [53] He seemed to be moving in the direction taken by Feuerbach and Strauss, and, though he never became a materialist, he began to have doubts about idealism.

In his *Aesthetics,* Vischer had seen the idea as a spiritual energy that animated and arranged beautiful objects. Since that spirit was also immanent in man, man's aesthetic experience arose from recognizing in objects the spirit that was within himself; in a sense, the sharing of spirit explained the process by which men had an aesthetic experience. Here was the Hegelian philosophy of aesthetics and Hegel's view of the necessary relationship between subject and object that was so essential to the Young Hegelians. In later years, when Vischer had doubts about the idealistic foundations that underlay his *Aesthetics,* he had to deal with the problem of explaining the aesthetic experience. For if objective reality were not permeated with divine spirit, how did the individual experience its beauty, how did he communicate with it, how, in short, did he have an aesthetic experience? A universe without spirit seemed but a conglomeration of facts, and such a universe seemed to be the only possibility allowed by the advances of science after 1850. It was this new universe that Vischer was trying to understand and explain by writing the specialized and narrower books aimed at answering specific questions, in pointed contrast to his earlier system, *Aesthetics.*[54]

53. "Kritik meiner Aesthetik," *Kritische Gänge: neue Folge* (Stuttgart, 1861–73), 6:111–12.

54. For an excellent discussion of Vischer's aesthetics and his reinterpretation of Hegel, see Willi Oelmüller, *Friedrich Theodor Vischer und das Problem der nachhegelschen Aesthetik* (Stuttgart, 1959); and Hermann

If Vischer had to reinterpret his Hegelian aesthetics for his new life, he had also to reinterpret his political views. Earlier, Young Hegelian humanism led him, as it led Ruge, to liberalism and democracy. If man was to be the philosophical measure of judgment, he ought also to be the political measure. Like most of the Young Hegelians, Vischer accepted Hegel's designation of the state as spiritual. The state had the obligation to provide for freedom, the highest goal of man. To provide for that freedom, the state had first of all to throw out Christianity which, by its teaching of dualism and transcendence, was a titanic impediment to the attainment of freedom. Then the state had to undertake the education of its citizens, education toward reason and spiritual freedom. The state, then, as a spiritual institution, was an instrument in human progress through education.[55]

As a young man, Vischer did not identify the Hegelian state with Prussia, as did Strauss and Ruge. On the contrary, as a member of the National Assembly in 1848, he was a firm opponent of Prussian leadership. He felt it a personal duty to stand for election to the Assembly, and, once chosen, he was from the first an opponent of the Prussian party.[56] He defended the *grossdeutsch* solution to German unity, the admission of all German states into a new united Germany that would have a democratically elected central government. He voted against the election of Archduke Johann of Austria as imperial vice regent and shared the other positions taken by the moderate left with whom he sat in the National Assembly. He spoke against the creation of a *Volkswehr*, he urged the removal of Christian education from the schools, he opposed offering the crown to the king of Prussia. Though Vischer was

Glockner, *Friedrich Theodor Vischer und das neunzehnte Jahrhundert* (Berlin, 1931).

55. Cf. Fritz Schlawe, *Friedrich Theodor Vischer* (Stuttgart, 1959), pp. 215–22.

56. For Vischer's own account of his activities in 1848, see "Mein Lebensgang," *Altes und Neues*, 3:321–26.

not one of the most important members of the Assembly, he was loyal to it. When it went as a rump session to Stuttgart in May, 1849, he went with it, and he remained with it until it was dismissed at the point of bayonets. His political life over, he returned home. He had favored democracy, the creation of a republic, the union of all Germans under a liberal government. Each of these dreams was destroyed. "The whole world appeared to me as gray as the grim autumn day when I went back, alone, to Tübingen," he wrote.[57]

Before long, Vischer adjusted to the autumnal weather. He was apologetic for his earlier political views, especially for his support of a "cosmopolitan, sentimental republic." [58] He was especially horrified at his earlier support for democracy when he saw as its results "the downfall of the French government in a coup d'état [by Napoleon III], the Commune, and the madness in Spain." [59] He sought to dismiss his performance in the events of 1848 as the exuberance of youth. "I was drunk on the wine of the times," he wrote, "and as foggy as the rest of the world." [60]

He resided in Zürich for eleven years after 1848. Like other intellectuals who lived in Switzerland—Burckhardt and Nietzsche, for example—he came to question seriously the value of democracy and to stress the threats that a democratic society posed to culture. Where he had once seen the Hegelian state best exemplified as a democracy, he returned to Germany in 1866 fully disillusioned with democracy and ready, like Bauer, Strauss, and Ruge, to identify the Hegelian state with Prussia. He maintained that, even in 1848, in issues of conflict between national unity and personal freedom, he uniformly supported national unity. He became obsessed more and more with the need for preserving law and order—a feat, he believed, democracy was unable to perform—and he turned to

57. "Mein Lebensgang," p. 327.
58. "Mein Lebensgang," p. 323.
59. "Mein Lebensgang," p. 322.
60. "Mein Lebensgang," p. 319.

Prussia and the *kleindeutsch* solution to German unity. In 1870, he glowed with patriotic pride over the achievements of Bismarck and the Prussian army; in the following year he exulted in the foundation of the German Empire. His liberal friends from the old days regarded him as a traitor to their cause, but that did not matter to Vischer. In 1872 he wrote "The War and the Arts," an essay that glorified the effects of the war on German culture. There was an ethical and social meaning in the war, he argued, for it united men in fellowship and patriotic fervor. Out of the great forces that were aroused and released by the war, great cultural strength and progress were certain to occur.[61] It was not, then, the democratic or republican state that embodied the spiritual qualities of humanity and educated its citizens in these qualities, but the assertive, bureaucratic state. Vischer did not abandon the Hegelian basis of his political thought, but he did transfer his cultural loyalty from an ideal democracy to Prussia.

Vischer, then, in his career after 1848, though still clinging to the philosophical background of his youth, sought to accommodate that background to the natural science and politics of the world in which he found himself. When he died, on September 14, 1887, it seemed that he had spent the last thirty years of his life apologizing for the opinions he had held the previous thirty years. Even if they were opinions for which he should have apologized, his preoccupation seemed overscrupulous at best and timeserving at worst.

The youthful Vischer, the Vischer who was a Young Hegelian publicist, is the center of interest here. In his early life and in his career prior to 1848, he was a writer for the *Hallische Jahrbücher* and a clergyman who abandoned Christianity for the Young Hegelian earthly paradise.

Vischer was born on June 30, 1807, in Ludwigsburg, the same Württemberg village in which Strauss, his life-long friend, was born. Like all the Young Hegelians, he was born into a

61. For Vischer's political views, see Friedrich Reich, *Die Kulturphilosophie Friedrich Theodor Vischers* (Leipzig, 1907), pp. 75–81.

middle-class family. His father was a clergyman, leaning towards liberal theology, who died in 1814 while ministering to the German armies during the Wars of Liberation. Young Fritz attended the gymnasium in Stuttgart where he developed the infatuation with art that remained with him all his life. He was intent upon becoming a painter, but his mother and family friends dissuaded him. Instead, they urged that he follow his father's example and become a clergyman. Complying with their wishes, he entered the seminary at Blaubeuren in 1821, where his friendship with Strauss developed and where he came to know his favored teacher, F. C. Baur.[62]

In 1825, Vischer, along with Strauss, entered the University of Tübingen to continue his theological studies. Life at the university has already been described in connection with Strauss: studies under F. C. Baur, the private reading of Schleiermacher and Hegel, the fascination with the problem of the relationship between theology and philosophy. In later years Vischer criticized the training he received in theology, for it concentrated on the past, the previous forms of the developing spirit, rather than the new forms. "We learned to know the old world," he wrote, "not the new one." [63] This was one of the standard Young Hegelian criticisms of theology. For the recognition of the new forms, philosophy, not theology, was to be their tool.

Vischer received his degree in 1830 and accepted a position in the small village of Horrheim. He became a preacher with great doubts about the truth of Christianity, doubts arising mostly from the private reading he and his friends did in philosophy. "However feeble our foundation may have been," he wrote about his reading of Hegel and other philosophers, "dualism was once and for all overthrown. I was and remain a monist, a pantheist." [64] The monism of Hegel's philosophy seemed to all the Young Hegelians to rule out the possibility

62. Schlawe, *Vischer*, pp. 1–18.
63. "Mein Lebensgang," p. 256.
64. "Mein Lebensgang," p. 266.

of remaining with Christianity. Other doubts about Christianity, all of them based on the Hegelian philosophy, began to trouble Vischer in the privacy of his vicarage: he denied the possibility that God was a person; he surrendered belief in personal immortality. Here were important steps away from Christianity, steps taken independently by Strauss and Feuerbach.[65] To answer the doubts that engulfed his mind, Vischer turned, interestingly enough, not to scripture, or to the fathers of theology, or to Luther, but to Hegel. "My morning study," Vischer wrote, "was Hegel, always Hegel." [66] By choosing to find his answers in Hegel's philosophy, he had, in fact, elevated philosophy above theology before he made his final commitment.

He was happy to get away from his preaching when he was called to Maulbronn as a tutor in 1831 and to Tübingen in 1833. By 1833 he had already decided that philosophy was the highest form of the spirit, that it was superior to theology, and that theology had to submit to its superior judgment. "I had now for all times the solution: philosophy above all!" [67] He had come to this conclusion after he went, like Strauss, to study at Berlin, at the university where the master's influence still abided. Though Hegel was dead, Vischer studied under some of his important students: Hotho, Henning, Michelet, and Gans. Now, however, that he had made his choice for philosophy, he examined himself carefully to see whether he ought not also throw over his clerical vocation. In a questioning mood, he wrote to Mörike about the problem that was troubling him. "I have absolutely no theological blood," he wrote, and he wondered "whether you do not really offend the law of life" if, despite all doubts about Christianity, "you remain in the theological calling." [68]

65. Cf., Schlawe, *Vischer*, pp. 43–75.
66. "Mein Lebensgang," p. 276.
67. "Mein Lebensgang," p. 280.
68. Vischer to Mörike, 13 September 1833, *Briefwechsel zwischen Eduard Mörike und Friedrich Theodor Vischer*, ed. Robert Vischer (Munich, 1926), p. 96.

Within a short time Vischer had his own answer to this question. He abandoned theology and the clerical vocation completely, realizing that "a good third of the best years of my youth were lost, squandered on stupid diligence in matters that have borne no fruit for my spirit and my life." [69] He arrived at this answer through the influence of Strauss, especially of Strauss's *Life of Jesus*, and the harsh treatment that the orthodox clergy gave to his friend. He wrote an important and impassioned essay for the *Hallische Jahrbücher* in defense of Strauss, declaring his own emancipation from theology: "With his work on the life of Jesus, Strauss has shown himself to be a worthy contributor to the mission of our century, which is the freeing of the spirit from the restraints of the written word." [70] The spirit was vibrant, developing, progressive, yet scripture tried to stabilize it in absolute form; the elevation of a moment in the development of spirit to the level of absolute truth did violence to the very nature of spirit. Strauss had liberated spirit, and the way was now open for the new world to emerge. "You are the representative of the spiritual freedom of our century," Vischer wrote to Strauss in admiration and excitement.[71] To Mörike he wrote that Strauss "has demonstrated what the modern spirit demands and how absurd it is to want to enforce once more the old, simple, commonplace truths and piety." [72] The Young Hegelian expectation of the emergence of the next step of spiritual development ran through Vischer's praise of Strauss.

Most of the Young Hegelians, though they renounced Christianity, still maintained an abiding interest in it by writing on church history and dogma. Strauss wrote a critique of dogma, Feuerbach explored the origins of religious experience, Bauer wrote again and again on the source of the gospel nar-

69. "Mein Lebensgang," p. 267.

70. "Dr. Strauss und die Wirtemberger," *Kritische Gänge* 1:3.

71. Vischer to Strauss, 2 September 1837, *Briefwechsel zwischen Strauss und Vischer*, 1:40.

72. Vischer to Mörike, 7 June 1837, *Briefwechsel zwischen Mörike und Vischer*, pp. 130–31.

ratives. Vischer, however, turned his attention more and more to aesthetics and literature, though he commented upon religion as it impinged on these two fields or threatened his liberty. In 1835, he accepted a position on the faculty of aesthetics and literature at the University of Tübingen. Even as an aesthetician he still admitted that his thought was essentially Hegelian, since Hegel's "philosophy was a key, an instrument" for the comprehension of aesthetic experience.[73] In fact, he lectured on Hegel at Tübingen in 1836–37.

While teaching at Tübingen, Vischer became a publicist for the Young Hegelians.[74] Ruge came to visit him in 1837, looking for writers to contribute to his new journal, the *Hallische Jahrbücher*. Vischer agreed to contribute articles to the journal and welcomed the opportunity to express his ideas in a publication devoted to the spiritual freedom that he and the other Young Hegelians prized. He wrote many important articles for the journal, among them his defense of Strauss, his essay on religion in art, his many denunciations of the current dominance of theology over philosophy, his demands that the state abandon Christianity and adopt humanism. His essays on aesthetics were important, for they urged that the function of art was to portray the world of the immanent God. In his articles, Vischer showed that he shared the assumptions and positions of the Young Hegelians on important issues, that he still accepted Hegel's philosophy as the basis of his thought, and that the new theology of the Tübingen School had impressed him deeply.

Vischer was pleased with the *Hallische Jahrbücher* because "it is a place where the freedom of the spirit makes itself felt." [75] Again and again he urged Strauss not to separate him-

73. "Mein Lebensgang," p. 298.

74. For the correspondence of Vischer to Ruge about essays he submitted for publication, see "Eleven Unpublished Letters by Friedrich Theodor Vischer," ed. Adolph B. Benson, *Philological Quarterly* 3 (1924): 32–47.

75. Vischer to Strauss, 4 November 1838, *Briefwechsel zwischen Strauss und Vischer*, 1:71.

self from the journal, reminding his friend that Ruge's editorial partner, "Echtermeyer is now emancipated and won for the left because of your efforts and my efforts." [76] In the end, Vischer as well as Strauss drifted from the journal because it raced too quickly into every radical position, moved far to the left of their philosophical tenets, and fell more and more under the influence of Bauer and the Berlin Young Hegelians. After 1842 Vischer did not contribute to the *Hallische Jahrbücher*, but submitted his essays, instead, to the more moderate *Jahrbücher der Gegenwart*, the journal founded by Eduard Zeller and his friends at Tübingen.

Vischer's career as a publicist for the Young Hegelians did not please his conservative colleagues on the Tübingen faculty. They were scandalized by his opinions, by his irreligiosity, by his hatred for theology, and by his avowed pantheism. Vischer became a full professor in 1844, and the inaugural lecture he delivered at that event precipitated a great tempest of criticism. In his lecture he denounced the "scholasticism" that he believed dominated university faculties, and proclaimed that aesthetics would liberate all learning from the control of theology. [77] The lecture offered a convenient opportunity for Vischer's conservative opponents to bring charges against him. Their complaint was submitted to the university senate and the Württemberg government, and after some delay it was decided against Vischer. In February, 1845, the university issued a grave warning to him to cease his attacks on the Christian faith and, as a disciplinary measure, it suspended him for two years from the lecture halls. Vischer resigned himself to the judgment and announced that "I shall turn my attention to aesthetics." [78] He, like Strauss and Bauer, had had a revealing experience of German academic life—it was more often

76. *Ibid.*
77. Schlawe, *Vischer*, 180–88.
78. Vischer to Strauss and Märklin, 17 February 1845, *Briefwechsel zwischen Strauss und Vischer*, 1:160.

the orthodox university faculties than the governments that initiated censorship and resisted academic freedom.

Despite Vischer's apparent resignation to his suspension, that suspension did not please him. He regarded himself, as he had long regarded Strauss, as a martyr for academic freedom. "From that moment on," he wrote, "an abiding hatred for pietism, the church, and the clergy burned in my soul." [79] Vischer's rejection of Christianity was only confirmed by his experience at Tübingen. It was no wonder that he regarded his call back to this university in 1866 as the reparation of an old injustice. By then, of course, he was no longer a radical.

Vischer once wrote that religion should be abolished as a separate area of study and its study be taken over by the humanistic disciplines that would treat it as a mere phase in human spiritual development. Exegesis would be taught as philology, church history would be taught as history, dogma would be taught as philosophy, and Christian morality would be treated as part of human ethics.[80] Religion, then, would be treated not as a supernatural realm, a realm of specific revelation and transcendence, but as an inherently human experience. Vischer's demand was fully in agreement with the Young Hegelian insistence that, because of the unceasing development of the spirit, Christianity was obsolete and had to be replaced by philosophical humanism. Christianity was the product of "the simple, quiet piety and objectivity of naive times" and had no meaning apart from those times.[81] Its study in modern times could only be justified when it was treated as one particular moment in the spiritual development of humanity.

Like the other Young Hegelians, Vischer was not an atheist

79. "Mein Lebensgang," p. 317.
80. "Mein Lebensgang," pp. 268–69.
81. Vischer to Mörike, 20 June 1837, *Briefwechsel zwischen Mörike und Vischer*, p. 134.

who denied the existence of God. Rather, he, like his colleagues, accepted Hegel's definition of God as immanent. He repeatedly announced that "I . . . remain a monist, a pantheist." [82] There was no distinction in his mind and thought between God and the universe. Perhaps "pantheism" is not the most fortunate term to describe his view, for it suggests that the universe *is* God, while Vischer and the Young Hegelians thought rather of equating God and the universe in the process of becoming. It was neither a static God nor a static universe that he accepted, but a vibrant, generating development:

> The world is not God in a static way, but, that God might continually improve his existence in it, it continually eclipses one temporary form with a new and better one. God is really this wondrous and holy restlessness . . . . One must say: "The being of God is the world." [83]

God, for Vischer, was the immanent force in a restless, developing, progressing universe. His atheism amounted to rejecting a personal, transcendent God.

As God was immanent, it made no sense to accept transcendence, God as a person distinct from the world. Yet Christianity did precisely that. "The Christian God is merely the work of fantasy or a phase of the ideal," he wrote, for it taught "faith in a transcendent being that belongs . . . to the teaching of fantasy." [84] He saw Christianity's treatment of Jesus as a striking example of its tampering with the progress of the spirit by insisting on transcendence. Jesus initiated a new step in the development when he proclaimed, in himself, the union of divine and human natures; the next necessary step was the recognition that all of mankind united divine and human natures. Christianity attempted to prohibit this step by raising Jesus himself to the level of transcendence, by

82. "Mein Lebensgang," p. 266.
83. *Auch Einer* (Stuttgart and Leipzig, 1879), 2:126.
84. *Aesthetik oder Wissenschaft des Schönen* (Reutlingen and Leipzig, 1846–57), 1:276.

separating him from the rest of humanity. "The magnificent character, the admirably noble, pure, free-thinking, benevolent, loving man, Jesus," he lamented, "we do not rest until he becomes a demigod, a son of God." [85] Vischer denounced the deification of Jesus. He rejected Christianity because, he argued, it was dualistic, because it had now become contrary to the truth of divine immanence. Only when men realized that the divine spirit was immanent in themselves would they be free. In this mood he declared: "Since I no longer believe, I have, for the first time, become religious." [86] Here was his acceptance of the Young Hegelian doctrine that man was God; here was the faith of the Young Hegelians.

Vischer described the faith in humanity as pure religion.[87] Following Schleiermacher rather than Hegel in this one regard, he believed that religion had its origin in feeling. It was feeling that united idea and reality, that united the individual with the whole and made him conscious of his connections with humanity. Because of this feeling of unity, the individual felt dependent on something beyond himself. Vischer's opinions never led him to the uncompromising individualism of Bauer and Stirner. What was beyond the individual was humanity—which was itself God—and the individual subjected himself to humanity in order to further its aims, to further the development of spirit. Concerning the feeling of dependence on humanity, Vischer wrote: "I am a nothing if I do not serve it [humanity]." [88] Because of his strong sense of mankind as a whole, he would not accept Bauer's view of the origin of the gospel narratives: Bauer treated them as "reflective and premeditated poetry" composed by an individual artist and failed "to appreciate the life of the *Volk* and all the stages of formation of the spirit." [89] Far more acceptable to him was

85. *Das Schöne und die Kunst* (Stuttgart, 1898), p. 156.
86. *Auch Einer*, 2:126.
87. Cf. Reich, *Vischers Kulturphilosophie*, pp. 38–49.
88. *Auch Einer*, 2:278.
89. Vischer to Ruge, 8 July 1842, "Unpublished Letters," p. 47.

Strauss's explanation of myths issuing from the womb of the species.

In explaining his views on pure religion, Vischer drew a sharp contrast between it and positive religion. Positive religion was theology; it transfered feeling into objectivity and demanded that this alienated feeling be worshipped as a transcendent divinity. Like Feuerbach, he argued that the projection of human ideals into objects apart from humanity was the origin of Christianity. He asked, then answered, the question about the origin of positive religion:

> But what is religion? What is and what is not its essence? We say to our opponents: myth is the darkening of pure religion; the projection of sense representations into the supernatural is your intention and teaching.[90]

Theology portrayed immanent truth as myths and objectified these myths as a transcendent God. In asking man to worship its God, theology demanded that man worship his own alienated spirit. Here was the great offense of Christian dualism.

Vischer's commitment to aesthetics was fostered because he believed theology had used art to create its gods. He accepted Hegel's description of the origin of artistic creation as the objectification of the spirit inherent in the artist. Hegel said human art was the beginning of the divine, and Vischer agreed. Vischer argued that the artist transferred the feeling for humanity, the essence of pure religion, into his creation, since

> all feeling requires that it be joined to a representation. . . . Therewith religion takes the representation for fantasy [and consequently] takes art into its service. The gods, to whom a body was already attributed by mythical fantasy, are figuratively placed before the eyes by art and become transfigured to ideal forms.[91]

90. *Altes und Neues: neue Folge* (Stuttgart, 1889), p. 228.
91. *Das Schöne und die Kunst,* pp. 154–55.

He crowned his argument with a quotation that all the Young Hegelians used: "A Greek defines the worth of art for religion with a simple phrase: 'The poets have given the Greeks their gods.' " [92] As Stirner associated the origin of a transcendent God with the process of artistic creation, so did Vischer. The basis for this view lay in the Hegelian philosophy.

Vischer's interest in aesthetics, however, had a deeper philosophical foundation than his concern for the misuse of art by theology. He accepted fully Hegel's affirmation that the absolute spirit expressed itself in three spheres: religion, art, and philosophy. Shuffling Hegel's order, he suggested that "religion is the first sphere of the absolute spirit" and, as such, deserved some attention.[93] But religion was the childhood form of the developing spirit, while philosophy was its highest form. The importance of art for Vischer was that it was the stage of spiritual development between religion and philosophy; it was the means by which religion and philosophy were mediated, by which theology was transcended. If the development of art and aesthetics could be understood and explained, then the passage from theology to philosophy could be demonstrated for all to see. If Vischer, with his *Aesthetics,* could show the exact process by which the spirit went from religion, through art, to philosophy, then men would have to accept the truth of the Young Hegelian position. Then would come the Young Hegelian apocalypse: the victory of humanism, the triumph of monism and spiritual immanence, the recognition of humanity as God. So that when Vischer, after his suspension from Tübingen, announced "I shall turn my attention to aesthetics," he did so with a profound sense of mission.

Aesthetics came to be, for Vischer, the abiding source of value in an historicist metaphysic that saw change, decay, and progress at the heart of reality. He felt neither frustration nor horror at a vision of ideas and institutions as ephemeral forms

92. Ibid.
93. *Aesthetik,* 1:161. Cf. *Das Schöne und die Kunst,* p. 166.

outmoded in time, because he found in aesthetics an experience of transcendence: man's artistic creativity fashioned the ephemeral forms, but that creativity was itself the source of continuing value and permanence. The one unchanging fact of history was man's ability to project his own ideals outward from himself into works of art that expressed the level of his spiritual development. Truly, the whole of human development, from art through religion to philosophy, was aesthetic because it meant man's creating his own world through the projection of his own consciousness and expressing it in the form of which he was historically capable. Thus primitive men personified the forces of nature; thus the Greeks fashioned their gods as images of themselves, both in poetry and sculpture; thus the Christians pictured, in both myth and painting, Jesus as the God-man. The poets and artists took the lead in this process—Homer and Hesiod, for example, created the Greek gods; Dante, Milton, and the painters of the Italian Renaissance created the modern Christian God. The aesthetic process was one of alienation, the human spirit projected from the artist into the plastic material which then itself became a fusion of spirit and matter that expressed the spiritual ideal of civilization at the time.

Vischer agreed completely with Hegel's suggestion that "art spiritualizes, it animates the mere outward and material object with a form that expresses soul, feeling, and spirit," so that matter, after its manipulation by an artist, became a "form full of the meaning with which spirit has infused it." [94] The process was, at the same time, the overcoming of alienation, a progressive fusion of human consciousness with matter that was itself the meaning of history. Thus for Vischer aesthetics was the key to human development, for man fashions his own consciousness in historical forms so that he might know as an object the spirit inherent in himself. He agreed with Feuerbach in seeing the forms of religion as creations of man, but he emphasized much more the positive aesthetics of such cre-

94. *Werke*, vol. 9, *Philosophie der Geschichte*, p. 493.

ation. The advantage in his own age was that a recognition of the aesthetic reality of the historical process was made possible by Hegel and the Young Hegelians. Now man could perceive all the ideas, forms, and institutions of history—religion, art, and philosophy themselves—as the record of the growth of human consciousness told in the progressive fusion of spirit and matter. The historical process was thus the essence of aesthetics and freedom. It yielded a transcendent principle from its own testimonial to relativism: the understanding that man communicated, in a religious sense, with the immanent spirit through aesthetic experience, that man knew himself through his art.

In 1845, on a lithograph of himself, Vischer wrote the following inscription:

> Our God is an immanent God; his dwelling is everywhere and nowhere; his life is only the entire world, his true presence is the spirit of humanity. The true mission of the new art is to glorify *this* God.[95]

It was this sense of mission that led Vischer to seek the victory of humanism in aesthetics. The inscription summarized his version of the Young Hegelian creed.

Ernest Renan, feeling himself both a victim and an agent in the religious criticism that pervaded the intellectual life of nineteenth-century Europe and made a continued belief in Christianity impossible for honest intellectuals, worried about the consequences of the widespread loss of religious faith. "An immense moral—perhaps even intellectual—degeneration will follow the disappearance of religion from the world," he wrote. "Religious people live on a shadow. We live on the shadow of a shadow. What will those who come after us live on?" [96]

Feuerbach and Vischer did not share his worry. They saw the true divinity as humanity, made manifest by the creative

95. Cited in Glockner, *Vischer und das neunzehnte Jahrhundert,* p. 270.
96. Ernest Renan, *Feuilles détachées* (Paris, 1892), pp. 17–18.

act by which men fashioned their ideals into gods. The creative process—whether artistic, religious, or philosophical—was that in which men objectified the spirit inherent in themselves. The loss of faith in Christianity was not to be lamented but to be welcomed as the casting off of an outmoded aesthetic form in order to accept a more encompassing one. The transition from Christianity to humanism meant both a recognition of the working of history and a movement to a higher and more inclusive spiritual form. Abandonment of the form of Christianity was, then, not a loss, but a progression forward in a process of which Christianity was but a part, a progression that kept the content of religion while it cast off the form.

Feuerbach and Vischer were, consequently, excited by the prospects of the future: the age of humanism was at hand to replace the old forms. To Renan's question—"What will those who come after us live on?"—they had clear and certain answers. In general terms, they saw the religion of humanity as the new faith of civilization. In specific terms, Feuerbach saw transcendent value embodied in the full range of man's creative activities that themselves exalted humanity; Vischer saw it specifically in aesthetics. Each thought a transcendent faith possible because he understood the time-bound, historicist quality of reality. Each faced the future with confidence precisely because he had an assured knowledge of the workings of the past.

5 Bauer, Stirner, and the Terrorism of Pure Theory

The terrorism of pure theory must clear the field.

—Bruno Bauer, 1841

Even after Hegel's death Berlin remained the center for the Hegelian philosophy, the academic locus for Hegelians right and left, the fourth Rome. Much of the important conflict within and against the Hegelian philosophy was fought in Berlin. In 1835, Altenstein prevailed over the university Hegelians by appointing Gabler, rather than Marheineke, to replace Hegel. After 1840, the Prussian government, directed by the anti-Hegelians, Frederick William IV and Eichhorn, sought to remove the Hegelian influence by appointing Schelling to Hegel's chair.

Not all the battles were fought between the Prussian government and the academic Hegelians. Equally important were the conflicts among Hegel's own followers, the epigones: the conflict over which of them should succeed to the master's chair, which of them was the true interpreter of the master, which of them was in error. Was Hegel a defender of Christianity, or was he an atheist? Did the Hegelian philosophy preach God becomes man or man become God? Such were the questions that the Hegelians needed to weigh. The Berlin Young Hegelians were prominent for their decisive answers.

Almost to demonstrate the truth of the observation that an opposition tends to take on the character of what it is opposing, the Berlin Young Hegelians quickly became the extreme wing of the Young Hegelian movement. The opposition to the Young Hegelians in Berlin was twofold: the philosophical faculty in the university, that was controlled by conservative Hegelians; and, after 1840, the government, that pursued the policy of suppressing the Young Hegelians in particular. Academic positions were therefore denied the Young Hegelians in the city they deemed philosophically and politically the capital of Germany.

The Berlin Young Hegelians expressed their opposition to what they regarded as the philosophical and political tyranny that oppressed them like all good disciples of Hegel, by using the Hegelian philosophy to demonstrate that they were the proper and correct interpreters of the master and that their opponents were consequently in error. To demonstrate their correct understanding of Hegel, they employed philosophical criticism and stressed the subjective element in the Hegelian philosophy.

Criticism was the method Strauss had used in his *Life of Jesus*, a philosophical method designed to demonstrate the contrast between the form and content of truth. The Berlin Young Hegelians used criticism as the total and complete method. Criticism was to be the negative principle necessary for progress, the principle that rejected outmoded forms, thus preparing the way for the new age, the Young Hegelian apocalypse. Christianity, the outmoded form, defined the state, the ideas, the academic life, the private life of men in the nineteenth century. Christianity dominated the academic establishment of right-wing Hegelians; it dominated the interests and policies of the Prussian government. Negative criticism to shatter that Christianity, to expose it, was thus necessary: with the new age at hand, the continuation of Christianity was unthinkable. The Christian dominance of the Berlin philosophical faculty and the Prussian government was such an outrage for the Berlin Young Hegelians that only their continued and relentless use of criticism could awaken the world and ease its passage to the next stage of progress, the age of humanism, the total union of divine and human spirits.

As characteristic of the Berlin Young Hegelians as their use of relentless theoretical criticism was their development of subjectivity from Hegel's philosophy. Bauer argued for the isolation of the private critic; Stirner taught anarchic subjectivity. Yet their emphasis on subjectivity was not simply an assertion of preference, a summons to ignore the objective world, a retreat from the rigors of the external world; their assurance was much greater. Hegel had taught that the philosopher, the subject, must put himself in tune with the development of objective spirit and repeat its patterned progress in his own consciousness. Thus, the subject did not merely assert its own importance arbitrarily; it was itself the development of absolute truth. That equation of subject and object gave the Berlin Young Hegelians their absolute assurance. Bauer became in his own mind criticism incarnate; Stirner refused to countenance any authority external to himself. The Berlin Young Hegelians combined, in this way, the subjective emphasis and the method of absolute criticism derived from the Hegelian philosophy. As the trumpet of Joshua shattered the walls of the heathen, so the critical method and the subjective identification with that method would shatter the empty shell of Christianity and expose the new era. Such was the passionate and assured expectation of Bauer and Stirner, the leading figures of the Berlin Young Hegelians.

One of the most vigorous critics of Strauss's *Life of Jesus*—a critic Strauss deemed it necessary to answer at length—was Bruno Bauer. At the time of his criticism, Bauer was a young teacher on the theological faculty of the University of Berlin, an associate of the conservative Hegelians who gave little indication of holding any but orthodox Christian views. He had been thoroughly educated in theology and seemed to have a promising career, blessed by the Prussian minister of education, Altenstein, and the celebrated Hegelian theologian, Marheineke. Almost suddenly, and certain without warning, he became an atheist and a belligerent foe of theology. Where he had once criticized Strauss, he soon passed into the radicalism that frightened Strauss. Where he had once insisted that Jesus's existence was a philosophical necessity, he came to deny that Jesus ever existed. Where he had once been a theologian, he became, in the descriptive phrase of Ruge, "the Robespierre of theology." [1] In abandoning theology for atheism, Bauer became an intellectual Penelope, unravelling at night what he had woven during the day.

In the old Thuringian city of Eisenberg, then part of the Duchy of Saxony-Altenburg, Bauer was born on September 6,

1. Ruge to Ludwig Ruge, 26 September 1842, *Briefwechsel und Tagebuchblätter*, 1:281.

1809. He too came from a middle-class family; his father was a porcelain painter. In 1815, Bauer's father was called to the Royal Prussian Porcelain Factory, and the family moved to Charlottenburg. There Bauer began his theological studies at the gymnasium and, in 1828, entered the University at Berlin. At Berlin, Bauer became, almost at once, a disciple of Hegel, his antipathy to Schleiermacher increasing as his devotion to Hegel grew. He proved an outstanding student and, in 1834, was offered a teaching post at the university. Overcoming his father's opposition—the elder Bauer had long dreamt of his son's becoming a pastor—Bauer accepted the post.[2]

Unfortunately, little is known of Bauer's private life. He seemed to thrive at the university, enjoying the cultural life of Berlin. He became a member of the "Doktorklub." In the roily atmosphere of cigar smoke and Hegelian argot at the coffee house where the members met, they discussed the religious implications of Hegel's thought and heard both the radical and conservative views of Hegel's philosophy expounded.[3] What the effect of all these debates was on Bauer, it is not possible to say. Generally throughout the 1830s, however, he was considered an ally of the conservative Hegelians, though he was certainly aware of the radical Hegelian position and friendly with exponents of it. As late as 1839, Ruge listed Bauer along with other conservative Hegelians, the "dromedary, Göschel, and the camel, Erdmann," as one of the reactionaries in philosophy.[4]

Bauer's publications also indicated his allegiance to the conservative Hegelians. Reviewing Strauss's *Life of Jesus* for the Hegelian journal, the *Jahrbücher für wissenschaftliche Kritik*, he criticized both Strauss's methods and conclusions. His major criticism was that Strauss failed to recognize the philosophical necessity in the appearance of Jesus. Bauer argued that in his

2. For the best account of Bauer's early career, see Dieter Hertz-Eichenrode, *Der Junghegelianer Bruno Bauer im Vormärz* (Berlin, 1959).
3. Hertz-Eichenrode, *Bruno Bauer im Vormärz*, pp. 30–31.
4. Ruge to Rosenkranz, 2 October 1839, *Ruges Briefwechsel*, 1:181.

person Jesus summarized all previous development, all the heathen principles and Hebrew revelation, and at the same time brought a new step in revelation, the union of divine and human natures in his person. Jesus, then, was the necessary conclusion of previous revelation and the necessary revelation of the next step in the development of the spirit. His appearance, indeed his reality, was a philosophical necessity.

> The man [Jesus], in whom the union of divine and human natures has appeared, has as his mother a virgin and his father a spirit: this is the absolute necessity of the divine and the human natures. His being is the result of the meeting of susceptibility and creative necessity, and all physiological questions are done away with in this meeting.[5]

Strauss's criticisms were irrelevant because Jesus was a philosophical necessity; he was needed in the development of self-consciousness, both to give purpose to revelation and to reveal the union of divine and human spirits. Hence, arguments about whether the gospel events really happened were completely irrelevant. The stories were philosophical necessities, and that was all that mattered.

Other publications of Bauer's showed the same sympathies. He did a series of studies on the theology of the Old Testament in the *Zeitschrift für spekulative Theologie*. In these he pronounced the conservative Hegelian views that Hegel's philosophy justified Christian dogma, that Hegel united theology and philosophy permanently, that Hegel saw Judaism as a special revelation, and that in Hegel's system faith and knowledge could coexist.[6]

Bauer's most important publication in his conservative period, however, was his *Religion of the Old Testament in the Historical Development of its Principles*, a two-volume study

5. *Jahrbücher für wissenschaftliche Kritik* 9 (1835): 896.
6. Martin Kegel, *Bruno Bauer und seine Theorien über die Entstehung des Christentums* (Leipzig, 1908), pp. 5–7, 10; and Hertz-Eichenrode, *Bruno Bauer im Vormärz*, pp. 10–22.

of the Hebraic principle, published in 1838. By the Hebraic principle Bauer meant the teaching of the absolute otherness of God, the teaching that God was totally separate from his creation, from his universe, from man. In tracing the history of that principle, he dismissed the early history of the Bible, the events prior to Abraham, as myths.[7] His major interest, however, lay in tracing revelation from Abraham through the prophets, from the teaching of monotheism to the announcement of a messiah. The final step in Hebraic development came with the prophets who foretold a messiah who would be the union of divine and human natures.[8] The progress of revelation from Abraham to the prophets meant both the fulfillment and the end of the Hebraic principle. For the Hebraic principle taught that God was separate from his creation, but the next step in revelation was to be the appearance of the messiah who would, in fact, unite God with his creation by uniting, in himself, divine and human spirits. Hence, the last step in revelation within the Hebraic principle was the dismissal of that principle. Israel had fulfilled its purpose; it had no future, it had no further use. Its end came with the destruction of the Hebraic principle by Jesus, who united divine and human natures. Jesus's existence, apart from all questions of history, was a philosophical necessity.

Bauer in all his public pronouncements was a conservative Hegelian and Christian; his private thoughts and personal counsels, though, are not known. His scholarly work was well-received, especially by the theologians who appreciated his attack on Strauss. Altenstein, the Prussian government minister who had arranged Hegel's appointment in 1818 and the appointment of Hegel's successor in 1835, became intent on placing Bauer in an important theological post.

The advancement of Bauer at Berlin was unlikely, as he had attacked one of the Berlin theologians, Hengstenberg, in a

7. *Die Religion des alten Testamentes in der geschichtlichen Entwicklung ihrer Principien* (Berlin, 1838), 1:9–77.

8. *Die religion des alten Testamentes,* 2:292–446.

bitter and polemical pamphlet.[9] But a sudden vacancy appeared at Bonn, and Altenstein decided to appoint Bauer to fill it. The Bonn theological faculty had no Hegelian on it, and the Prussian minister, an admirer of the Hegelian system, saw the opportunity of supplying the need. In his support of the Hegelian philosophy, he wanted to infiltrate the conservative theological faculties with disciples of Hegel. Bauer's appointment was unpopular with the Bonn faculty for precisely the reason that prompted Altenstein to make it, and he was treated with great suspicion even from the start. The theologians at Bonn were furious at having to accept as a colleague a man who openly counted himself a disciple of Hegel rather than of Schleiermacher and Neander.[10] Bauer arrived in the Rhineland city in the autumn of 1839 to assume his post, filled with hope and apprehension.[11]

Almost at once a conflict between Bauer and the Bonn faculty broke out. His enemies at Bonn believed that the best way to strike at him was to refuse to pay him for his trip and his inaugural lectures and to make no promises about future payment. The stratagem was the most effective they could have employed: Bauer had for several years been living a penurious existence, surviving only by selling a part of his private library and by working for Frau Hegel, preparing an edition of her husband's *Philosophy of Religion*. He needed money desperately and appealed to Altenstein to help. Fully realizing his plight, he wrote to his brother that "my situation is precarious in the highest degree." [12]

9. Kegel, *Bauer und seine Theorien*, pp. 20–22.
10. See Bonn's judgment of Bauer. *Gutachten der Evangelisch-theologischen Facultäten der Königlich Preussischen Universitäten über das Licentiaten Bruno Bauer auf dessen Kritik der evangelischen Geschichte der Synoptiker* (Berlin, 1842), p. 61.
11. For the story of Bauer's appointment and career at Bonn, see Max Lenz, *Geschichte der königlichen Friedrich-Wilhelms-Universität zu Berlin* (Halle, 1910–18), vol. 2, part 2, pp. 25–39.
12. Bauer to Edgar Bauer, 21 October 1839, *Briefwechsel zwischen Bruno Bauer und Edgar Bauer während die Jahre 1839–1842 aus Bonn und Berlin* (Charlottenburg, 1844), p. 10.

His situation grew even more precarious as it dragged on, unresolved. Before long both Frederick William III and Altenstein died and were replaced by the two virulent opponents of the Hegelian philosophy, Frederick William IV and Eichhorn. Bauer's plight seemed more hopeless as the new Prussian regime sought to thwart the influence of Hegel and remove Hegel's disciples from important posts. It was now up to Eichhorn to settle the conflict between Bauer and the Bonn faculty.

In the meantime, Bauer wrote a study of the gospel of John and submitted it to the ministry of education in order to elicit official support for his cause in Bonn. If he could demonstrate his theological scholarship, he thought, perhaps he would be able to hold his position. The arrival of his book at the ministry produced only consternation and resentment: Eichhorn was now firmly persuaded that Bauer was a dangerous man, a threat to Christian beliefs.

Bauer's study of John, *Critique of the Evangelical History of John,* distinguished this gospel from the synoptic gospels.[13] The synoptic gospels were intended to be histories, while the author of the gospel of John was a reflective artist who read back into the person of Jesus certain philosophical views of a later period. The gospel of John, then, was a work of artistic creation—not, of course, an intended deception—whose author used Jesus as the vehicle to express his particular point of view. The Jesus in this gospel was not the historic Jesus, but a creation of an artistic imagination that sought to use a personality to explain a philosophical conception. To find the historic Jesus, as all theologians presumably wanted to do, demanded exclusive concentration on the synoptic gospels, for the real Jesus could not be discovered in this artistic creation.

Bauer's rejection of the gospel of John as an historical record convinced Eichhorn that he was a threat to orthodox

13. See Kegel, *Bauer und seine Theorien,* pp. 25–32; and Hertz-Eichenrode, *Bruno Bauer im Vormärz,* pp. 48–49.

Christianity, and seemed to justify the attempts to remove the Hegelian influence from the theological faculties. For was not the result of Hegel's philosophy infidelity and unbelief?

Bauer wrote another essay in 1840, *The Evangelical State Church of Prussia and Knowledge*. This, since it appeared anonymously, did not militate against his position. It was, however, significant in his development and in the history of the Young Hegelians. The pamphlet was a study of church-state relations, especially of the union of the Lutheran and Reformed Churches in Prussia in 1817. In that union, he argued, each church ceased to exist, immersing itself in a higher spiritual form, the rational state. The Prussian state, having absorbed the churches in recognition that they were not something apart from its own mission, now embodied all spiritual life and progress. The Prussian state, not one of the Christian churches, was now the only form in which reason, freedom, and the good of the human spirit could have real existence. These transcendent categories were now all translated into realities inherent in the state, for the spirit had now to develop within the state. The Christian churches had surrendered all their spiritual claims to the rational state. Here, clearly, Bauer spoke as a disciple of Hegel.

He continued in the pamphlet to remind the state of its true spiritual calling; having recognized itself as the state of reason, Prussia had to fulfill its responsibilities. Bauer predicted a coming conflict between philosophy and theology. In this battle, Prussia, the rational state, had no choice but to protect philosophy. If Prussia, in aberration and betrayal of its own mission, did ally with orthodox religion against philosophy, philosophy would have to oppose the state and try to restore it to its true spiritual calling. The rational state had to support philosophy, the expression of its spiritual progress. Prussia had always stood for progress and learning, especially since the great period of Prussian reform when it first became the rational state. Bauer expressed great hope that the new king,

Frederick William IV, would fulfill Prussia's mission in this great turning-point of history.[14] In this hope, Bauer, like all of the Young Hegelians, was to be sorely disappointed.

Eichhorn considered Bauer's case with greater patience and toleration than might have been expected. He determined to pay Bauer a salary and allow him to continue at Bonn if he would promise to maintain scholarly objectivity in his lectures. Bauer agreed, but his promise was as easily broken as made: it proved impossible for him to be indulgent toward views other than his own.

The storm that had centered on Bauer and his views, the storm that seemed to have been neutralized by Eichhorn's modest solution, suddenly burst forth again in June 1841 with an increased fury. For Bauer published his most famous work, *Critique of the Evangelical History of the Synoptic Gospels,* an attack upon the historicity of the gospels, and he sent a personal copy of the work to Eichhorn!

In his study of the gospel of John, Bauer had promised to write a work on the synoptic gospels in order to discover the historic Jesus. His *Critique of the Evangelical History of the Synoptic Gospels,* the fulfillment of that promise, was, like Strauss's *Life of Jesus,* a combination of Hegelian philosophy, theology, and the critical method. Though his work never attained the popularity of Strauss's work, it still stands as one of the most important of the quests of the historic Jesus in the nineteenth century. It was also a dramatic pronouncement that Bauer had left his conservative colleagues and joined the Young Hegelians.

Bauer once gave the opinion that theology had to be "engaged in answering the questions that Strauss has raised." [15] It was against the background of Strauss's questions that Bauer wrote his study of the synoptic gospels. Though he finally op-

14. Kegel, *Bauer und seine Theorien,* pp. 32–34; and Hertz-Eichenrode, *Bruno Bauer im Vormärz,* pp. 55–59.

15. *Jahrbücher für wissenschaftliche Kritik* 14 (1840): 223.

posed several of Strauss's important conclusions, Bauer was in complete accord with him on one vital question: they both treated the gospels as human documents, products of human creativity and consciousness, not as the inspired works of men to whom divine revelation had descended. Their agreement was weighted with important religious implications—to them the word of God was the word of man.

Bauer, like Strauss, rejected the notion of a transcendent God who intervened in particular moments of history to reveal his truth to man. As good Hegelians, they both believed in a continual revelation within human history of the immanent spirit. Therefore, they viewed the gospels in terms of their human origins, in terms of the time and place in which they were written. "The gospels," Bauer concluded, "were written by men and their content together with their form has gone through a human self-consciousness." [16]

Bauer refused to accept Strauss's conclusion that the gospel writers merely recorded the tradition of their community. It did not matter, he argued, whether scholars concluded that the authors of the gospels "had written down the history given to them under the inspiration of the Holy Ghost" or whether "the evangelical history has built itself on tradition," since "both are the same in principle, for they are equally transcendent, and the freedom and immortality of self-consciousness are impaired in each." [17] For Bauer, tradition, as much as inspiration, would have been a force in control of the authors of the gospels. In taking possession of them in order to have itself recorded, it would have destroyed the individual creativity of the recorder. Tradition would have made the evangelist a tool, as much as inspiration would have, and, in so doing, would remove the faculty of self-consciousness. No, Bauer said, each gospel was the product of an individual crea-

16. *Kritik der evangelischen Geschichte der Synoptiker* (Leipzig, 1840–1843), 1:xvi.
17. *Kritik der evangelischen Geschichte*, 1:vii–viii.

tive self-consciousness working, not with some vague myth as Strauss would have it, but with reflection, creative reflection on real experiences.[18]

Bauer's emphasis, then, was on the personalities of the evangelists and on their gospels as works of literature. As John had written his gospel to affirm a particular point of view, so did the authors of the synoptic gospels. Each of the gospels was a literary work, an artistic creation, the product of an individual self-consciousness that aimed to demonstrate the philosophical viewpoint of its author. Each story, each supposed saying of Jesus, all of the characters and events in the gospels were influenced by the creative reflection of the authors. The object of reflection, however, was not the person of Jesus but the experiences of the early church. Conflicts arose within the early church, and the writers of the gospels, in order to express their opinions in those conflicts, stated their positions as religious tenets that they read back into the person and sayings of Jesus. None of the process, of course, involved fraud. Each evangelist was merely expressing religious truth in an artistic form, since "only the subject, the individual self-consciousness can bring it [truth] into form." [19]

Showing himself better trained in the methods of historical research than Strauss, Bauer sought to determine the priority of the gospels, to determine if any of them was based upon another. He accepted the hypothesis then current in German theology that Mark was the original gospel and that the other two gospels were based upon it, often using literary enlargements upon ideas found in Mark.[20] He concluded that all knowledge about Jesus was based, not on tradition—for that was philosophically impossible—nor on three independent gospels—for their dependence was clear—but upon one single gospel. The troubling question was whether the gospel of

18. *Kritik der evangelischen Geschichte*, 1:71.

19. *Kritik der evangelischen Geschichte*, 1:69. Cf. Albert Schweitzer, *The Quest of the Historical Jesus*, pp. 145–53.

20. Schweitzer, *Historical Jesus*, pp. 140–41.

Mark, like that of John, was also a literary creation, not a factual and eye-witness report but the artistic creation of a reflective author.

Bauer answered that the gospel of Mark, like the other gospels, was also an artistic creation, a literary account born from its author's reflection on the early conflicts within the church. The philosophical point of view from which Mark wrote his gospel was the messianic mission of Jesus. In Hebraic prophecy, "the messiah was only an ideal product of religious consciousness," not a particular person.[21] Mark wrote his account to demonstrate that Jesus was the Logos. Yet, in Jesus's own time, Bauer argued, there was no general expectation of the messiah; the only evidence for such an expectation came from the gospel of Mark itself. "Before the appearance of Jesus and before the developments of the Christian community," he wrote, "the reflective conception of 'the messiah' did not prevail, . . . there was no Judaic christology." [22] The Jews were not expecting the messiah. The idea of the messiah emerged in the early Christian community, and Mark, in writing his gospel, cast back into the person and the historical time of Jesus his own reflective conception of the messiahship.

What, then, could be known of the historic Jesus? Very little, in Bauer's view. Jesus could only be known through one original gospel, and that gospel was an artistic creation to present the author's philosophical viewpoint. Bauer did not now argue, as he did later, that Mark had invented the person of Jesus. He still accepted Jesus's existence, but he regarded the evangelists in the same category as Homer and Hesiod who, according to Herodotus, created the Greek gods.

Although Bauer realized he might be condemned for being negative, as Strauss was condemned, he regarded negative criticism as essential to the attainment of truth. For "criticism is the last act" of the Hegelian philosophy, and only through

21. *Kritik der evangelischen Geschichte*, 3:14.
22. *Kritik der evangelischen Geschichte*, 1:xvii. See also 2:409–10.

negation was progress possible.[23] Criticism helped to bring a higher step in the development of truth, by rejecting the historical accretions onto Christian truth. Speculative philosophy was to establish the tenets of the Christian faith in a new form, not in the form chosen by the evangelists. Criticism would reject the old forms of Christianity, not its content. "In the beginning," Bauer wrote, describing his work, "contradictions appear to dominate—but it would be a shoddy work that did not move through inner, living contradictions. At the end will be found the positive resolution." [24] His logic was that of Hegel, perhaps even that of Strauss.

The positive resolution that Bauer presented was based on Hegel's view of self-consciousness. All the Young Hegelians used this view in opposing Christianity and in developing their philosophical humanism. Hegel's view and the use made of it by the Young Hegelians have already been discussed, but Bauer's use of self-consciousness might be stated here for the sake of clarity. Hegel's disciples accepted his argument that self-consciousness united both subject and object, that the subject and object of consciousness were parts of a whole. Like all the Young Hegelians, Bauer believed that God and religion were the objects while man was the subject. Man, then, in so far as he was self-conscious, was both the subject and the object of his consciousness. But man had objectified his own spirit as divine, had alienated his own spirit from himself and worshipped it as transcendent. On the basis of Hegel's philosophy, Bauer knew there could be no difference between subject and object—in a religious sense, no difference between man and God—and that if man subjected himself to something external, he was surrendering to his own alienation and doing violence to his own freedom. If religion taught that there was some-

23. *Kritik der evangelischen Geschichte,* 1:xxi.
24. *Kritik der evangelischen Geschichte,* 1:xxiii n. Cf. Hertz-Eichenrode, *Bruno Bauer im Vormärz,* pp. 36–37; and Kegel, *Bauer und seine Theorien,* pp. 30–32.

thing separate from man to which he owed reverence, religion was a challenge to self-consciousness and freedom:

> The religious spirit is that cleavage of self-consciousness in which the essential preciseness of itself steps over against consciousness as one of its distinct powers. Self-consciousness must naturally go astray before this power—for it has thrown forth out of itself its own content and as long as it asserts itself as a subject for itself, it must feel itself to be nothing before that power, and thus it must assert itself as nothing.[25]

Self-consciousness demanded the unity of subject and object on the basis of an act of knowledge. Religion, in teaching God separate from man, was denying that unity and thus denying the act of knowledge. The worst offender in Bauer's eyes was Judaism, for teaching the absolute otherness of God.

The Christian revolution had ended the Judaic separation of God from man. Here was its great positive contribution. Whether Jesus existed was problematical, a matter of indifference. What was important was that the authors of the gospels had, by philosophical reflection, attained to the truth of the union of God and man. That they chose to express this truth in terms of Jesus was a comment only on the form in which they represented this truth. The truth of the union of divine and human spirits, the content of the gospels, was untouched by rejecting the form in which this truth was represented. Error came in when Christians raised the gospels to absolute authority and objectified Jesus as the unique manifestation of God in history. By subjecting themselves to the gospels, they subjected themselves to the form, but not the content, of truth. By subjecting themselves to Jesus, they once more made themselves victims of their own alienated spirit. Christianity taught the union of God and man. Men had centered that union on a person unique in history and denied that union to all other men. Thus Christianity, which began

25. *Kritik der evangelischen Geschichte der Synoptiker*, 1:25.

by ending man's alienation from himself, ended by reestablishing the alienation. It was now the task of philosophy to make men aware of the truth that humanity united divine and human natures, that in humanity, not in one unique person, subject and object were united.

This study of the synoptic gospels was what Bauer submitted to Eichhorn to convince the Prussian minister that he should be advanced on the theological faculty of Bonn. Perhaps it was no wonder that the theologians were aghast at such audacity. Bauer's conclusions were quite extraordinary for a man who wanted to retain a theological appointment. He contributed to the implications of the works of scholars like Strauss that the gospels were the work of mere men. What was more, he insisted that Christianity was obsolete and had to make way for a philosophy of humanism that saw all humanity as the union of divine and human natures.[26]

Eichhorn showed far greater patience than might have been expected, certainly far greater toleration than Bauer ever showed for those with whom he disagreed. He believed that Bauer's work "puts forth views that attack the essential part and certitude of the Christian truth at its innermost foundations," but rather than condemning the book and its author, he determined to ask the judgment of the theological faculties of all the Prussian universities.[27] In August, 1841, he sent a letter to the theological faculties asking for their answers to two questions: first, was Bauer a Christian; and second, should he be allowed to teach on a theological faculty.[28] The faculties were slow to respond, and their answers, once in, were neither uniform nor unequivocal. The Bonn faculty, where Bauer's enemies were strongest, wanted his license to teach withdrawn; the Königsberg faculty, though convinced of the fallacy of his views, did not think he should be forbidden to teach. Halle,

26. Cf. Hertz-Eichenrode, *Bruno Bauer im Vormärz*, pp. 49–55.
27. *Gutachten der Evangelisch-theologischen Facultäten*, iii.
28. *Gutachten*, pp. iii–iv.

Breslau, and Griefswald were evasive. The Berlin faculty was divided. Faced with these judgments, the Prussian ministerial council met and decided, in March, 1842, to forbid Bauer to teach.[29]

Bauer returned to Berlin after his dismissal, bitter and vengeful. During the months between his appointment to Bonn in 1839 and his dismissal in 1842, a gradual change of attitude began to possess him, a change difficult to explain that brought him to blatant atheism. Who can account for the subtle shifts, the personal moods, the movements of mind and heart that led him step by step farther left in the Hegelian spectrum? By a gradual process—apparently without external influence—Bauer had become a Young Hegelian.

His progress had been continually to the left: from his study of the Old Testament, to his attack on Hengstenberg, to his critique of the gospel of John, to his rejection of the historicity of all the gospels, to his virulent atheism. As early as 1840, Edgar Bauer wrote breathlessly to his father that "Bruno now believes in nothing." [30]

Now that Bauer had arrived at irrepressible atheism and had lost his freedom to teach, he would lose nothing by revealing his opinions to the public. Besides, he was never one to keep his ideas to himself. He openly declared his connections with the Young Hegelians. "The Young Hegelians," he wrote, "are the true Hegelians, the legitimate Hegelians." [31] He wrote two books on Hegel, *The Trumpet of the Last Judgment on Hegel, the Atheist and Anti-Christ* and *Hegel's Teachings Concerning Religion and Art,* in which he claimed that atheism was the true consequence of Hegel's philosophy. Bauer also began to

29. Lenz, *Friedrich-Wilhelms-Universität,* vol. 2, part 2, pp. 35–39.

30. Bruno to Edgar Bauer, 20 January 1840, *Briefwechsel zwischen Bruno und Edgar Bauer,* p. 31.

31. *Die Posaune der jüngsten Gerichten über Hegel den Atheisten und Antichristen: ein Ultimatum* (1841), in Hertz-Eichenrode, *Bruno Bauer im Vormärz,* p. 67.

look to Ruge's journal as an ally and published articles in its pages while praising it for "having declared open war." [32] Ruge was quick to respond to his new ally, favorably reviewing his publications. Early in 1842, after his dismissal, Bauer began contributing articles to the *Rheinische Zeitung,* thus allying himself with the Rhineland Young Hegelians. The government might prevent him from teaching, but he had found two publications that were receptive to his ideas.

Bauer's formal connections with the Young Hegelians went beyond his friendship with Ruge and his writing for the *Hallische* and *Deutsche Jahrbücher* and for the *Rheinische Zeitung.* Perhaps more important to him was his membership in the circle of Berlin Young Hegelians, the "Freien." Here Bauer found an audience for his opinions, and colleagues, if not friends, with whom to debate. His brothers, Edgar and Egbert, were members of the group, as were Stirner and Rutenberg; frequent visitors to the ranks were Marx, Ruge, Herwegh, Engels, Hoffmann von Fallersleben, and other radicals from the vicinity of the Prussian capital. Hippel's Weinstube, impromptu gathering place for the "Freien," formed a convivial, if contrasting, background for the earnest discussions of religion and Hegelian philosophy. The conviviality formed only a surface unity: the circle was never more than a gathering of strong personalities who were momentary companions, and it was on the basis of personality that the circle shattered and divided. For how could a group of dogmatists, each vying for leadership and attention, unite to form a close party? Bauer was disillusioned with the "Freien" shortly after his return to Berlin society, yet there seemed to be no other progressive group in Berlin, and he remained with them while condemning them as "beer literati." [33] When the group finally dissolved, he was not sorry.

32. Bruno to Edgar Bauer, 6 May 1841, *Briefwechsel zwischen Bruno und Edgar Bauer,* p. 136.
33. Bauer to Ruge, 15 June 1842, cited in Hertz-Eichenrode, *Bruno Bauer im Vormärz,* p. 90.

Berlin society offered other opportunities for a clever man like Bauer. He returned to the salon of Bettina von Arnim who gained the opposition of the Prussian government by her publication of *This Book Belongs to the King* in 1843, a work vaguely socialist that urged the king to alleviate the misery of the poor, grant "freedom," and encourage the "free spirit" in religion and politics. Bauer's two brothers, Edgar, the outspoken supporter of Bruno's views, and Egbert, the wealthy brother who opened a publishing firm to print the works of his brothers, frequented the salon with him. "The three little leaves of a clover" was the descriptive phrase used by the Prussian police to describe the brothers Bauer.[34]

Bruno Bauer had returned to Berlin after his dismissal from Bonn with a mistaken assurance. He believed that his dismissal announced the great crisis that all the Young Hegelians were expecting, the conflict between progressive theory and reactionary practice; he expected that the Berlin radicals would use his case as a rallying call. Even in Bonn he waited for "the progressives in Berlin" to adopt his ideas and "swerve to the left" in their religious views.[35] His expectation, however, proved unwarranted. When he returned to Berlin only a few other Young Hegelians consorted with him, and these showed little inclination to accept his unquestioned leadership; he returned to Berlin and the Young Hegelian apocalypse seemed as remote as ever. In this situation, Bauer grew more bitter, more outspoken, more extreme. He came to identify the reaction with Christianity, and he soon demanded the complete elimination of all religion. His opinions were made all the more astonishing by the violence of his language. He abandoned scholarly forms and wrote polemically, sarcastically, passionately.

34. Report to Frederick William IV, 6 June 1844, in *Bettine von Arnim und Friedrich Wilhelm IV: ungedruckte Briefe und Aktenstücke,* ed. Ludwig Geiger (Frankfurt, a.M., 1902), pp. 58–59.

35. Bruno to Edgar Bauer, 15 March 1841, *Briefwechsel zwischen Bruno und Edgar Bauer,* p. 48.

Ruge wrote excitedly that "Bruno Bauer . . . and Feuerbach have or will proclaim the Mountain and will raise the banner of atheism and mortality." [36] Bauer waved that banner with unlimited enthusiasm. Christianity had become his chief hate, and with passionate intensity he worked to overthrow its power. Not that Christianity had taught false doctrine. In that sense Bauer was not anti-Christian. Christianity was a moment of truth in the development of the human spirit, it was true for the time and place in which it appeared, but it was a religion preserved in a transitional form. The transitional had become absolute and prevented the progress of truth—here was the great sin of Christianity.[37] Like Hegel, Bauer saw Protestant Christianity as the highest possible development of religion, but, now under the guidance of Feuerbach, he denied that religion was the highest spiritual development. He insisted that self-consciousness emancipate itself from its own creation, religion, in order to have the freedom for its own development. Increasingly he absorbed the Hegelian absolute spirit into his own person and spoke only of the self-consciousness of the subjective spirit, outside of which there was no spiritual power. Development for him meant the increasing perfection of the human spirit to the point where it ended human self-alienation completely. As a disciple of Hegel, he insisted on a monistic philosophy and continually denounced the worship by men of spiritual categories external to themselves, categories they have themselves created. There was no spiritual existence outside of man. "If I have exposed the lies and hypocrisies of theology," Bauer asked, "must I invent new ones?" [38] Any spiritual category apart from man was a result of his own alienation and destroyed human freedom.

Bauer's publications revealed his passionate hatred for Christianity and his urge to replace it with a philosophy of human-

36. Ruge to Stahr, *Ruges Briefwechsel,* 1:239.

37. Cf. Schweitzer, *Historical Jesus,* pp. 153–57.

38. *Die gute Sache der Freiheit und meine eigene Angelegenheit* (Zürich und Winterthur, 1842) , p. 201.

ism. In the book he wrote in immediate response to his dismissal from Bonn, *The Good Cause of Freedom and My Own Affair,* he publicly announced that he was an atheist and defended atheism as the only position that freed man from the tyranny of religion. His atheism was that of all the Young Hegelians: it did not deny God, it denied the possibility of a spiritual existence apart from man. He denied a transcendent God. Religion, he charged, was preventing the emergence of human freedom, for in religion the human "spirit is separated from man and placed in heaven" and the result has been "confusion, barbarity, and inhumanity." [39] The self-alienation of man had to be ended by the acceptance of the philosophy of humanism. When religion was destroyed, "it is then a question of humanity, and humanity will be everything." [40] His message, like that of all the Young Hegelians, was that Christianity, no longer true for the times in which he lived, had to be replaced by humanism.

An even more forceful, if vituperative, critique of Christianity came from his pen in 1843, *Christianity Exposed.* Seized by the censors before it was published, this book never appeared publicly until 1927. Yet it is important to mention it here as an indication of Bauer's views and a measure of what he must have been broadcasting to the "Freien" and to every habitué of Bettina von Arnim's salon. In a letter to Julius Fröbel, who was to publish this work, Bauer summarized its contents for him: "I demonstrate that religion is a hell composed of hatred for humanity and that God is the bailiff of this hell . . . ." [41] Condensing all his hatred for religion in this study, he once more denounced religion as the alienation of the human spirit from man and charged that it could linger on only because

39. *Die gute Sache der Freiheit,* p. 203.
40. *Ibid.*
41. Bauer to Fröbel, 2 August 1843, in Ernst Barnikol, "Bruno Bauers Kampf gegen Religion und Christentum und die Spaltung des vormärzlichen preussischen Opposition," *Zeitschrift für Kirchengeschichte* 46 (1927): 5.

man was weak, despondent, poor, and unhappy. Courage and philosophical criticism would put an end to it.

Bauer believed that this book would "decide the question of religion once and for all." [42] In that expectation he was grievously disappointed. For all his philosophical assurance, for all his exhortations, Christianity refused to succumb to his implacable blows. Like Strauss and Feuerbach, he had again and again to return to criticizing religion and, like them, he died knowing that his great mission, the replacement of Christianity with humanism, remained unaccomplished.

One thing only, beside self-conscious humanity, Bauer seemed to allow autonomous existence—the principle of criticism. Criticism involved the application of Hegelian philosophy to current theological and philosophical positions in order to determine the diversity between spirit and reality in them. Its ultimate purpose was to work for the reconciliation of man with his spirit. Bauer had used the critical method in his study of the gospels, not profaning the sacred, but determining their true content; and he dismissed the forms in which their stories were expressed as historical, not absolute, creations. Criticism, then, sought to explain the development from the past to the present and to cast off the historical forms in which developing truth had been expressed. It was for him intimately connected with the development of consciousness, and its purpose, though seemingly negative, was to aid in the development of subsequent steps of truth. "Without passing through the fire of criticism," he explained, "nothing will emerge into the new world . . . ." [43] And he asserted even more forcefully that criticism was the means for ending the alienation of man from himself: "Criticism is the crisis that breaks the delirium of humanity and lets man understand himself once more." [44] The

42. "Bruno Bauers Kampf gegen Religion," p. 4.
43. *Die Judenfrage*, cited in Hertz-Eichenrode, *Bruno Bauer im Vormärz*, pp. 45–46.
44. *Die gute Sache der Freiheit*, p. 204.

Young Hegelian apocalypse, the crisis through which Bauer believed his generation was passing, would be informed and propelled by criticism.

There was no doubt that Bauer had inflexible faith in the principles of criticism. "Religion," he cried, "do you hear me? —religion will be absolutely destroyed by criticism." [45] Part of that dogmatic faith rested on his insistence that theory, not empirical reality, was the ultimate truth. Unlike Strauss and Feuerbach, he was a Young Hegelian who preserved the monistic philosophy as an uncompromising idealism. For him the ideal was the only true reality—history, after all, developed in the realm of thought, in the self-consciousness—and "theory has given us freedom, . . . theory has revealed to us our own inner essence and has given us the courage to be ourselves and to unite ourselves with our own essence." [46] Theory, then, the theory of criticism, would end the self-alienation of man. For that reason, "the terrorism of pure theory must clear the field." [47] Ruge's description of Bauer as the Robespierre of theology seems a sound character analysis.

Because of Bauer's increasing insistence upon the theory of criticism, he finally broke all connections with the "Freien," with Ruge and his journalistic Hegelianism, with all parties. He explained in 1843 that "everyone must now be separated and each must operate on his own hand." [48] Since the critic must deal with pure theory, he must stand independent of all parties, all groupings, all assumptions. The critic could not belong to the society, the philosophical causes, the world of thought that he criticized; he had to stand apart, condemned to loneliness because of his calling. "The critic," he wrote, "does not belong to any party, nor does he want to belong to

45. *Die gute Sache der Freiheit*, p. 201.
46. *Die gute Sache der Freiheit*, p. 224.
47. Bauer to Marx, 28 March 1841, *MEGA*, part 1, vol. 1, section 2, p. 247.
48. Ruge to Marx, 4 June 1843, *MEGA*, part 1, vol. 1, section 2, p. 309.

any party—he is lonely, lonely in that he has immersed himself in opposition, lonely in that he has set himself apart."[49] It can only be speculation to what extent this attitude was influenced by his connections with Stirner, the anarchist among the "Freien," or to what extent it was merely the unavoidable resolution of his absolute idealism, his personal dogmatism. One thing, however, was clear: Bauer, in his own eyes, had become criticism incarnate.

Bauer once wrote that "the creed of atheism . . . will split and dissolve parties and then create new ones."[50] Now that he had resolved to stand alone in the empty realm of criticism, the fate of parties no longer mattered to him. Those among the Prussian opposition who cared about parties realized the unhappy effect Bauer's views had in splitting that opposition. Bauer's conflict with the Prussian government over both his academic appointment and the censorship of his books had become a political issue. The liberals in Prussia who supported Bauer found that, though they intended their support to be taken as a defense of academic freedom against the strong hand of the government, they had allied themselves with atheism. At best they found themselves uncomfortable in a politically unpopular alliance that went far beyond their modest demands for the separation of church from state. Religionists who might otherwise have allied with the liberals could not find it in their consciences to defend Bauer. What was worse, Bauer insisted upon turning all issues, all political questions, into religious issues. The liberals wanted political action; Bauer wanted the destruction of religion: their definitions of freedom seemed entirely different. The cleavage seemed to worsen as the Weinstube soirées urged spiritual liberation and the liberal groups urged political reforms.[51]

49. Bauer in *Allgemeine Literatur Zeitung*, cited in Hertz-Eichenrode, *Bruno Bauer im Vormärz*, p. 103.

50. Bauer to Ruge, 6 December 1841, *MEGA*, part 1, vol. 1, section 2, p. 263.

51. See Barnikol, "Bruno Bauers Kampf gegen Religion," for the splits in the Prussian opposition that resulted from Bauer's views.

Bauer had been quite right in seeing atheism as a divisive force.

The liberal support of Bauer's cause was unfortunate for a further reason: Bauer, whatever may be said of him, was not a liberal. The liberals supported the separation of church and state. Bauer, on the other hand, applauded the union of the two and the absorption by the state of the spiritual life of its citizens. For him the secular state was nonsense. The liberals generally favored some sort of franchise and exhibited some concern over the condition of the people. Bauer had disdain for the mass of people, for majority rule, for any such numerical principle that would swamp the power of the independent critic. Popular rule in his mind was equal to ignorance and materialism, the destruction of culture, the end of the critical philosophy, and, hence, the denial of freedom. The liberals favored political and social reforms. Bauer believed in pure, theoretical criticism, in abolishing bad forms, not reforming them. Bauer was, and continued to be, an absolute idealist.

Another issue over which Bauer clashed pointedly with the liberals was the question of Jewish emancipation. The liberals, generally supporting civil liberties, supported Jewish agitation for the removal of political and social liabilities and for the toleration of their religious practices. Bauer quickly and violently attacked the whole movement for Jewish emancipation, first in an essay in the *Deutsche Jahrbücher* in 1842, then as a pamphlet, *The Jewish Question*, in 1843. His basic opposition to Jewish emancipation lay in his insistence that no group whose spiritual principles differed from those of the state deserved the protection of the state; in a sense they were not members of the state, since they based their lives on something outside the state. To grant the Jews special rights because of their religion was to encourage a dualistic state, to suggest that man's spirit was separate from his body. The liberal state, then, was a threat to freedom, for, in seeing man's spiritual life as distinct from the state, it committed the sin of dualism. Besides, Bauer was not about to defend the rights of Judaism when he saw in its basic position, the separation of God from the universe, the opposition to human freedom, the alienation he so detested. The Jews were so reactionary that, not only would they not accept the atheism and humanism of the new dispensation, they would not even accept the old Christian revolution that ended the division between divine and human natures. Did such a reactionary minority, such opponents of freedom, have the right to be protected by a state that should emancipate all men from the tyranny of religion? Bauer's anti-Judaism had deep philosophical roots in his acceptance of the Hegelian definitions of the state and of religion.

Bauer admitted that "the question of emancipation is a general question, the most important question of our time . . . ." [52] That emancipation did not mean the freeing of one religious group; it meant the freeing of all mankind from religion. Christians were not free, why should they free the Jews? If Jews wanted emancipation, they should adopt atheism and the critical philosophy and work for the emancipation of humanity; it was as human beings, not as Jews, that they could have freedom. Once again, Bauer saw freedom as a religious issue; once again, the liberals were aghast.[53]

One incident, strikingly revealing the opposition between Bauer and the liberals, took place in the autumn of 1841 in Berlin. Members of the opposition in Prussia were feting the south German liberal, Welcker, and they asked Bauer, the martyr for academic freedom, to attend the testimonial. At the dinner Bauer rose and called for a toast to the Hegelian philosophy of the state, the most excellent, energetic, and liberal view of the state in existence. Bauer smilingly observed that on this toast, "Welcker practically choked." [54] Bauer al-

52. Bauer, *Die Judenfrage* (Braunschweig, 1843), p. 61.

53. For Marx's review of Bauer's views on Jewish emancipation, see *Deutsch-Französische Jahrbücher*, 1–2 (1844):182–214.

54. Bauer to Ruge, 24 December 1841, *MEGA*, part 1, vol. 1, section 2, p. 265.

ways believed in the spiritual nature of the state—the Hegelian state—a view the south German liberals would never accept.

When the Revolution of 1848 came to Germany, Bauer, the critic who had renounced party connections, stood apart and watched it scornfully. Ruthlessly applying his criticism to the revolutionary movement, he mocked it as a fraud, a farce, an inevitable failure that was comic, not tragic. It was led by the "Bürger," a derisive term Bauer used to describe the middle-class revolutionaries who were revolutionaries in spite of themselves, men who wanted to preserve the old forms of society but to place themselves at their head. In his view, the "Bürger" was a "half-educated person who decks himself out in the rags of a threadbare, aristocratic finery," a man who "creates no new image and fails to destroy the old." [55] For the revolution to succeed, the old world had to be destroyed, its ideas and images shattered. Only then could the new world, the world all the Young Hegelians were awaiting, emerge. The "Bürger" failed to realize this truth and used "empty phrases, . . . conferences, deliberations, and negotiations" to preserve what had no right any longer to existence—"the old world, its wisdom exhausted, has nothing more to endow." [56] The "Bürger" did not understand the philosophical necessity that demanded the creation of a new idea or image that would unite all parties and divisions, that would end the separation of class from class, state from state, man from man. The fate of the National Assembly was only too clear an example of the "Bürger's" failure to find some all-embracing principle that would unite all apparent divergencies.[57] Bauer's final estimate of all the events of 1848 and 1849 was expressed in one piercing verdict: "The entire revolution was a fraud." [58]

55. *Die bürgerliche Revolution in Deutschland seit dem Anfang der deutsch-katholischen Bewegung bis zum Gegenwart* (Berlin, 1849), p. 25.
56. *Die bürgerliche Revolution*, pp. 25–26.
57. See Bauer's *Der Untergang des Frankfurter Parlaments: Geschichte der deutschen constituirenden Nationalversammlung* (Berlin, 1849).
58. *Untergang des Parlaments*, p. 279.

In Bauer's eyes one unifying principle did emerge victorious from the revolution—absolutism. The existing governments that withstood the revolution were the real victors, their absolutism the unifying idea of the future. It was "absolutism in which the revolution found both its end and its form," and the state that best exemplified absolutism was Russia.[59] Russia seemed for Bauer the hope of the future. He had lost faith in Prussia because of its treatment of him, a treatment in which it was only too clear outmoded Christianity dominated the interests of the state. The year before the revolution he had published his *Russia and Teutonism* in which he despaired of Germany's future, lamented Prussia's sterility, and looked to Russia as the future leader of humanity and civilization. The revolution seemed only to confirm his views. Russia, the spiritual state in which Christianity was subservient to the state, the state that was founded on the unifying principle of absolutism, did not falter before the fraudulent force of the revolution. It was Russia that destroyed the revolution; it was Russia that held the future hope of humanity. At odds with his colleagues in nearly everything, Bauer was at odds with them in his admiration of Russia. There was generally among the German intellectuals a hatred and dread of Russia: in the words of one liberal journal, it was "the flaming hatred of Russia" that stirred the hearts of most German intellectuals.[60]

Bauer's pessimism about Prussia and his admiration for Russia were changed by the successes of Bismarck. It was not, however, an abandonment of principles by Bauer, dazzled by success and deafened by the drumbeats of nationalism. He had always been an opponent of nationalism and he continued to be. He had, long before, seen Prussia as the bearer of a mission. What he admired about Bismarck was that the Prussian statesman seemed to recognize and perform this mission, the introduction of a new era. Bismarck seemed to institute everything

59. *Untergang des Parlaments,* p. 305.
60. *Kölnische Zeitung,* 25 March 1848, cited in L. B. Namier, *1848: the Revolution of the Intellectuals* (London, 1944), p. 49.

that Bauer had wanted. His *Kulturkampf* seemed to be Prussia's adoption of the task of destroying Christianity. His emancipation of Germany from Austria seemed to be a victory for the rational state. The great burst of literary and artistic production under Bismarck seemed to be the recognition by the state of its spiritual role. Bismarck's creation of a centralized absolutism seemed to be the institution of the unifying ideal so long needed. No wonder that Bauer spoke of "Bismarck's bearing, . . . his anguish, his *Weltschmerz*, . . . his energetic service to the state." [61] Bauer did not betray himself in his final devotion to Prussia. For years he had called upon Prussia to lead the way to the new era and now, for the first time, Prussia seemed to be performing that mission. His philosophical vision of the Hegelian state seemed to be transforming itself into reality, and his elation over seeing his life-long dream fulfilled was only natural.

Bauer had still not found peace. Religion was, and remained until his death, a gnawing problem for him. The opposition would not listen to him; Christianity would not die. He would have to turn to his pen once more. Shortly after the Revolution of 1848, still bothered by the question of the historic Jesus, Bauer wrote his *Critique of the Epistles of Paul*. The Tübingen School had already pronounced the epistles of Paul to be authentic. That did not matter to Bauer. He denied their authenticity and placed their origin at the end of the second century. The letters, he concluded, were written by an author reading the conflict between Judaism and heathenism into the past.

Still dissatisfied, he published, in 1850–1851, his famed *Critique of the Evangelical Gospels and the History of their Origin*, denying the historical existence of Jesus. He had been near that denial for some time, perhaps even as early as 1841. He argued that there was one original gospel on which all the others were based, though the text of that original no

61. *Zur Orientirung über die Bismarck'sche Ära* (Chemnitz, 1880), p. 311.

longer existed. The author of that original gospel was a reflective, creative artist living in the second century, a man who considered the philosophical conflicts among Judaism, Hellenism, heathenism, and sought to establish some positive view out of all these, to express the Christian revolution of the union of God and man in some symbolic form. He thus took the philosophical categories he wanted to establish and attached them to an historical figure of his own creation, Jesus. Jesus, in short, was the creation of an artist to symbolize the great philosophical insight of the union of divine and human natures. To be true to the original Christian revolution, Bauer argued, men had to reject the gospels both as records of absolute truth and as historical records and to accept the new form of truth, philosophical humanism, the union of divine and human natures in all of humanity. "All progress in history has only been possible through criticism," and, consequently, Christianity had to be criticized, exposed, and replaced by humanism.[62] The world had changed, but Bauer's message was still the same.

Even with this work Bauer did not find peace. Growing older, he grew more cantankerous. In 1874, in his *Philo, Strauss, and Renan and Primitive Christianity*, he charged that the authors of the gospels based their work on Philo's combination of Greco-Roman philosophy and Judaism. Three years later, he published his *Christ and the Caesars: the Origin of Christianity in Roman Greece*, a summary of all his previous views. Here he charged that Jesus was created by a member of a philosophical group in the Roman Empire of the second century. The original evangelist used the ideas of Seneca, the stoics, Philo, Judaism, Hellenism, heathenism, Josephus, and the general thought of his time.

Still not satisfied, Bauer published another study in 1880, *The Original Gospel and the Opponents of the Book: Christ and the Caesars*, where he again argued that Jesus was created

62. *Kritik der Evangelien und Geschichte ihres Ursprungs* (Berlin, 1850–51), 1:x, xvi.

by an artist who combined the ideas of Seneca, Philo, stoicism, Judaism, and Roman centralization. The more Bauer wrote, the less impact each succeeding book seemed to have. One thing only was clear: the desert of his solitude was still strewn with the mirages of his youth.

Having worked in his last years in the family tobacco shop, Bauer died in 1882 without having found either tranquillity or happiness. All his life he had made just one demand, based on his Hegelian philosophy—that Christianity be abandoned for humanism. It was just that demand, as Strauss and Feuerbach also learned, that the world would not satisfy; hence Bauer's bitterness, frustration, unhappiness. Always an idealist, Bauer believed that the application of philosophical criticism would bring the advent of the new world of humanism. When it did not, he continued more vehemently to identify his own self-consciousness with Hegel's absolute spirit and to become, in a very real sense, criticism incarnate. Having shown to his own philosophical satisfaction that Christianity was no longer true and having applied his criticism toward the emergence of a new world of philosophical humanism that did not appear, he found himself

> Wandering between two worlds, one dead,
> The other powerless to be born.

How often an author's use of a pseudonym has indicated his adoption of a new personality. Mlle. Dupin adopted the *nom de plume* "George Sand" and with it the character of a masculine, emancipated woman. Friedrich von Hardenberg chose the name "Novalis" and converted to Catholicism in his romantic protest against the Protestantism and rationalism of his background. The Young Hegelian, Johann Kaspar Schmidt, also wrote under a pseudonym. He was a quiet, mildmannered man, detached and reflective. As "Max Stirner" he was a passionate egoist, an outspoken anarchist who condoned selfishness and crime, attacked the notions of religion, the state, the family in violent language. As Schmidt he was, in any measurement of worldly success, a failure. As Stirner, he was the notorious exponent of anarchism.

Johann Kaspar Schmidt was born in Bayreuth on October 25, 1806.[63] As is the case with Bauer, little is known of his private life and thoughts, of the tortuous path that led him from his academic career to anarchism. There is no collection of private letters, there is no extant picture of him except for a pencil sketch done by Engels at Hippel's Weinstube. It is really only as Max Stirner that his personality has had an historical significance; as Schmidt he has faded into obscurity.

Stirner was born into a lower middle-class Protestant family; his father was a maker of musical instruments. Part of the unhappiness that was to pursue Stirner all his life came early to him when his father died shortly after his birth. His mother remarried two years later, and the family moved to West Prussia. Young Stirner, however, returned to Bayreuth for his youthful education. Coincidentally, the director of the gymnasium where he studied was Georg Andreas Gabler, the philosopher who was Hegel's immediate successor at Berlin.

Stirner went to the University of Berlin for his training in theology and philosophy. What his intentions were, what career he was anticipating, is not known. He showed interest in theology, attending the lectures of Schleiermacher, Neander, Marheineke, and he heard Hegel lecture. Even then he was plagued by the ill health that punctuated his entire life, and he left Berlin for the University of Erlangen in 1828 where he continued his studies in theology and philosophy. Still in frail health, he was forced to undertake a long rest tour of Germany, and, in 1829, he entered the University of Königsberg. There he attended no lectures; for reasons of health and finances, his studies were again interrupted. His mother's mental illness further distracted him, and it was not until 1832, still beset by his own illness, that he returned to Berlin to complete his studies.

63. The standard biography of Stirner is John Henry Mackay's *Max Stirner: sein Leben und sein Werk* (Treptow bei Berlin, 1910).

In 1835, the year Strauss published his *Life of Jesus*, Stirner took the examinations to obtain a license to teach in Prussia. He failed to pass them. For a year's probation, he went to teach at the Königliche Realschule in Berlin, but he left the position shortly after accepting it. In 1837, hope appeared that he might begin to lead a normal life, when he married the daughter of one of his former landlords. Whatever happiness he derived from his marriage was short-lived. His wife died in childbirth less than a year after their marriage.[64]

Stirner obtained a teaching position in 1839 that seemed, temporarily, to satisfy him: he began to lecture at Madame Gropius's school for young ladies in Berlin. Teaching, Stirner was, for one of the few times in his life, free from financial worries. He was living in Berlin, a city he knew from his student days, frequenting the coffee houses and taverns, acquiring for himself the reputation of being a dandy. He sought the company of intellectuals and litterateurs—and Berlin had many such men wafting about its wine shops. Though he came to be acquainted with many young intellectuals, he never became personally close to anyone. He would talk about philosophy, but not about himself or his private thoughts. He never allowed to any man the one benefit of friendship, the entry into the privacy of his soul. Throughout his life he had neither a close friend nor a personal enemy.

In 1841 Stirner became a member of the "Freien," that group of Young Hegelians and radicals who met at Hippel's Weinstube. How he became a member is not known. He soon belonged to the inner core, the organizing center of the "Freien," along with the brothers Bauer, Buhl, Meyer, and the others. He seemed friendly to all those who frequented Hippel's, yet he was reserved. He never engaged in the philosophical brawls that ended with over-turned tables and chairs, he never used the appeals to cynicism and vulgarity that the others cherished. He sat aloof and calm, smiling knowingly through the cigar smoke, inserting an occasional word into

64. Mackay, *Max Stirner,* pp. 45–62.

the animated discussions. He was willing to talk about philosophical matters, but he never spoke about himself.[65]

Through his contact with the "Freien" Stirner first began to publish his essays.[66] Through the Berlin group, he came to know the editors of the *Rheinische Zeitung,* the Young Hegelian newspaper printed in Cologne, and he published several important articles in it. Interestingly enough, he never published in Ruge's *Hallische Jahrbücher,* the major organ for the Young Hegelians. In publishing his articles in the *Rheinische Zeitung,* he used the pseudonym "Max Stirner." Ever since his school days he had borne this name because of his inordinately high forehead, and it was the name by which he was known among the "Freien."

As his first article for the Rhineland Young Hegelians, Stirner wrote "The False Principle of Our Education, or Humanism and Realism" in April, 1842. The essay was an important indication of his autonomous development and a forecast of his later work on individualism. He rejected both humanism and realism as authorities external to the individual that actually limited his freedom. To Stirner, true freedom was internal; external authority merely negated internal freedom by demanding that the individual surrender his obedience to it. "Whoever is a complete man," he wrote, "needs to have no authority." [67] Each man was to be the complete measure of himself. To fulfill his capacities, he had to have complete freedom of will, a freedom that disdained external authority as tyrannical. "The idea and moving-force of our time is the freedom of the will," he argued, "so the creation of a free personality must hover before pedagogy as its beginning and goal." [68] A free man could only emerge when his

65. Mackay, *Max Stirner,* pp. 99–107.
66. For a discussion of Stirner's published essays, see Mackay, pp. 107–122; and Henri Arvon, *Aux sources de l'existentialisme: Max Stirner* (Paris, 1954), pp. 19–41.
67. "Das unwahre Prinzip unserer Erziehung oder der Humanismus und Realismus," *Kleinere Schriften,* ed. John Henry Mackay (Berlin, 1898), p. 27.
68. "Das unwahre Prinzip," p. 28.

will was disentangled from all authority alien to man himself. Stirner thus decreed that "the goal to which our time must be directed" is "the necessary destruction of knowledge not founded on will and the raising up of self-conscious will that is consummated in the glory of a free person." [69] Already Stirner's abiding concern for the freedom of the individual personality and the individual will was evident. Equally evident was his Young Hegelian concern for man's alienation from himself.

Stirner's second important essay, "Art and Religion," appeared in the *Rheinische Zeitung* in June, 1842. In this article, he firmly announced that he was on the side of Young Hegelian atheism, the atheism that did not deny divine spirit but denied a transcendent, personal God. Bruno Bauer published two books—*The Trumpet of the Last Judgment on Hegel, the Atheist and Antichrist* in 1841 and *Hegel's Teachings Concerning Religion and Art* in 1842—in which he claimed that Hegel was an atheist and that atheism was the true consequence of his philosophy. Stirner's article agreed totally with Bauer's claim.

"Hegel," Stirner began, "put art before religion." [70] Hegel, he went on, had a profound insight when he realized that as an artist created a work of art he was transforming the ideal within himself into an external object or form. Thus, sculpture, painting, poetry, were not external and objective. They were, in fact, the ideal, the spiritual, alienated from man and embodied in the object of art. As there was no spirit apart from man, so there was no art apart from man, since spirit was the foundation of art. All artistic creation, then, came from within. When man viewed a work of art, he had to realize that the ideal he recognized in it was the ideal immanent in himself, for in the artistic creation, "man stands alienated from himself." [71]

Stirner further credited Hegel with the same insight into

69. "Das unwahre Prinzip," p. 30.
70. "Kunst und Religion," *Kleinere Schriften*, p. 35.
71. "Kunst und Religion," p. 36.

the origin of religion. Man created religion by alienating the ideal within himself and embodying it in some external form. This external form he defined as subject, called it a "god," and then subjected himself to it. He thus became a prisoner of his own alienated spirit, tyrannized over by his own creation. "Here," Stirner sadly observed, "lie all the tortures and battles of thousands of years." [72] He reminded his readers that Homer and Hesiod created the gods for the Greeks—the Young Hegelians, and Hegel himself, never tired of pointing this out: "artists have founded religion." [73] The artist alienated spirit into his created object, and man made that alienation permanent by turning the object into a subject, into God. "Art is the beginning, the *alpha* of religion," Stirner wrote. "Without art and the creative artist, religion would never have originated." [74]

Here were all the important elements of the Young Hegelian attack on religion. Religion represented the alienation of man's spirit from himself and the enthronement of that spirit in God, yet spirit was meaningless apart from man, for spirit was immanent. It was important that Stirner assigned the origin of these views to Hegel's philosophy.

At this point in his intellectual development, Stirner's philosophical relations with other Young Hegelians were evident. Feuerbach's *Essence of Christianity* expressed conclusions that were similar to those of Stirner. The idea that religion was the self-alienation of man, that man created God, was essentially Feuerbach's message. Now Stirner was pronouncing the same homocentric origins of religion.[75] Yet, on his own avowal, he regarded Hegel's philosophy as the source of his views. Influence is, at best, elusive and subtle to trace. It was indeed probable that Stirner came to his views independent of any

72. "Kunst und Religion," p. 37.
73. "Kunst und Religion," p. 41.
74. Ibid.
75. Matteo Lucchesi, *Die Individualitätsphilosophie Max Stirners* (Leipzig-Reudnitz, 1897), pp. 77–82.

mediator between Hegel and himself or that Feuerbach only pointed out what to him was obvious. There is no way to know.

Similarly, Stirner seemed close to many of Bruno Bauer's views.[76] Bauer's view of the independence of the absolute critic especially seemed similar to Stirner's outspoken egoism. A certain comradeship did exist between the two men, and it was possible that influence was exerted across one of the tables at Hippel's Weinstube. The question, however, is whether Bauer influenced Stirner towards individualism, whether Stirner influenced Bauer, or whether there was a mutual influence of one on the other. Once more the elusive question of influence lies unanswered.

The "Freien" had several women among their members, and one of these women, Marie Dähnhardt, caught the fancy of the lonely Stirner. She was the picture of the emancipated woman. An avid reader of George Sand's novels, she patterned herself after the French authoress by supporting female emancipation and the elimination of distinctions between men and women. Influenced by the character of the heroine of Gutzkow's *Wally the Skeptic,* she had abandoned Christianity, broken with her family, and fled to the freedom of Berlin. Once in the city, she frequented the taverns and coffee houses, fraternized with the rootless literati, and smoked cigars. A strange bond of affection developed between Stirner and her, and they were married late in 1843. Their wedding was the fantastically bohemian masque that might have been expected. When the preacher arrived at Stirner's apartment to perform the ceremony, he found the groom and the guests—Bauer, Buhl, Wilhelm Jordan, and other members of the "Freien"—playing cards in their shirtsleeves. The bride, arriving late, refused to wear wedding garments; there was no bible available for use in the ceremony. The crowning moment came when they realized they had forgotten to procure wedding rings. Bruno

76. Kurt Adolf Mautz, *Die Philosophie Max Stirners im Gegensatz zum Hegelschen Idealismus* (Berlin, 1936), pp. 25–46.

Bauer obligingly removed two brass rings from his purse, and the couple was finally united in holy matrimony.[77]

For a short time Stirner was probably happy. Because of his own teaching position and his wife's private income, he had no financial worries. He had a wife who was as emancipated from social restraints as himself. He had a circle of comrades with whom he could discuss philosophy and quaff earthly spirits.

Suddenly, in 1844, he resigned from his position at Madam Gropius's school for young ladies. The reasons for his sudden resignation are not now known. Shortly afterward, the rumor began to be passed around Hippel's Weinstube that Stirner was preparing a major book for publication. It was impossible to determine the accuracy of the rumor, since Stirner never talked about his work and never asked any of the "Freien" to read his manuscript. Not until the book, the notorious *The Unique One and His Property*, actually appeared did the "Freien" know the rumors were true.

The Unique One and His Property was a highly personal book, written in a vigorous, passionate style suggestive of that used by Fichte in his *Vocation of Man*, that used by Kierkegaard, that later used by Nietzsche. It was Stirner's private, violent reaction against all those forces and abstractions that were plunging man toward the depersonalization that Stirner dreaded and feared. Many of the views that he expressed here were developed from his earlier essays, especially his defense of the right of the individual will to its own development, free from external authority. Many may have been born from the personal failure of his career and the frustrations of his life.

Stirner's *The Unique One and His Property* was passed easily by the censors. The book was too absurd, they said, to be dangerous.[78] Among many radicals it immediately attained a popular reputation, and its notoriety, though perhaps mo-

77. Mackay, *Max Stirner*, pp. 122–29.
78. Mackay, *Max Stirner*, p. 137.

mentary, was widespread. Ruge wrote enthusiastically that "it is the first readable book in philosophy that Germany has produced." [79] Of its readability there was never any doubt. Stirner emptied the torments of his soul into *The Unique One and His Property*. Throughout it he was never caught in heavy style or pedantry; he was always inspired, always panting. Nonetheless, like those romantic artists who refused to have their creative spirit bound even by their own creation, Stirner dismissed his book as "clumsy." [80]

The Unique One and His Property was divided into two parts: the first was "Man," the second was "I." The first dealt with alienation, the favorite complaint of the Young Hegelians. The second part dealt with reconciliation, Stirner's answer to how spirit and man were to be united, how alienation was to be ended. [81] Stirner began with an affirmation of the primacy of the ego, the free individual driven by his own will. "My concern," he wrote, "is neither the divine nor the human; it is not the good, the just, the free, *etc.*, but solely what is mine; and it is not general, but—*unique, as I am unique.* Nothing is more to me than myself." [82]

In a mood similar to Rousseau's, Stirner observed that the ego was born free, but everywhere it was in chains, because of the human tendency of self-alienation. Enlarging upon his essay, "Art and Religion," he argued that man had a penchant for alienating his own spirit from himself as in some artistic creation, and then turning his alienated spirit into his own master. Man, instead of maintaining himself as an individual, submerged himself into a general spirit whose locus was outside and alien to himself. Religion was the flagrant example of

79. Ruge to his mother, 17 December 1844, *Ruges Briefwechsel*, 1:386.
80. Cited in G. Edward, "Die philosophischen Reaktionäre," in *Die Epigonen*, ed. Otto Wigand (Leipzig, 1846–48), 4:150.
81. Cf. Arvon, *Max Stirner*, pp. 46–54.
82. *Die Einzige und sein Eigenthum* (Leipzig, 1845), p. 8. An English translation by Steven Byington has appeared as *The Ego and His Own* (New York, 1919). Italics here and in all subsequent citations are in the original.

man's projecting his own spirit out of himself and then bowing to his creation. "The spirit is your ideal, the unattained, the other-worldly: spirit is for you—God, 'God is spirit.' " [83] Yet man has failed to realize that spirit was not alien to himself: "You alone are the one who is higher than you—*i. e.,* you are not only creature, but likewise your own creation." [84] Man created God, created all ideals from his own spirit; when he bowed to worship his own creation, he sanctified his self-alienation and destroyed his freedom. Here was the great offense of religion.

At first, Stirner shared the position of all the Young Hegelians on religion—Strauss, Bauer, Feuerbach, Ruge, Vischer, all were generally in agreement. Stirner did not stop there. He turned his criticism against all external authorities, against all abstractions, against everything that lay outside the ego. Where the other Young Hegelians had summoned humanity and the spiritual state to replace the deposed God, Stirner denounced these as new gods and cried, instead, for the individual ego to stand alone, unsupported by external phantoms.

In denying all external authority over the ego, Stirner broadened the definition of religion to mean any authority, any abstraction, any truth that men wanted to raise above the individual. "As long as you believe in truth," he declared, "you do not believe in yourself, and you are a—*servant,* a—*religious man.*" [85] All abstractions, all movements, all social and political issues that purported to be more than the individual were for Stirner religions to be condemned equally with Christianity.[86] Humanism, nationalism, socialism, the state, the family, reason, mankind, freedom, and so on, were all religions in that they were external authorities created by the alienation of man's own spirit and essence. To Stirner they were "fixed ideas," and to the Young Hegelians a "fixed idea"

83. *Der Einzige,* p. 42.
84. *Der Einzige,* p. 50.
85. *Der Einzige,* p. 473.
86. Mautz, *Philosophie Max Stirners,* p. 44.

was by definition tyrannical in view of their teaching of historicism. "What, then, does one call a 'fixed idea'? An idea that has subjected man to itself . . . . Yes, the 'fixed idea,' that is the truly sacred." [87] And *"everything sacred is a tie, a fetter."* [88] Any idea or structure or philosophy that claimed to transcend the ego was a religion, a new god; all were created by man's self-alienation, all claimed mastery over man. What was worse, they all demanded that the ego sacrifice itself for them, that it surrender itself to the betterment of humanity, the state, freedom, and the rest. To Stirner that was a monstrous demand. The ego could not be asked to sacrifice itself, for there was nothing beyond the ego.

The Young Hegelians generally supported the philosophy of humanism. Stirner scoffed at humanism as a new god that demanded the individual sacrifice himself to it: "In our days, . . . they have not realized that man has killed God in order to become—'sole God on high' . . . . God has had to give place, not to us, but to—humanity." [89] He specifically condemned Feuerbach and Bauer for setting up a new god, humanity, to replace the Christian God. In such an exchange, the individual was no better off. Humanism "is a religion because it separates my essence from me and places it above me, because it exalts 'humanity' in the same manner that any other religion exalts its God or idols." [90] Stirner would not be tempted into adopting the god "humanity." Similarly, he was not enticed into adopting the god "state" as most of the other Young Hegelians had. "The state is a *despotism* whose sole purpose is to limit the individual, to master him and subordinate him." [91] Stirner would tolerate no despotism.

Having defined all the panaceas—the social and political movements, the ersatz religions, the philosophical answers—

87. *Der Einzige*, pp. 57, 59.
88. *Der Einzige*, p. 384.
89. *Der Einzige*, p. 203.
90. *Der Einzige*, p. 230.
91. *Der Einzige*, pp. 257, 298.

offered in the nineteenth century as mere new gods, perpetuations of man's self-alienation, Stirner answered that man must smite down these new gods with ferocity and recognize that nothing lay outside the ego, its power and its will:

> The thoughts had become corporeal for themselves—they were ghosts, like God, emperor, Pope, fatherland, *etc.* If I destroy their corporeality, I then take them back into myself and say: "I alone am corporeal." And now I take the world as what it is to me, as mine, as my property: I relate everything to myself.[92]

Stirner's answer, in brief, was the answer of all the Young Hegelians: man could be free only when he ended his self-alienation and restored spirit to himself.

Stirner's method of ending man's self-alienation was different from that of the other Young Hegelians. Instead of the humanism they offered, he offered the subjective, egoistic, and willful individual; instead of their mankind, he offered the individual man. "Bring out from yourselves what is within you," Stirner cried, "bring it to the light, bring yourself to revelation." [93] He demanded that the ego recognize nothing as existing independent of itself, that "I, as creator, create everything." [94] Like the romantics, he insisted that the ego created the world.

For Stirner, the end of alienation would come when the ego took back to itself its creation, when it absorbed the world back into itself. The ego was to absorb everything, make everything its property, Stirner said. "What, then, is *my* property? Nothing but what is in my *power!* To what property am I entitled? . . . Everything over which I can exercise enough power so that it cannot be torn from me." [95] There was no law outside the ego; and the ego, driven by will, should seek to take back the whole world for itself.

92. *Der Einzige,* p. 20.
93. *Der Einzige,* p. 212.
94. *Der Einzige,* p. 8.
95. *Der Einzige,* pp. 339–40.

Such a philosophy of egoism would seem to leave as alternatives solipsism or the unending clash of egos. On this point, Stirner was not clear. At times he seemed to envisage a union of egos in which each ego would defend itself against encroachments on its power.[96] At other times, he seemed to speak for solipsism. "No one is *my equal*," he wrote, "but I regard all others equally as my property . . . . I am not an ego among other egos; I am, rather, the sole ego: I am unique." [97] In such statements as this, Stirner seemed to have assumed the role of absolute ego, as Bauer seemed to have assumed the role of absolute criticism.

Stirner gave no picture of the future that he anticipated. Preferring aphorism to analysis, he chose to end his work with the resounding rejection of authority: "All things are nothing to me." [98] He specifically renounced any claim to picturing a future for man, since by that act he would have set up another external ideal, another "fixed idea," another god that would demand the ego's sacrifice.[99] His aim was to liberate the ego; he would not, like Feuerbach and Bauer, then go on to limit it by establishing a new authority.

Stirner was not merely an eccentric anarchist, a worldly failure who sought to compensate for his frustrations by advocating the destruction of the world—there was a profoundly philosophical base to his thought.[100] Beneath it all lay the philosophy of Hegel. Like all the Young Hegelians, Stirner accepted the divine spirit as immanent in man. Externalized in an objective form, it was tyrannical. Whereas Feuerbach and Strauss insisted that the spirit was immanent in all of humanity, Stirner insisted that it was immanent in only the individual, the ego. In this insistence he was close to Bauer

96. Cf. *Der Einzige*, p. 258.
97. *Der Einzige*, pp. 415, 483.
98. *Der Einzige*, p. 491.
99. Cf. *Der Einzige*, pp. 426–83.
100. Cf. Wilhelm Cuypers, *Max Stirner als Philosoph* (Würzburg, 1937), p. 1.

when Bauer rejected Strauss's idea of community as the creator of myth and, instead, regarded the individual authors of the gospels as the creators. On these two issues of romanticism and of the Hegelian philosophy, the *Volk* as creator and the individual as creator, the Young Hegelians took sides. Interestingly enough, Stirner insisted that Hegel taught the supremacy of subjectivity, that his philosophy was not objective idealism. In Hegel, he argued, "the triumph of mind" was achieved, for in his philosophy "reality, the world of things, had to conform to thought, and no concept was without reality." [101] However much the Young Hegelians took postures of their radicalism, they still consciously argued within the assumptions of the Hegelian philosophy.

Needless to say, Stirner's *The Unique One and His Property* created great agitation in Germany. The liberals were scandalized, the socialists infuriated. Feuerbach and Moses Hess wrote indignant replies. The "Freien," little knowing what kind of book Stirner had been writing, found his egoism less attractive when they were themselves denounced for setting up new gods. Bruno Bauer felt deep resentment, but he maintained an outward civility toward Stirner. Stirner blissfully disregarded most of the agitation and spent much of his time editing and translating the works of Adam Smith, Blanqui, and others for the multi-volume *The National Economists of France and England.*

Stirner soon tired of the editing work and threw it up. Marital problems began to dominate his life. His second marriage had never been successful. Neither he nor his wife found the expected freedom in family life. They separated in 1846, and Frau Schmidt went to London. By 1870, she presumably had found that assurance that her life in Berlin was unable to grant her: she converted to Catholicism.

Stirner was left alone in Berlin, without a wife, without money, his connections with the "Freien" strained. His reputation prevented him from obtaining another teaching job.

101. *Der Einzige,* p. 97.

He appeared in society less and less, preferring to nurture his own ego and dispassionately observe the world that was his own. When the Revolution of 1848 swept through Berlin, Stirner was detached, unconcerned, uncommitted. Unmoved, he watched the whole event from Hippel's through cigar smoke and the distorting lens of a freshly-drained wine glass. Like Bauer, he would have nothing to do with the revolution.[102]

Stirner did try, in his *History of the Reaction* (1852), to discuss the revolution and the reaction that had smothered Europe since the Vienna Settlement. He denounced Burke, Prussia's reactionary policies, and the "Christocracy" that dominated Europe. This work proved dull and uninteresting; it lacked the vigor, the protest of desperation that inspired his *The Unique One and His Property*. Its publication was scarcely noticed.

Stirner spent the next few years in desperate struggle with poverty and illness. Never sound in health or finances, he passed from one illness to another and evaded one creditor after another. On June 25, 1856, Stirner died, leaving behind, in the world that was his own, debts and the notoriety of the author of *The Unique One and His Property*. These were the legacies, respectively, of Schmidt and Stirner.

Stirner saw freedom for himself only in the collapse of all external authority. "The fall of peoples and of humanity," he exulted, "will invite *me* to my ascension."[103] It might prove tempting to seek in psychoanalysis the explanation for his egoism, his hostility to external authority, his worldly failures in marriage, employment, and friendship. He bears, in this regard, much resemblance to the portrait of Baudelaire composed by Jean-Paul Sartre. Both Baudelaire and Stirner had strikingly similar lives: their fathers died when they were small children, they developed an exaggerated fondness for their mothers that was disrupted by their mothers' re-marriage,

102. Mackay, *Max Stirner*, pp. 210–13.
103. *Der Einzige*, p. 285.

they found great difficulty in sustained work, they found personal friendships virtually impossible even though both were recluses longing for companionship, their lives were burdened with physical illness. Sartre has concluded that this life experience revealed itself in Baudelaire as a shattering and consuming sense of self-consciousness. He "felt and was determined to feel that he was unique; and he pushed this sense of uniqueness to the point of extreme solitary enjoyment and of terror." [104] Perhaps the explanation of Stirner's ideas, his own sense of uniqueness, also lies within the domain of existential psychology.

What is equally important is that his ideas can be understood as a philosophical extension of the Young Hegelian metaphysic and an interpretation of Hegel's philosophy.[105] The closeness of his stance to Bruno Bauer's itself indicated Stirner's philosophical position. His work was directed toward defining and then answering the question that formed the Young Hegelian vision: the results that man must draw from his recognition that philosophy and religion were now incompatible. Stirner saw both the premises and answer to that question in personal terms. The process of alienation—the very meaning of history—showed him that man's propensity to project and objectify his own spirit was the source of the tyranny that denied him freedom. The demands of monism, of returning spirit to man as the act of freedom, led him to equate Hegel's spirit with his own ego and philosophical criticism with his own logic, to contain the entire process of history as a subjective experience. Ever fearful of creating any object external to his own mind that would act as a restraint upon him, he could do nothing else but claim everything as

104. Jean-Paul Sartre, *Baudelaire*, tr. Martin Turnell (New York, 1967), p. 18.
105. Cf. Carl August Emge, *Max Stirner: eine geistig nicht bewältigte Tendenz* (Wiesbaden, 1964), pp. 7–12; and S. Jankelevitch, "L'unique et le surhomme: Le problème de la personnalité chez Stirner et chez Nietzsche," *Revue d'Allemagne* 5 (1931):27–40, 216–43.

his own creation and call it back to its place of origin, his own mind. His humanism was a subjective and individual experience that disallowed alienation to the point of asserting that reality could be only his own ego and the world it conceived, though with the self-warning that his own ideas must not be allowed to tyrannize over him.

"I, therefore, am the kernel that is to be freed from the husk—free from all confining shells," he rejoiced. "What remains when I have been freed from everything that is not I? Only I and nothing but I." [106] His version of historicism judged everything relative except his ego. Thus he feared Christianity, but he feared, perhaps even more, the transcendent substitutes for it that those philosophically closest to him created: the state, humanity, politics, culture. He offered in response to both his philosophical perception and his fears a dynamic titanism in which his own ego became the absolute.

Bruno Bauer once wrote that "the terrorism of pure theory must clear the field." His formula expressed both the method and expectation of the Berlin Young Hegelians. Deprived by academic and political circumstances of any true influence in forming the world and its institutions according to their understanding of the Hegelian philosophy, they had to be content with the role of subjective critics, armed with the truth, who could shatter the theoretical foundations of the old world.

Bauer and Stirner agreed, as did all the Young Hegelians, that they were experiencing the beginnings of the apocalypse which would replace the old Christian world with philosophical humanism. In their private visions they disagreed about the form the new world would take. Philosophical unity for the Young Hegelians was always a mirage because of the wide divergences in private vision of the new world.

Bauer and Stirner did agree on one point. Each saw the role of the subjective critic as essential to the appearance of the new world. Subjectivism was not an arbitrary imagining, but

106. *Der Einzige*, p. 215.

an absolute assurance of the philosopher's self-conscious identification with truth. To demonstrate by criticism the errors of the old forms, the folly of preserving the old forms at a time of historical change was to be sufficient. The political action of Ruge was to be disdained, the social action that was the growing concern of such younger associates as Marx and Engels was to be scorned. "The terrorism of pure theory" would be enough.

The perils of such a view were clear. Perhaps Bauer recognized them in his desperate aim to identify his stance with absolutism, with Russia, with Prussia. The posture of pure theory and absolute subjective criticism held the temptations of delusion, madness, and solipsism. The need to actualize that posture in some objective form was, therefore, compelling. Bauer faltered at the consequences of his own thought, seeking to avoid the inevitable titanism to which his own logic led him. He found no absolute in the anchors he grasped at, and he moved closer and closer to the uncompromising position of Stirner. That he sought some principle, some object, some institution to keep him from the consequences of that position indicated his awareness of its perils as well as his own philosophical needs. At best, he succeeded only in compromising the purity of his own thought.

Stirner never grasped at an anchor. He scorned the other Young Hegelians for erecting absolute principles as new gods, and he regarded Bauer's faltering before the consequences of immanence as a betrayal. For Stirner the philosophy of immanence meant that the individual must redeem his own existence and his own freedom without the support of an absolute. It meant his uncompromising and total commitment to a titanism with himself the absolute. There is truth to the judgment of Stirner that Albert Camus has pronounced:

> This bitter and imperious logic can no longer be held in check, except by an I which is determined to defeat every form of

abstraction and which has itself become abstract and nameless through being isolated and cut off from its roots.[107]

That, for Stirner, was the very virtue of his position. He never faltered in bringing "the terrorism of pure theory" to its absolute conclusion.

107. Albert Camus, *The Rebel*, tr. Anthony Bower (New York, 1956), p. 64.

6 Arnold Ruge and the Politics of a Young Hegelian

Our poetry has had its time; and if German life is not to stand still, then we must entice the talents, that now have no object, into the world of reality and the state where a new spirit can be poured into new matter.

—G. G. Gervinus, 1840

Heinrich Heine once described the members of Young Germany as men who "draw no sharp distinction between living and writing—who never separate politics from scholarship, art from science—and who are at once artists, tribunes, and apostles." [1] The same might have been said of the Young Hegelians. For among the German intellectuals of the 1830s and 1840s, there was no idea that a great man did great things in a specialized field. Such professionalism was not a part of their way of life. The intellectuals all grasped firm hold of a weltanschauung that was a world view in every sense of the word: it comprised all knowledge, all art, all politics, and all philosophy. The intellectuals believed they could grapple with any problem that touched on the life of man and the universe. There was no knowledge, no province outside their scope. With this confidence, they were indeed "tribunes and apostles."

The most prominent of the Young Hegelians in the category of "tribunes and apostles" was Arnold Ruge. Ruge was trained in theology and philosophy; he wrote on religion, art, literature, philosophy, and politics; he was a journalist and essayist; he was a teacher; he was the leader of a philosophical party; he was a politician. He could not be described as a specialist, he did not believe in professionalism. He believed, rather, that his weltanschauung provided the key to understanding all phases of life.

As an intellectual, Ruge assigned to himself great responsibility. For he was the keeper of the spirit, responsible for its proper transmission to all of society. His weltanschauung provided him with confidence and faith—the confidence that inspired him with a sense of mission, the faith that demanded that he devote his life to its propagation. In this missionary mood, Ruge asked, and answered, a vital question:

> What do I want? Characters, real men, real conflict and real partiality, but engaged in the serious battle over the question of

1. "The Romantic School," in *The Poetry and Prose of Heinrich Heine,* p. 720.

freedom. If we could have these things in Germany, it would be worthwhile once more to continue living.[2]

His mission was to transform the philosophy of Hegel, as he understood it, into a philosophy of action and change.

One of Hegel's leading disciples, Karl Rosenkranz, though not himself a Young Hegelian, once declared that "Ruge is perhaps the greatest aggressive journalistic talent that we Germans, at least, have possessed." [3] Ruge deserved this praise for his services as editor of the *Hallische Jahrbücher* and the *Deutsche Jahrbücher*. Driven by the sense of mission and vocation to propagate the views of the party he sought to organize, he provided a vigorous forum for the writings of the Young Hegelians. Though he failed to form the group into a durable philosophical party, his failure was certainly not a reflection on his great energy and ability.

Ruge was more than an editor and journalist: he regarded himself as a philosopher. He saw a philosopher, however, as responsible for translating the liberating ideas of philosophy to the world of reality. The philosopher, after all, was the most effective man in political life, for "it is the philosopher who knows when the situation is ripe, who sits at the loom of time." [4] Beyond recognizing and guiding contemporary events, the philosopher had also to work with the people, to convince them of the soundness and wisdom of his position. He insisted that philosophers "must be obliged to come out of abstract literature and interest men in public and political matters." [5] The role of the philosopher for Ruge, then, was not only to think, but also to act and inspire others to action as well.

Ruge envisioned himself as the philosopher in politics,

2. Ruge to Fleischer, 27 May 1845, *Briefwechsel und Tagebuchblätter*, 1:396–97.

3. Karl Rosenkranz, *Neue Studien* (Leipzig, 1875–78), 2:293.

4. *Deutsche Jahrbücher* (1842), p. 1543.

5. Ruge to Prutz, 25 January 1843, *Briefwechsel und Tagebuchblätter*, 1:297.

and he intended to fulfill the obligations that he defined as part of that role. First as a journalist, then as a member of the National Assembly, he sought to awaken public consciousness to the realities of political life. He was the intellectual in politics—the "grim doorkeeper of the Hegelian philosophy," as Heine dubbed him. His career as an intellectual and as a politician must be investigated to show how he sought to translate his Young Hegelian metaphysic into a positive political program.

Arnold Ruge was a Pomeranian, but by birth a Swedish subject, born on the island of Rügen on September 13, 1802. He came from a family of tenant farmers, and he was always proud of his middle-class origins.[6] Young Arnold attended the gymnasium in Stralsund and, in 1821, matriculated at the University of Halle with the intention of studying theology. He was, however, soon disappointed. "The theologians know nothing," he declared. "Their subject is the Bible, but this . . . is only the fantasies and conceptions of the Jews."[7] In his disappointment, he later recalled, he renounced Christianity. "I gave up theology and turned my attention to philosophy."[8]

Ruge made another choice in his university days that affected the entire course of his life—his involvement in political activity. He joined student political organizations, although they had been banned by the Carlsbad Decrees. When he transferred to the University of Jena, he continued his participation in these organizations, joining one of the new Burschenschaft groups and speaking openly against the Holy Alliance. The Prussian government was not slow to respond to the challenge: it arrested and tried Ruge and other leaders

6. Herbert Strauss, "Zur sozial-und ideengeschichtlichen Einordung Arnold Ruges," *Schweizer Beiträge zur allgemeinen Geschichte* 12 (1954): 163–65.
7. *Aus früherer Zeit* (Berlin, 1862–67), 2:11.
8. Ibid.

of the political group. Ruge was sentenced to fifteen years' imprisonment for his activities, but royal clemency reduced the sentence to five years.

Ruge accepted his fate with resignation. Imprisoned in the Prussian fortress of Kolberg, he devoted his full energies to the vigorous study of philosophy. When he was released, he became a teacher in Halle and, shortly after, began to give lectures at the University of Halle on philology and ancient philosophy. Interestingly enough, the Prussian government allowed him to teach, despite his conviction for political offenses, while it would not allow religious critics like Bauer to teach. Religious criticism was, apparently, more dangerous than political opposition.

At Halle, Ruge became friendly with a group of philosophers that included Echtermeyer and Rosenkranz. "Echtermeyer," he recalled, "spoke continuously with me about philosophy," and the two men often discussed the founding of a literary journal.[9] Echtermeyer's great interest was the Hegelian philosophy, and he encouraged Ruge to read deeply in Hegel. Ruge obliged his friend. He was happy to catch up with the years of German philosophy that had passed him by when he was in prison. He remained thankful for his years at Halle, "where I met every day with inspired disciples of and profound experts in the Hegelian philosophy." [10] After 1833, Ruge had the opportunity to devote himself to an intensive study of Hegel's philosophy, for his first wife suddenly died, and he turned to his books to find solace.

In his seclusion Ruge sought in Hegel's works the answers to many questions. As a student he had rejected Christianity, but he still lacked the positive faith he believed was necessary to replace it. Hegel provided him with that faith. "From 1833 to 1837," Ruge recalled, "I occupied myself partially with the study of the Hegelian philosophy, partially with the conflict between its principles and the religious and political develop-

9. *Aus früherer Zeit*, 3:339.
10. *Aus früherer Zeit*, 3:344.

ment of our time." [11] Hegel's philosophy was not only a positive faith, but a guide and inspiration to action as well.

Ruge's reading of Hegel was that of the Young Hegelians; he saw not the Hegel of Christianity, but the Hegel of humanism. He concluded that Hegel's philosophy of immanence denied the transcendence of Christianity and left Christianity totally unacceptable to the modern world. Further, he insisted that Hegel demonstrated that men created their gods by alienating the immanent spirit from themselves and projecting it into objects apart from themselves. The only philosophy possible within the Hegelian context, he concluded, was the philosophy of humanism, the view that recognized the spirit immanent in man, the view that accepted the divinity of humanity.

There was one point, however, on which he felt that he disagreed with Hegel: the question whether the philosophy of humanism ought to be reserved for the cultural elite. Ruge insisted that this philosophy be spread to all the people, the humble as well as the educated. His democratic views applied to philosophy as well as to politics. When he finally emerged from his retirement, he was charged with a sense of mission to publicize the philosophy of humanism. "We must now proceed to free the world," he announced.[12]

Ruge seemed to have no forum in which to express his ideas. He wrote an article condemning the journals that did appear in Germany because they were not the organs for Young Hegelian humanism,[13] and he was pleased with Echtermeyer's suggestion that they found a new journal to serve their ideas. It was then that Ruge undertook his trip to recruit contributors to the new journal. In 1837 the *Hallische Jahrbücher* was born.

The history of Ruge's and Echtermeyer's journal has already

11. *Aus früherer Zeit,* 4:441.
12. *Aus früherer Zeit,* 4:127.
13. See Ruge's "Unsere gelehrte kritische Journalistik," *Blätter für literarische Unterhaltung,* 11–12 August 1837, pp. 905–07, 909–10.

been discussed and need not be repeated. What is of interest here are the opinions and views of Ruge, the standpoint of the man who edited the major Young Hegelian organ and sought to form the group into a party.

Ruge once wrote that "the criticism of the old system develops from within the Hegelian philosophy. It remains with great thoroughness with theology, comes later to the examination of religion itself, and has only in isolated assaults been able to reach politics and immediate reality." [14] This outlined his own path. For him the philosophy of Hegel could not rest merely with the rejection of Christianity; it had, inevitably, to lead to reforms in the social and political life of Germany. If Feuerbach was satisfied to affirm humanism and draw no political conclusion from his affirmation, Ruge was not. His acceptance of humanism in philosophy meant that he had also to accept its consequences in politics. For him, political humanism meant only one thing—political democracy. Progress from religious criticism to political action was necessary to free man first philosophically and then politically. The philosophy of criticism knew no limitations.

Ruge agreed with all the criticisms the Young Hegelians made. He drew from Hegel a view of religion in its historical development from natural religion to Christianity, and it was the human experience in religion, not the divine offering, that he discussed. In this sense, Ruge's views were closer to Bauer's than to Strauss's. He saw the first period of religious development as that in which man both revered and feared natural forces as the expressions of some divine will. In the second period man "created and worshipped personal gods," "the poets were the fathers of the gods." [15] The poets created the gods by alienating the immanent spirit of man in the form of their creations, thus objectifying human ideals. In Ruge's view, Homer and Hesiod created the Greek gods, but Dante

14. *Zwei Jahre in Paris*, 2:15–16.

15. *Acht Reden über Religion "an die Gebildeten unter ihren Verehrern"* (St. Louis, 1868), p. 13.

and Milton were equally important in creating the Christian God. In seeing artistic creation as the intial alienation of man, his argument was nearly the same as those of Feuerbach, Vischer, and Stirner. Ruge saw the third period of religious development as the period of "speculation by the priests about the personal gods, the period of the priest as theologian." [16] Theology emerged to perpetuate man's alienation from himself, to teach a transcendent God, to demand that man worship his own alienated spirit.

Ruge's view of religion seemed to combine the views of Strauss, Bauer, and Feuerbach, though how much he borrowed from them and how much he developed independently cannot be known for certain. He also shared with them the insistence that the next step in spiritual development was humanism, the end of transcendence and the recognition of the divinity of humanity. For the divine spirit was immanent in humanity: human history, thus, was divine revelation, the study of man was the study of God. Condemning Christian transcendence, Ruge wrote:

> Sacred history is a fable that was supposed to have happened once in Palestine. Secular history is true history, the true incarnation, the true revelation. For it is the development of the contemporary human world, accomplished by the knowledge and the will of its members, in which all secrets of the gods, of nature, and of spirit will be opened to daylight and exposed.[17]

The history of mankind was the history of the developing spirit; any view that attempted to separate man from spirit, to perpetuate man's self-alienation, impeded progress. It was progress that Ruge wanted, progress to the humanist and rational state. He believed Christianity was his greatest enemy in the achievement of that goal because it insisted on separating God and man and thereby "obstructs knowledge and the secular life of the state in Europe." [18] There was no question

16. *Acht Reden*, pp. 13–14.
17. *Acht Reden*, p. 51.
18. *Acht Reden*, p. 14.

in his mind that Christianity had to be overthrown in order to make human freedom possible. Freedom was only possible with humanism, and humanism and Christianity "are unrelenting foes," for "truth cannot be reconciled with fable." [19] Christianity, an old form of the developing spirit, had to give way to the new form, humanism. "The total freeing of man," Ruge declared, "is the same as the suppression of religion." [20] The chief conclusion Ruge drew from his humanism was that he had a grave responsibility to translate humanism into the areas of social and political questions outside its purely philosophical setting. One of his major charges was that German thought tended to be too abstract and theoretical, disdaining action as petty. It was precisely that action on which Ruge insisted. For if the liberating ideas of philosophy were left in their own realm, distinct from the realm of political action, they could not work towards human freedom. If the philosophers, poets, and intellectuals could not "remove immediately the reality that stands between us and our wishes . . . ," Ruge wrote, "they are surely not the founders of a new and free state—indeed, they only create our ideals as they once created the gods for the Greeks." [21] He intended to remove that reality, to promote human freedom by political action based on "immanence (as opposed to transcendence), the reality of the world, the real existence of men and nature . . . ." [22]

For Ruge Christianity was indeed dead, but he rejected atheism with the same determination. Atheism was merely another religion, a negative theology, but no less a theology for being negative. No Young Hegelian denied God—they only denied a transcendent, personal God. Moreover, Ruge did not see the crisis of his time as the question of religion versus irreligion, but the question of what form religion

19. *Acht Reden*, p. 51.
20. *Zwei Jahre in Paris*, 2:290.
21. *Die politischen Lyriker unserer Zeit* (Leipzig, 1848), p. 113.
22. *Zwei Jahre in Paris*, 2:61–62.

would take. Man's needs had to be satisfied by positive assertions, not negations. Atheism was a negation; it could not be the positive program man required. Ruge believed in the forces of idealism and truth, human freedom, and the religion of humanity. "The enthusiasm for the realization of free, self-respecting, rational individuals," he wrote, "the humane supposition that reason guides every man—this is religion and conscience." [23]

Ruge was a democrat, a humanist, and a rationalist. He believed passionately that his ideas had to be spread to the people, that he had to fight the political battles that Bauer and Feuerbach fought in religion. He urged participation in "the battle of true religion with religious illusions, of living philosophy with the abstract . . . , and of practical problems with the illusory and fantastic." [24]

Ruge was especially distressed by the political condition of Germany during his lifetime. Since 1815, Germany had been "experiencing a time of death and decay." [25] Such an unhappy political condition, Ruge said, was caused by the a-political character of the Germans, their preference for abstract ideas and theoretical freedom over practical politics. In the atmosphere of Germany, he claimed, Indian mysticism and religious penitence predominated, people withdrew from the world instead of entering it actively and purposefully. Germans existed within a system that placed terror and control above the principle of humanity, that ruled not by popular sovereignty but by the methods of the police state. The German people refused to place "politics over thought, practice over theory, and the external world over the inner existence," and consequently, "since the Reformation, they have had no thoughts at all in political matters." [26] Too consistently, Ruge

23. Ruge to Fleischer, 13 December 1845, *Briefwechsel und Tagebuch-blätter*, 1:400.
24. "Selbstkritik des Liberalismus," *Gesammelte Schriften* (Mannheim, 1846–48), 3:97–98.
25. "Selbstkritik," 3:81.
26. "Selbstkritik," 3:91–92.

cried, the Germans were willing to subject themselves to authority, to refuse to accept the responsibility for making their own decisions: Luther rejected one authority only to establish another; the Wars of Liberation merely exchanged one tyranny for another. This passivity in accepting the dictates of authority was more than Ruge could bear:

> To the Germans political life is not their essential business, but a theft which they commit, a boldness which they have not really dared, a loss of time to their essential private business. Indeed, politics affect them, but only in the same way that the weather affects them . . . ; and when they want good politics, as when they want good weather, they look silently and trustfully towards heaven.[27]

Ruge felt it was his calling to bring the Germans to an awareness of their political situation, to turn their eyes to earth. The aim of the Young Hegelians was, after all, to interest men in this world.

Ruge argued that the same tragic preference for the abstract over the practical debilitated German liberalism. He condemned its preference for theoretical freedom rather than practical reforms and workable solutions to political and social problems. He did not see liberalism as an aggressive and dynamic force actively and vigorously engaged in pitched political battles—liberalism in Germany merely gazed down from its theoretical heights and wished victory for those involved in the fight for freedom. Liberals thought about democracy, sympathized with freedom, and theorized about good politics, but they refused to act to bring them about. Liberalism was a failure, Ruge argued, precisely because it did not act to "return political consciousness" to man, nor to "liberate us from theory, from the position of the observer" in political life.[28]

Ruge fought against the values and settlements of Restora-

27. "Selbstkritik," 3:92.
28. "Selbstkritik," 3:86.

tion Germany. He vigorously assaulted what he regarded as the two cultural supports of reaction—romanticism and the historical school of law. To him the great epoch of recent history was the Enlightenment, the period in which humanity and human reason were the guiding principles.[29] The romantic movement worked against all that the men of the Enlightenment cherished: it yearned for the unattainable, sought the irrational, consumed its energy in quest of Novalis's blue flower. Romanticism, Ruge declared, regarded humanity as trivial, the critics of religious mysteries as shallow, and the state as a mysterious being. It served as the great intellectual defense for the forces of reaction, for Restoration Germany. By its preference for imaginative flights, romanticism encouraged a political quietism amenable to any form of government; by its stress on the beauty of otherworldliness, it made the practical political achievements of this world seem cheap and petty. Romanticism stood in the way of freedom and progress:

> I call our romantics the writers who, through the medium of our culture, oppose the epoch of the Enlightenment and the Revolution and who fight against and condemn the principles of a freed humanity in the areas of science, art, and ethics.[30]

No wonder that his *Hallische Jahrbücher* declared war on romanticism.

The other great enemy that Ruge's journal attacked was the historical school of law and its major exponents, Savigny and Leo. Ruge charged these two with supporting the reactionary regimes of Restoration Germany. The historical school of law criticized the efforts of the French Revolution; it refused to submit legal institutions and constitutions to the penetrating eye of reason; it refused to consider human

29. Cf., Hans Rosenberg, "Arnold Ruge und die 'Hallischen Jahrbücher,'" *Archiv für Kulturgeschichte* 20 (1930): 282–83.

30. "Unsre Classiker und Romantiker seit Lessing," *Gesammelte Schriften,* 1:11.

attempts to reform the legal system. For all these reasons, Ruge took up his attack against the school he saw as a major support of Restoration Germany.

Ruge's program was not all negative; he was not merely a man in opposition. His fervent faith in democracy, reason, and humanism formed the positive credo that he followed all his life. He believed that he had to work to create among the German people a new consciousness that would replace their a-political attitudes. Liberalism had failed in this essential act of creation. The new consciousness of Germany was to be formed by the political writers and philosophers, much as Voltaire, Lamennais, and Rousseau had reformed the French consciousness. Here, again, was the mission of the intellectual. The reform, however, had to be a reform of men, not of institutions. The failure of liberalism, he noted, was that it expected the world to change merely because the political institutions were reformed. In fact "the reform of consciousness is the reform of the world, and no god can stop it." [31]

The new consciousness that Ruge hoped to rouse in Germany was that of political democracy, the recognition of individual worth, the acknowledgment of popular sovereignty:

> In order to save itself from death and ensure its future, the German world needs nothing but a new consciousness that, in all areas, will raise up the freedom of man to a principle and [the rule by] the people to a goal—in brief, the transformation of liberalism into democracy.[32]

To accomplish the transformation of political consciousness, Ruge demanded widespread popular education, transferal of military decisions to the people, and the election of a popularly controlled government with a free judiciary. Then the basis for freedom would be achieved—"the elevation of all men to the dignity of men." [33]

31. "Selbstkritik des Liberalismus," *Gesammelte Schriften*, 3:110.
32. "Selbstkritik," 3:116.
33. "Selbstkritik," 3:115.

Ruge looked to France as the great example of a nation that developed a new spirit under the guidance of her intellectuals. He hoped the Germans would emulate the French example. In learning the necessity of political courage and action, "the French have fortuitously found the freedom of our time." [34] The French insistence on individual liberty and human reason had to be transported across the Rhine and combined with the liberating German philosophies. Ruge wanted to create a new spirit for Germany, but not nationalism. He recognized that a national spirit aroused in Germany would take an anti-French form, and opposition to France meant a rejection of the ideals of freedom that France had developed. Perhaps even more important, Ruge regarded nationalism as the partner of reaction. "Without the overthrow of patriotism," he declared, "Germany can never be won for freedom." [35] Like Stirner, he regarded nationalism as an "earthly religion," a product of human self-alienation in which man was asked to sacrifice himself to a national state, "an entirely general, vague and fantastic abuse." [36] Ruge, the cosmopolitan, stood with all men who shared his ideals of humanity, freedom, and reason.

Though Ruge determined to avoid the unfortunate results of German nationalism, he defended the necessity for a state in the Hegelian sense. He believed firmly in state sovereignty and saw the state as the great protector of individual freedom, the organization within which the individual could best define his moral being, his freedom, and his purpose. "Whoever wants freedom," he observed, "must want the sovereign state; and whoever wants the sovereign state must want its terms." [37] To Ruge the Hegelian state had to be democratically organized. To be the true Hegelian state, the state of reason,

34. "Selbstkritik," 3:91.
35. Ruge to Fleischer, 9 July 1844, *Briefwechsel und Tagebuchblätter,* 1:361.
36. *Zwei Jahre in Paris,* 2:302–03.
37. "Selbstkritik des Liberalismus," *Gesammelte Schriften,* 3:116.

it had to be based on the idea of individual human equality. The state could not take sides politically, could not defend the interests of one class or one group; it had to stand above the conflict and represent the interests of everyone within its sovereignty. Ruge opposed the states of Restoration Germany because they represented the interests of the old feudal orders; he quarreled with Marx because Marx insisted that the state had to be controlled by a social class for its own interests. The true Hegelian state was the impartial locus of each individual's freedom and moral life.

All his life Ruge had identified Prussia with his state of freedom and reason. Not that Prussia was at the time democratic, but it had the potential for democracy. During the period of reforms earlier in the century, it moved towards rationality; during the Wars of Liberation, it moved towards democracy in winning popular support. In the 1830s, in 1848, in the Bismarckian period, Ruge supported Prussia as the only German state that could provide the locus within which the individual could define his freedom and morality.

Ruge demanded the right of political opposition within the state structure, especially parliamentary opposition parties like those in Britain. He argued that the principle of opposition was necessary for the life and progress of the state. Since the state was a living structure, the political opposition formed as significant a part of the structure as the government itself. The negative element was vital to all development and progress, as Bauer, Strauss, Stirner, and Feuerbach had said. "Without criticism," Ruge wrote, "there is no development and without development no life." [38] In order to ensure progress and development, Ruge called for the formation of a democratic party. He hoped to escape the abstractions that philosophical liberalism developed by creating a political organization that would work for the practical reform of social and political conditions. Ruge wanted to escape from the con-

38. *Deutsche Jahrbücher* (1842), p. 2625.

fines of theory, he did not want to be an intellectual who slammed his study door on the world. Party organization, practical problems, a sense of political realism were the means he would use to bring vital changes to Germany. The winning of freedom meant work, and Ruge set himself to that task.

Ruge's intentions of forming the Young Hegelians into the cohesive core of a party of political action were frustrated. The Prussian government suppressed the *Hallische Jahrbücher;* the Saxon government suppressed its successor, the *Deutsche Jahrbücher,* in 1843. His publishing venture with Marx in Paris, the *Deutsch-Französische Jahrbücher,* also failed. Ruge felt a strong sense of disillusionment as he was continually frustrated in his plans for the spiritual liberation of Germany. "This generation was not born to be free," he wrote sadly. "Our people has no future; what sense is there in our calling?" [39] He lived for awhile in Switzerland, then in Leipzig. When the revolution came to Leipzig, in 1848, Ruge's buoyant optimism returned, and he set out once more, with the same dreams, to work for a democratic Germany.

The revolution in Germany followed the news of events in France. Throughout much of Germany the revolution came almost too easily—in the excitement of revolutionary demands the old order was carried along in the sweep of events as were the momentary victors. "They were indeed remarkable days," Ruge recalled, "when each mail brought us news of another victorious revolution, when no despotism was spared the general political earthquake." [40]

The two leading revolutionaries in Leipzig were Robert Blum and Arnold Ruge. Though they were willing to cooperate with one another, there was little personal friendliness

39. Ruge to Marx, March 1843, in Marx's *Die Frühschriften,* ed. Siegfried Landshut (Stuttgart, 1953), pp. 159–60.
40. "Episoden aus dem Jahre Achtundvierzig," *Briefwechsel und Tagebuchblätter,* 2:22.

between them. They were rivals for dominance in Leipzig, for popularity, and, ultimately, for election to the National Assembly.

Almost from the beginning, Ruge was unhappy with the revolution in Leipzig because it failed to bring the political democracy he believed was necessary. A dual sovereignty existed in Saxony, a "royal liberalism" in which reforms were granted by the traditional authorities without the recognition of popular sovereignty. The people did not rule in Saxony; the king still ruled, granting a few reforms to maintain his control. Ruge accused the revolutionary movement "of standing reverently before the throne, a revolution with written petitions . . . ." [41] He charged the politicians with failure to demand political democracy and abolition of royal authority. Especially odious to Ruge was Robert Blum, for he "embodied the muddled impulse for royal liberalism," he refused to strive for democratic institutions to replace the monarchy, and he failed to exercise purposeful leadership towards popular sovereignty. [42]

To counteract the distressing situation in Leipzig, Ruge undertook two important projects: he began to deliver political speeches, and he founded a new journal. Popular speaking was a new medium for him, but he entered into it with his accustomed vigor, seeking to channel the popular revolutionary excitement toward the achievement of popular sovereignty. He held meetings, distributed pamphlets, organized political banquets on the French model; he told the people they had to "take the political situation into your own hands." [43]

Ruge's new journal, *Die Reform*, appeared at the same time in Berlin, where it became the organ of the Berlin radicals. More and more impressed with the revolutionary

41. "Episoden," 2:28.
42. "Episoden," 2:28–31.
43. *Grenzboten*, 4:159, cited in Walter Neher, *Arnold Ruge als Politiker und politische Schriftsteller* (Heidelberg, 1933), p. 163.

movement in Berlin, Ruge came to place his hopes for the future of the German revolution on the success of the Berliners in casting off the autocratic rule of king and army.[44] When news of the March Days in Berlin reached Ruge, he went immediately to the Prussian capital. There he attended popular demonstrations and radical meetings; there, he happily realized, his views and his journal were popular. No wonder he formed the conviction that "here in Berlin will be decided the future of Germany." [45]

Through his journal, Ruge made his political position clear. He called for complete freedom of the press, open courts with jury trials, respect for civil liberties, popular education financed by the state.[46] He recognized that a major part of the revolution was a movement for German unification, a movement to create a national state, yet he did not think national unification should be amplified into the major issue of the revolution. To him the most important achievement had to be political freedom; unity was meaningless, indeed, dangerous, unless preceded by freedom for all citizens. The question, he argued, was not "how large a state to set up," but rather "how free its institutions will be, how easy they will be to administer." [47] As a democrat he cared primarily for individual freedom, not for national extension.

Because he was associated with neither of the Leipzig political parties, Ruge was not a delegate to the *Vorparlament* that met in Frankfurt in March and April. Robert Blum represented Leipzig. Ruge came increasingly to resent the prominence of Blum, a man he could not respect; he scornfully referred to him as the "political pope" and the "dictator." [48] He especially regretted that the people, in whom he placed a democrat's faith, took Blum to their hearts as a hero

44. Cf., Neher, *Ruge als Politiker*, pp. 167–68.
45. "Episoden," pp. 37–39.
46. *Akademie*, 1848, cited in Neher, *Ruge als Politiker*, pp. 165–66.
47. *Grenzboten*, 1848, cited in Neher, *Ruge als Politiker*, p. 167.
48. "Episoden," p. 41.

and looked to him for guidance. When the *Vorparlament* called for elections to a German national assembly, Ruge lamented that "now, in place of the revolution for freedom, stepped the impulse for the rebirth of Germany." [49] He feared that national glory rather than philosophical freedom would become the solitary goal of the revolution. Nonetheless, he determined to stand for election to the National Assembly from Leipzig.

In preparation for the elections, Ruge published a political manifesto. He demanded that the National Assembly, in its initial meeting, recognize itself as the sovereign political authority of Germany, dominant over all princely authority. He urged that it select a president, an executive for all of Germany, create a republic, and assume for itself the functions of a democratic body.[50]

Ruge considered himself a man of the people, most qualified to be a delegate to the National Assembly. He entered into the Leipzig elections with great vigor, but, since he stood outside the official party structures, neither party favored his election. In one of the wild political meetings, Ruge assaulted the moderator and threatened to call a public demonstration against the party. Despite his threats, he received the endorsement of neither party in Leipzig. Disheartened by his rejection, he spent the evenings drinking with Bakunin—Bakunin was visiting with his old friend, Ruge, while passing through Leipzig on his way to the Pan Slavic Congress in Prague—cursing the philistines of Leipzig and the seeming victory of mediocrity.[51]

Bakunin was not one to abandon his friends. He decided Ruge ought to be a delegate from Breslau and contacted his friends in that city to support Ruge's candidacy. In a close election, Ruge won the right to represent Breslau in the National Assembly. He felt indebted to Bakunin and happily

49. Ibid.
50. Cf. Neher, *Ruge als Politiker*, p. 172.
51. "Episoden," pp. 43–45.

observed that at least in Breslau "the free intelligence of ideas ruled instead of the papal dignity of Blum." [52] Once again Ruge showed his disdain for those who disagreed with him. He sought to make the political reality of Germany conform to his philosophical vision. When he found that some did not agree with him, he had to decide that they were either villainous or irrational. Such choices did not allow him to be the effective politician he fancied himself.

The German National Assembly convened for its first session on May 18, 1848. On May 19 it elected Heinrich von Gagern president. Ruge, who voted for him, later regretted that vote when he realized that Gagern did not agree with his political vision. Nonetheless, the early sessions seemed industrious and purposeful, and Ruge was impressed with the early burst of activity. He wrote proudly to his wife that "the Assembly has declared itself sovereign and, like a new-born child, has given forth its first cries of life." [53]

The National Assembly soon began to bog down in official procedure and parliamentary delays. Ruge became impatient with the delays, with the slowness of the Assembly and the seeming halt to progress. He published an article in *Die Reform* criticizing the delays. He wanted decisive and immediate action; he feared the forces of reaction would regain control if the National Assembly failed to maintain the initiative. "We have been victorious," he declared, "and now we do not know what we should do with that victory." [54]

Ruge and his friends knew what to do with that victory. He and the few other democrats in the Assembly—notably, Wilhelm Zimmermann, Franz Zitz, and Julius Fröbel, the friend of the Berlin "Freien"—formed a faction called the Donnersberg, named for the place in which they gathered for private meetings. The program of the Donnersberg called

52. "Episoden," p. 48.
53. Ruge to Frau Ruge, 28 May 1848, *Briefwechsel und Tagebuchblätter*, 2:13.
54. *Die Reform*, 10 June 1848, cited in Neher, *Ruge als Politiker*, p. 176.

for the recognition of the National Assembly as the sovereign authority for all Germany, and it urged that the military power of the states be placed under the control of the Assembly. It demanded a republican constitution based on the principles of liberty, equality, and fraternity; it insisted on popular sovereignty expressed by freely chosen and responsible representatives.[55]

The first constitutional problem that confronted the National Assembly was the creation of the central executive power. The parties of the right and center favored a royal executive who would be chosen by the princes. The parties of the left wanted the Assembly to elect the executive. Ruge, of course, agreed with the left. He argued that the Assembly, the expression of the people, had the authority to elect an executive, an authority the parties of the right and center were still reluctant to remove from the hands of the princes.

The debate on this constitutional issue was stormy and energetic. Ruge delivered a particularly brisk speech during the debate, passionately urging the Assembly not to surrender its power to the princes, not to tolerate an executive that was not responsible to it. "The German nation is united here in the Paulskirche," he shouted.[56] His speech was interrupted several times by shouts of protest from the right, especially from Prince Lichnowsky, soon to be murdered by a mob, and Arndt; it was also interrupted by Gagern, who asked him not to criticize fellow members of the Assembly. Ruge ended his speech with a passionate plea that the Assembly create a republic for Germany.

Ruge's speech changed no opinions. Gagern proposed the compromise that was accepted: the Assembly would choose the

55. See Veit Valentin, *Die erste deutsche Nationalversammlung* (Berlin, 1919), pp. 27–34; Ludwig Bergsträsser, "Parteien von 1848," *Preussische Jahrbücher,* 177 (1919): 187–91; and Rudolf Haym, *Ausgewählter Briefwechsel* (Berlin, 1930), pp. 40–41.

56. *Stenographischer Bericht über die Verhandlung der deutschen constituirenden Nationalversammlung zu Frankfurt am Main,* ed. Franz Wigard (Frankfurt, 1848–49), 23 June 1848, 1:480.

executive, but the executive would be a prince not responsible to the Assembly. Archduke Johann of Austria was chosen as the executive. The members of the Donnersberg, however, refused to accept the compromise. When Ruge was asked for his vote, he shouted: "I will not vote for an executive who is not responsible to the Assembly!" [57] Archduke Johann's election was a major event in Ruge's progressive disillusionment with the National Assembly.

The other major issue with which Ruge concerned himself as a delegate to the National Assembly was the Slavic Question. This issue involved the fate of the Slavic minorities in Germany—the Poles in Prussia and the Czechs in Bohemia—at the establishment of the new German state. Should these minorities be invited into the German nation, or should they be excluded to found their own nation or to join a larger Slavic state?

When Czech nationalists in Bohemia ignored the German National Assembly and attended the Pan Slavic Congress in Prague instead, a shock of disbelief spread through the Assembly. Arndt seemed to speak for the majority when he cried: "Where will we be if we give each little individuality an equal right to life?" [58] Ruge, however, did not share the aggressive nationalism of some of his colleagues. In a moving speech, he pointed out that the Czech decision reflected a general European movement of the Slavic peoples to associate themselves democratically in a federated system of states. The National Assembly, he pleaded, must do nothing to interfere with the right of a national group to choose its own course:

> If we fight against the Slavs, then it will mean that the National Assembly wants to destroy freedom, and, gentlemen, we are gathered in the Paulskirche to establish freedom, not to destroy it. [59]

57. *Stenographischer Bericht*, 24 June 1848, 1:521.
58. *Stenographischer Bericht*, 5 June 1848, 1:214.
59. *Stenographischer Bericht*, 7 June 1848, 1:240.

The Assembly did not listen to Ruge; it passed a resolution on July 1 asking Austria to force the Czechs to elect representatives to the National Assembly.

The Polish Question was the other aspect of the Slavic problem that inflicted itself upon the National Assembly. The problem centered on whether to accept a part of the Grand Duchy of Posen into the German nation and to seat the delegates from Posen in the Paulskirche. The expansionists and military nationalists wanted to include as much territory as possible; the left wanted a free and independent Poland.

The two most important speeches in the debate over Poland were those by Wilhelm Jordan and Arnold Ruge.[60] Jordan was a friend of Bruno Bauer's and a member of the "Freien." Many times he had opposed Ruge's wishes in Hippel's, and now he opposed Ruge in the National Assembly. "To try to re-establish Poland only because its collapse fills us with appropriate sadness," Jordan shouted, "that is what I call feebleminded sentimentality." He attacked the generous disposition toward Poland as a policy of weakness and cowardice: "A people does not have the right to existence merely from the fact of existence—this comes only through the strength to assert itself as a state among other states."[61] To Jordan the urge for national honor was more important than the existence of Poland.

Ruge had always seen nationalism as a danger to be avoided, and he remained true to that early vision. In his speech to the National Assembly, a speech Sir Lewis Namier called "the funeral oration of German revolutionary idealism,"[62] Ruge defended the rights of an independent Poland. He called the Poles "apostles of freedom" and called upon the Assembly to "take up this mission" of freeing Poland. In the name of humanity and justice he summoned the Germans to create

60. See Marx's analysis of this debate in *MEGA*, part I, vol. 7, pp. 312–17, 324–37.
61. *Stenographischer Bericht*, 25 July 1848, 2:1144–46.
62. Namier, *1848* (London, 1944), p. 89.

a free nation on the borders of reactionary Russia. He insisted that Germany assume the responsibility for the restoration of Poland, for "our intervention must break the way for the reconstitution of Poland." [63] The Assembly did not listen to him: it voted to absorb Posen, and accepted the Posen delegates into its membership.

Ruge was infuriated by the decision against Polish independence, and his anger was another important element in his growing disillusionment with the National Assembly. Grieving under his disillusionment, he wrote:

> The Frankfurt Parliament is so hopeless that it costs me a great effort not to quit it. The resolution against Poland is a true outrage for which the Germans will atone . . . . They have thrown a glove into the face of the revolution.[64]

The speech of which Ruge was proudest in his Assembly career was his famed speech urging European disarmament.[65] He proposed that a congress of peoples be summoned to effect general European disarmament. His great hope was the union of the three great powers, France, Britain, and Germany, which he believed were all sympathetic to international peace. The political tradition of Britain, the revolutionary tradition of France, the philosophical tradition of Germany all combined would bring an era of international peace and justice. He argued that his proposal was not utopian, because all the nations of Europe would soon be governed democratically. A true democrat, he believed that governments controlled by the people would never war with one another, that universal democracy meant universal peace.[66] His sentiments were not shared by his colleagues; they presumably felt that

63. *Stenographischer Bericht*, 27 July 1848, 2:1184–88.

64. Ruge to Josephine d'Alquen, 1 August 1848, "Briefe von Arnold und Agnes Ruge aus den Revolutionsjahren," *Süddeutsche Monatshefte*, September 1912, p. 733.

65. Cf. Ruge to the Peace Conference, 15 August 1850, *Briefwechsel und Tagebuchblätter*, 2:116–17.

66. *Stenographischer Bericht*, 22 July 1848, 2:1098.

more pressing matters needed their attention, and they rejected his motion to call a European peace conference by a vote of two to one. For a man who so long had insisted that practicality be the guide to political life, Ruge's activities must have seemed strange to the rest of the Assembly.

Ruge's disillusionment with the Assembly, overwhelming by late September 1848, was accompanied by an increasing interest in the revolutionary activities in Berlin. There, the radicals and democrats in the Prussian Assembly were far stronger than at Frankfurt; there his journal, *Die Reform,* was the official organ of the extreme left; there, indeed, lay his hopes for the accomplishment of democracy in Germany. "Frankfurt is dead," he wrote, but in Berlin, "everything is invigorated anew." [67]

Ruge informed his wife that he was leaving Frankfurt for Berlin, for in the Prussian capital popular sovereignty was asserting itself:

> Berlin is in victory. The Berlin parliament is the true National Assembly. It must succeed, and it will be sovereign. Its victory is a revolution, while the victory of this Assembly [Frankfurt] is a victory of reaction.[68]

From Berlin on October 1, he wrote to the National Assembly to ask that a temporary replacement be named for him while he engaged in organizing the democratic movement in the Prussian capital. The National Assembly refused his request; it demanded that he either return to Frankfurt at once or resign.[69] Ruge chose the latter and severed all physical connection with the Assembly he had already abandoned spiritually.

As a parliamentary figure Ruge had inspired neither admiration nor respect in most of his colleagues. His frequent

67. Ruge to Frau Ruge, 9 September 1848, *Briefwechsel und Tagebuch-blätter,* 2:15.

68. Ruge to Frau Ruge, 22 September 1848, *Briefwechsel und Tagebuch-blätter,* 2:18.

69. *Stenographischer Bericht,* 11 November 1848, 5:319.

absences, his pedantic and dogmatic speeches, his radical democratic position, and his disdain for those who disagreed with him were not the characteristics of a subtle and effective parliamentarian. A contemporary caricature pictured him in a tall, pointed cap, lecturing to the Assembly, and titled him a "learned Jack Sausage." [70] The caricature represented the common view of Ruge as a ludicrous and doctrinaire pedagogue. One of his colleagues complained that his speeches were like those of a school teacher scolding misbehaved children. With his lofty manner, he claimed, Ruge failed to present his ideas clearly:

> The faded-blond Pomeranian with high shoulders and head bent forward began to spin his continually disconnected threads. He cannot spin an entire thread, for his positive capacity and devotion lack all form. He does not speak, he crams one contradiction next to another . . . . His whole being is humorous, even though he is rarely witty.[71]

Another of Ruge's colleagues also remembered him as a pedantic lecturer before the Assembly, a man who spoke with "pretensions of infallibility":

> Is not Ruge, the philosophical doctrinaire, on the tribune? If the rostrum is a professor's lecturing table, is it not reasonable that the Assembly is an attentive and patient student body attending a lecture? [72]

The simple truth was that Ruge, for all his demands for practical and realistic political programs, was totally dogmatic. Reality had to conform to the metaphysical image he held. He was the school teacher lecturing, insisting that the world make reality conform to the new form of spiritual development.

70. For a reproduction of the cartoon, see Hans Blum, *Die deutsche Revolution, 1848–49* (Leipzig, 1898), p. 275.

71. Heinrich Laube, *Das erste deutsche Parlament* (Leipzig, 1849), 1:248–49.

72. Rudolf Haym, *Die deutsche Nationalversammlung bis zu den Septemberereignissen* (Frankfurt, 1848), 1:78.

Ruge left the National Assembly for Berlin because he believed that there his metaphysical image would be realized. The Prussian king had abandoned the city to a liberal ministry; the Prussian Assembly had many radicals and democrats as members. Joyful over the radical strength in Berlin, over the popularity of his *Die Reform,* he wrote that in Berlin "the extreme left is nobler in construction; democracy must be victorious and will be established here." [73] Once again philosophical necessity, rather than political insight, prompted his prediction.

A committee of political figures clustered about Ruge included the most prominent radical democrats in Berlin: Johann Jakoby, Stein, Lipsky, Stephan Born, Oppenheim, d'Ester, and Agathon Benery. Ruge avidly entered into the political turmoil of Berlin; he was in the position of prominence and leadership that he always cherished. He called for the gathering in Berlin of democratic elements from all over Germany. This gathering, a new national assembly, would honestly express popular sovereignty. For Ruge, Berlin was the German Paris. Reflecting her husband's views, Frau Ruge wrote in October:

> It is much talked of that the opposition groups of all German parliaments and of the National Assembly will gather together in Berlin, and it is expected that, as the true representatives of the people, they will set up a constitutional assembly and will be supported by the people.[74]

Ruge had misread the current of the times when he foresaw the victory of democracy in Berlin. Even as he made his prognostication the forces of reaction were massing and unifying. Most people in Berlin, Engels has suggested, feared democracy, for democracy suggested mob rule, disorder, social up-

73. Ruge to Josephine d'Alquen, 8 October 1848, *Süddeutsche Monatshefte,* p. 734.
74. Frau Ruge to Josephine d'Alquen, 11 October 1848, *Süddeutsche Monatshefte,* p. 735.

heaval. Popular sympathy was not with Ruge. More important, the chief obstacle to the achievement of Ruge's cherished democracy was the Prussian army.

The desire for military intervention in Berlin to restore order came after the wild meetings of the Democratic Congress were held in the city, meetings so stormy that the presiding officer had to use a brace of pistols rather than the more conventional gavel to maintain order.[75] Ruge addressed the first session of the Congress. He outlined the danger to revolutionary Vienna from the troops of the reaction under Windischgrätz and predicted that the "fall of Vienna would be the fall of Berlin."[76] He planned to organize a mass demonstration and present a petition to the Prussian Assembly demanding its support of the revolutionaries in Vienna. On October 31, he led a huge mob of demonstrators to the theater in which the Prussian Assembly met. The mob invaded the meeting place and swarmed through the building.[77] Such disorder finally shattered Frederick William's patience—he called upon the reactionary Count von Brandenburg to form a ministry, and he summoned the army to Berlin to restore order. Ruge's mass demonstration, intended to prevent the victory of the reaction, actually occasioned it.

The reaction in Prussia quickly put an end to the work of the revolutionaries. Ruge's *Die Reform* was suppressed, and he was ordered to leave Prussia. He was reluctant to go, for he saw in Prussia's revolution the genesis of the German nation, a nation of free individuals who were free, in the Hegelian sense, because they existed within a rational state structure. Destroy the reaction in Prussia, institute democracy, and Prussia would form the core of a free Germany against reac-

75. Gustav Lüders, *Die demokratische Bewegung in Berlin im October 1848* (Berlin, 1909), pp. 95–109.

76. See Ruge's *Die preussische Revolution seit dem siebenten September und die Contrerevolution seit dem zehnten November* (Leipzig, 1848), p. 36.

77. *Die preussische Revolution*, pp. 37–52.

tionary Austria. Prussia, he believed, had a latent democratic structure, a tradition of a devoted bureaucracy, a state structure within which individual freedoms could be defined. Ruge explained his position to the Prussian minister, Manteuffel. "In spite of November 9," he said, "Prussia is still the left wing of Germany." [78] Manteuffel, distrusting anyone so long associated with the democratic left, refused to listen to him.

Ruge left Berlin for Leipzig in search of old friends and old dreams. He found neither. "There is only romantic nonsense now," he lamented; "there is no Prussian desire for honor, no Prussian politics any longer in Berlin." [79] Like another victim of the revolution, Metternich, Ruge sailed in exile to England.

Ruge's exile lasted until his death in 1880, but he preserved an interest in continental affairs. He joined with Mazzini, Ledru-Rollin, and Darasz in forming the European Democratic Committee. He also expressed pleasure over Bismarck's victories in 1866 and 1870; his stand was gratefully repaid by the Bismarckian government with an annual pension. Ruge had not become a nationalist; he had not rejected his democratic principles. What pleased him about the Prussian military victories was that the two powers defeated were major opponents of freedom. To Ruge, Austria had always been the epitome of reaction, the author of repression, the enemy of Young Hegelian humanism. Napoleon III's France had, in Ruge's eyes, perverted the French ideals of freedom and destroyed the French Revolution. Thus, he applauded the victories of Sadowa and Sedan.

There was another important reason for Ruge's exultation in Prussian victory. All his life he had seen Prussia as the state that would accomplish the German revolution, that is, would create a democratic state within which human freedom could be defined and defended. In the 1830s and 1840s he

78. Ruge to Josephine d'Alquen, 2 February 1849, *Süddeutsche Monatshefte*, p. 738.

79. Ruge to Frau Ruge, 21 April 1849, *Briefwechsel und Tagebuchblätter*, 2:69.

saw the multiplicity of German states practicing tyranny, repression, and denial of human rights. It was the rational bureaucratic state, the Hegelian state, which had the potential for the democracy that best supported the rights of individuals. Prussia had long had implicitly democratic institutions; now that it had unified Germany and ended the tyranny of small states, its democratic potential, he believed, would develop into reality.

Ruge's political career, like his journalistic career, had but one purpose—the victory of the philosophy of humanism in all areas of life. Throughout both his careers he maintained his basic principles. Revolutions often cause men to do contradictory things, but Ruge's ambiguities were more an intrinsic part of his philosophy than a conflict of loyalties and ideals. His great criticism of German liberalism was that it was too abstract, too theoretical. He sought to overcome this weakness by entering active political life in order to translate the liberating ideals of philosophical humanism to the tyrannized realm of politics. Ultimately, he wanted reality to conform to his ideal—perhaps that was his failure.

The Germany of the 1830s and 1840s was a world in which ideas and words had as much claim to reality as any material object. Hence, Ruge could demand the sweeping aside of all mundane reality and tradition in the name of reason and ideals. For "the reality of freedom," after all, "was the inwardness and extension of philosophy." [80] Freedom, then, was a metaphysical ideal to which reality was to conform; freedom was the Hegelian philosophy. "Doctrinaire" and "dogmatic" were two descriptive terms applied to Ruge by both friend and enemy, terms that truly defined his refusal to compromise the metaphysical image he hoped to translate into reality. That dogmatism was the heart of the Young Hegelian philosophy. All the Young Hegelians—Strauss, Bauer, Feuerbach, Stirner,

80. Ruge to Haym, 16 July 1841, *Briefwechsel und Tagebuchblätter*, 1:233.

Vischer, Ruge—were dogmatic; the legacy of the Hegelian philosophy gave them their assurance.

Ruge was more conscious than any of the Young Hegelians of the need to avoid demanding that reality be made to conform to abstract theory. Indeed, his criticism of German liberalism was, specifically, that it exalted theory above practice. To understand Ruge—and to understand all the Young Hegelians—it is necessary to realize that he did not regard his own emphasis on philosophy as exalting theory over reality. His philosophical views, his Young Hegelian humanism, were not abstract theories for him but actual representations of reality in its spiritual foundations. If there was a contrast between the Young Hegelian apocalypse and the political, social, and philosophical realities of Germany in the 1830s and 1840s, the error was with the world, not with the metaphysical image. Hegel had shown the nature of reality; the Young Hegelians had grasped that reality was changing, with spiritual progress in advance of the institutional and worldly forms that it embodied. All Ruge's demands in the *Hallische Jahrbücher,* all his energy as a journalist, all his activity as a politician were simply his attempts to fulfill his mission of showing the world that it must adopt new forms to accommodate the change in the spiritual foundations of reality. Humanism, the rational state, and political democracy were the worldly forms now required. Ruge's special mission as an intellectual—one who comprehended the basis of reality because of his mastery of the Hegelian philosophy—was to instruct the world to alter its forms in order to adapt them to the change in spirit.

That mission required action in journalism and politics. For Ruge, publication for the elite or the academic world was not enough; the democratic demands of philosophical humanism required popular and mass appeal. For a moment in 1848 the possibility of such successful appeal appeared, but for Ruge nothing short of the total alteration of the political forms of Germany, the total political realization of the Young Hegelian philosophy, could indicate success. Only the full Young

Hegelian apocalypse, in place of all the outmoded forms of reality, was acceptable.

Though Ruge failed to generate a unified Young Hegelian party, though he failed to achieve success in the Revolution of 1848, he did establish an important legacy for the subsequent bearers of the Hegelian apocalypse. That legacy was an appreciation of the need for direct and purposeful action on the part of the intellectuals who understood the Hegelian philosophy and sought to transfer its liberating effect to the world. Political passivity was no longer allowable, publication of the truth was no longer sufficient in itself. The philosophy of humanism now demanded that the activities of men were necessary to accomplish its victory. The realization that Christianity was outmoded and the realization that spiritual immanence demanded a worship of man were not sufficient unless those who held these truths sought actively to liberate the world by them.

Strauss and Feuerbach avoided aggressive political activity; Bauer and Stirner were content with the role of critics; but Ruge developed the need for direct action to liberate the world through philosophy. Since the reign of Frederick William IV and the Revolution of 1848 showed the power of the opponents of progress to delay the development of the spirit into worldly forms, the intellectuals must show their power to usher in progress. The progress to freedom, the Young Hegelian apocalypse, could be delayed by human action. If the world was to be made free, the action, not just the awareness, of the intellectuals was to produce that freedom.

Moses Hess, a younger intellectual much influenced by the thought of the Young Hegelians, once assessed Ruge's importance. Ruge, he argued, had formed the transition from thought to action, from philosophy to practical politics. Through Ruge's efforts, the great liberating philosophical ideas were brought to German political life:

> Though not so very original and creative, [Ruge] was always able to feel with proper tact what was true and in keeping with

the times, what was healthy and what was sick in the movements of his day; less a philosopher than a man of progress, he represented in his person the very essence of Young Hegelianism—which formed the transition between German philosophy and socialism, between thought and action . . . .[81]

Hess, of course, understood the Young Hegelians in terms of his own needs and, consequently, saw their importance as a transition to his own variety of socialism. Nonetheless, he showed a sound appreciation and understanding of Ruge's role. Ruge resolutely faced the question that each of the Young Hegelians set out to answer. He concluded that Christianity as the spiritual basis for civilization was now outmoded. Humanism was the new spiritual vision, the new foundation on which the new forms of civilization would rise. Reality was the spiritual vision of humanism and the forms derived from it; existing institutions, empty shells from which the spirit had vanished, were now the unreality that had to be rejected. Thus, he saw his responsibility in political action informed by humanism and directed towards making the institutions of society embodiments of humanism. The answer he offered for his age was political action, democratic political institutions, and popular sovereignty. He saw these as necessary and logical conclusions derived from philosophical humanism. He agreed with the other Young Hegelians in his basic philosophical vision, but he disagreed with them on the specific application and conclusion to be drawn. Like the others, he never doubted that he was right.

81. Moses Hess, *Sozialistische Aufsätze, 1841–1848*, ed. Theodore Zlocisti (Berlin, 1921), p. 111.

7 Conclusion: From Religion to Philosophy

The absolute is the spirit: this is its ultimate definition. To find this definition and to comprehend its meaning and content is, we may say, the absolute tendency motivating all culture and philosophy.

—Hegel

In 1873 the popular German writer, Paul Heyse, published his *Children of the World,* a novel that depicted the fate of its characters as part of the generation torn from traditional religious faith by the influence of the Young Hegelians. For this generation the "canonized myths and metaphysical legends" of Christianity were no longer true, but only a measure of "the degree of veracity existing in the creators of the poetic myths and their audience." This generation concluded that Christianity was dead and that it was "deeply immoral to pass out . . . fairy tales and legends as the foundation stone of our happiness when all educated minds believe in them as little as the Greeks at the time of Aristotle believed in the fables of Homer and Hesiod." In the new age philosophy had transcended religion, for "the elements of the century have shaken and gnawed at the dam constructed of the rotted debris of faith and have left scarcely one stone standing on another." [1] The sense of apocalypse was both irresistible and gratifying. The very spiritual basis of civilization had changed, and when the dam of Christianity was finally smashed, then the rush of change would destroy all the old, empty forms of life and new ones would emerge as the historical realization of the new spiritual reality, humanism.

The Young Hegelians were both creators and products of the spiritual vision that they bent all their efforts to serve. Convinced that the insight of Hegel's philosophy was the perception of the end of Christian civilization, they accepted the full consequences of living in an age that rejected the ideas and institutions of the past as inadequate for the present. That acceptance meant their own search for new beginnings, exploring to the depths the meaning of history and human experience, defining new methods and opening new fields of intellectual endeavor. Each of the Young Hegelians provided his own interpretation of the transition from Christianity to philosophy, a personal vision that, while it varied from the others,

1. Paul Heyse, *Kinder der Welt* (Berlin, 1890), 2:329–30.

was at one with them in being directed to answering the same question.

Wilhelm Dilthey urged historians not to be distracted from recognizing the fundamental importance of the inquiry into Christianity and its origins, into the whole question of religion, that concerned the intellectuals of nineteenth-century Europe. He was doubtless concerned that "the political and social problems of a violently changing time" might draw all the attention of historians and cause them to slight the critique of religion which, he felt, was of such resounding significance that it was, indeed, "one of the greatest achievements of human scholarship and investigation." [2]

Some of the accomplishments resulted from the fact that the critique of religion required "entirely new starting-points and methods of analysis." [3] Surely the Young Hegelians' work indicated the results in new methods and new points of view obtained from probing the depths, reopening all the questions, seeking new foundations. In attempting to comprehend the transition to the new age of philosophy, they made discoveries of subject and method that thinkers were compelled to accept for the rest of the century, and even thereafter: discoveries in psychology, aesthetics, philosophy, theology and religion; explorations into the meaning of history, myth, and the creative processes of the human mind. Perhaps they were not original in all these, but they did pursue them to the full extent of experience and ability with creativity and originality. They were willing to face the demands of the new age with confidence because they possessed a sure understanding of Hegel's philosophy. It was the confidence, not specifically that Hegel provided all the answers, but that his philosophy provided the framework within which to perceive the right questions—and to answer them.

2. Wilhelm Dilthey, "Ferdinand Christian Baur," *Gesammelte Schriften* (Berlin, 1921–36), vol. 4, *Jugendgeschichte Hegels und andere Abhandlungen zur Geschichte des deutschen Idealismus*, ed. Herman Nohl, pp. 403–04.

3. "Baur," p. 404.

Alexander Herzen once complained that Hegel's philosophy "led straight to the recognition of the existing authorities, led to a man's sitting with folded hands, and that was just what the Berlin Buddhists wanted." [4] For the Young Hegelians such a reading of Hegel was inconceivable: humanism, not passivity and quietism, was the essence of his philosophy. Each had his own understanding of the meaning of humanism, ranging from Strauss's aristocratic sense of culture, to Ruge's political democracy, to Stirner's unique ego, but each saw it as the form in which the alienation of spirit from man would finally be overcome.

Humanism was for the Young Hegelians a mode of action. It was not the sentimental love of the "people" that George Eliot and other earnest Victorians took it for. It was not prompted by charity or sentiment, pity or fancy. Indeed, Strauss, one of the most forceful and influential exponents of humanism in the nineteenth century, actually despised and feared the "people." The humanism of the Young Hegelians was a philosophical necessity. Humanity was divine; humanism meant worshipping man because man was God. And worship meant action.

The necessity of human action might seem a peculiar appendage to a philosophy that appeared to depict the process of history as deterministic and automatic. If asked whether the transition from religion to philosophy and the advent of humanism—both as the spiritual reality and as the ideal infusion of ideas and institutions—were inevitable, each of the Young Hegelians would doubtless have said yes. Why, then, was human action necessary, if the goal of its efforts was inevitable? Why were the Young Hegelians so eager to preach, to labor, and to sacrifice so much of themselves to try to bring about what was going to happen anyway?

There were several reasons for their insistence on action. First, they knew that they understood the meaning of history,

4. Alexander Herzen, *My Past and Thoughts,* tr. Constance Garnett (New York, 1928), 2:120.

and they based their metaphysic entirely upon it. History was developing toward a necessary goal, and their ideas were in line with its development. By allying themselves with the historical process, they were, in fact, its agents: they were assured of success. Secondly, their view of history was not, in the strictest sense, deterministic. They allowed, as did Hegel, an important role to chance, accident, luck, and personality in history. Though humanism must inevitably become the foundation for civilization, it was not inevitable for a particular time: human action was necessary to bring about the inevitable. They were painfully aware that human action could delay the inevitable, as the stubbornness and myopia of Frederick William IV, the Prussian bureaucracy, and the academic establishment demonstrated. The Young Hegelians were convinced by both their understanding of history and their own experience that men could hasten or delay the process of history. Thus, there could be no sitting around with folded hands waiting for the inevitable; there could only be purposeful action to effect the inevitable. The historical process predicated the emergence of humanism, but the historical process had to be the work of human hands.

Further, and perhaps most important, history was never for the Young Hegelians an abstraction that caused events. History took place only through human agency; it was concrete, specific, and human in all its forms. With their understanding of Hegel's philosophy of history, they perceived the historical process compounded only in terms of man's thought, action, and institutions, only in terms of man's inherent spirit and the objective forms in which he represented it. However inexorable and necessary the development of the spirit seemed, it was always the *Bildungsroman* of humanity. Without man history would not occur; without his action the historical process would not develop. The passivity of Berlin Buddhism, the mere contemplation of history, was not enough. Even knowing the owl of Minerva had taken flight was not enough. Action was the demand and the mission.

Each of the Young Hegelians understood the need for action that humanism required, but each understood his responsibility to action in his own way. For Strauss and Feuerbach that action meant educating the public to appreciate the historical change that had taken place, to reject the outmoded dualism of Christianity and adopt the divine immanence of humanism. It meant encouraging a sense of awe toward the works of man that exalted humanity. For Vischer it meant developing both the awareness and practice of aesthetic creativity with the aim of making all men conscious of fashioning their world in accord with inherent ideals. For Stirner and Bauer that action meant the ruthless application of the principle of criticism, the principle of the dialectic that would shatter the empty forms founded on dualism and allow the easy emergence of humanism. For Ruge that action took the form of politics in the effort to transform government into the conscious agent of humanism and history.

Only days before his death Hegel worried that "the loud din and stunning garrulousness" of the contemporary world might allow no respite to the philosopher "for participating in the passionless calm of the pure experience of thinking." [5] He had a presentiment of the world in which the Young Hegelians would live, and they seemed to agree that their world and dispassionate thought were not easily compatible. The history of the Young Hegelians is the story of the increasing involvement of the disinterested intellectual, the progressive awareness of the need to intrude thought into the world as action.

The influence of the Young Hegelians is worth a special study itself. It is, of course, a different issue from the intrinsic merit and intent of their thought: it involves how others understood and used their ideas, how subsequent thinkers applied their ideas to other circumstances and demands, how elements of their thought were accepted without a commitment to their total philosophy. A few suggestions about the

5. *Werke,* vol. 3, *Wissenschaft der Logik,* p. 23.

nature and extent of their influence are clearly useful in determining their stature and importance for the intellectual life of the nineteenth century. It is important, however, to note that influence often differs from intent and that no thinker can ultimately be judged by what those influenced by him made of his thought.

One area of the Young Hegelians' influence, often commented upon, was the seeming direct impact on a whole group of younger associates who developed a burning concern for social questions: Karl Marx, Friedrich Engels, Moses Hess, Lorenz von Stein, and Michael Bakunin. Some have suggested that these formed a second generation of Young Hegelians, continuing the work of the first generation to its logical revolutionary conclusions.[6]

Of the direct influence of the Young Hegelians on these men there can be no doubt. Each of them knew and was at one time associated with the Young Hegelians personally; each acquired his understanding of Hegel through the works of the Young Hegelians. The members of the second generation attained much of their metaphysical basis from these associations. They assumed the view of history adapted from Hegel by the Young Hegelians: history as a process moving toward a final goal of freedom, a process involving the progressive fusion of spirit and matter as the very definition of freedom. They accepted the view that true freedom meant living in accord with the historical process and requiring human institutions to conform to it. They were assured that humanism constituted the necessary foundation for the new age.

6. While there is no general study of these men as a group, several individual studies of value suggest connections to the Young Hegelians: Auguste Cornu, *La jeunesse de Karl Marx* (Paris, 1937); Franz Mehring, *Karl Marx* (Leipzig, 1923); Auguste Cornu, *Karl Marx und Friedrich Engels*, 2 vols. (Berlin, 1954–62); Gustav Meyer, *Friedrich Engels*, 2 vols. (The Hague, 1954); Auguste Cornu, *Moses Hess et la gauche hégélienne* (Paris, 1934); Edmund Silberner, *Moses Hess, Geschichte seines Lebens* (Leiden, 1966); E. H. Carr, *Michael Bakunin* (New York, 1937); and H. Nitzschke, *Geschichtsphilosophie Lorenz von Steins* (Munich, 1932).

They learned from the Young Hegelians that alienation meant a restraint on human freedom. Where the Young Hegelians saw alienation as a spiritual phenomenon, the projection of man's inherent spirit into external and objective forms, however, the generation of Marx and Engels saw those objective forms as man's economic products. Alienation for them meant the separation of man from his production.

They learned from the Young Hegelians the need for human action to effect the changes of history. That action, allied with the historical process, was assured of success, but success was not possible without the action. Consequently, they accepted from the Young Hegelians the vision of a great apocalypse that would usher in the new age of history. Bakunin's faith in a rapid and immediate transformation of human society and Marx's and Engels's assurance in the *Communist Manifesto* that a great revolution was at hand indicated the extent to which they accepted the apocalyptic thinking of the Young Hegelians. In short, their socialism—whether the communism of Marx and Engels, the state socialism of Lorenz von Stein, the anarchism of Bakunin, the blend of "philosophical socialism" by Hess—seemed a natural extension of Young Hegelian humanism.

It would be a mistake though, to see in such continuity either a necessary development or a true insight into the real intentions of the Young Hegelians. That Engels saw it this way was a reflection of his own needs and a judgment on his own intellectual origins rather than an objective analysis that needs to be accepted and repeated. Major differences existed between them and the Young Hegelians that indicated a vast array of different emphases, expectations, and concerns. The first difference stemmed from the fact that they were different generations, separated by ten years, that did not, consequently, share the same intellectual and historical experience. For the generation of Marx and Hess absorbed the Hegelian philosophy from the Young Hegelians rather than from Hegel. Its careful reading of Hegel followed thereafter. Hegel's philosophy was, for it, filtered through the intellectual prism of the Young Hegelians. The Young Hegelians developed a philosophy of humanism and action from Hegel's thought; the second generation accepted that philosophy as an assumption and built its own views upon it. Perhaps Marx summarized the difference well when he wrote, "Philosophers have hitherto interpreted the world differently. The issue is to change it." [7] The difference meant that the very question the Young Hegelians saw as the vital issue of their time—the consequences that men must draw from the fact that philosophy and religion were no longer compatible—was not, for the second generation, a vital issue any longer. The members of the second generation absorbed and transcended that question, moving to what they felt to be the real concerns of their own age.

The second difference between the Young Hegelians and those of the second generation specifically concerned with the development of socialism was that the second generation absorbed French ideas into the Hegelian metaphysic—the ideas, variously, of Saint-Simon, Proudhon, Fourier, of the political and social theorists of the French Revolution. The absorption of the French experience meant that the second generation was no longer heir only to the philosophical revolution inaugurated in Germany, but also heir to the political and social revolution inaugurated in France. Where the Young Hegelians relied on Berlin, the generation of Marx and Engels combined Paris with Berlin.

The younger generation absorbed still another revolutionary impulse into its metaphysic—the industrial revolution. For the Young Hegelians the sign of the approaching apocalypse was essentially a spiritual change from Christianity to humanism. The younger generation, however, saw the clear sign of the approaching apocalypse in the radical change of society resulting from the disruptions of industrial and economic transformation. Society, they felt, must now reflect the eco-

7. *MEGA*, vol. 1, part 5, p. 535.

nomic change of the industrial revolution as it once reflected pre-industrial conditions.

Consequently, the younger generation was motivated by the social question, the need to accommodate industrial change, the need to found the humanist society of freedom on the principles of socialism. The need was to establish socialism, a system that would end the alienation of man from his creations, his economic productivity. The Revolutions of 1848 revealed what the members of the younger generation had long known: the social question was the true point of division between them and the Young Hegelians. Two of the most impressive social analysts of the generation, Marx and Lorenz von Stein, both saw the June Days in Paris as the significance of the social question made manifest, the evident intrusion of industrialization in the historical process.[8] The significance of the social and economic change had long been stressed by the younger generation—witness, for example, Engels's study in 1844 of the condition of the working class in England—but now the significance was obvious for all to see.

It was precisely this social element that the Young Hegelians never accepted. Strauss and Feuerbach soon developed a profound distaste for the revolution, a distaste prompted in great part by the intrusion of the social question; Bauer and Stirner remained indifferent; even the involvement of Vischer and Ruge went no further than the political level, the demand for democracy. By 1848, Strauss's complaint that the demands of the time seemed to leave him behind could, perhaps, have been uttered by all the Young Hegelians.

The point was, of course, that the Young Hegelians were specifically, even exclusively, concerned with the historical transition from religion to philosophy, Christianity to human-

8. See Karl Marx, *Class Struggles in France, 1848–50* (New York, 1964), pp. 60–94; and Lorenz von Stein, *The History of the Social Movement in France, 1789–1850*, tr. Kaethe Mengelberg, (Totowa, New Jersey, 1964), pp. 319–429. Cf. Leonard Krieger, "Marx and Engels as Historians," *Journal of the History of Ideas* 14 (1953):381–403.

ism. They saw all the other issues of their time as derived from that transition, and they were never moved from their central concern. Their influence on those who developed their metaphysic into socialism, however deeply it extended, was always distinct from their intention.

Calling Marx, Engels, Lorenz von Stein, Bakunin and Hess the second generation of Young Hegelians is, thus, misleading. It suggests a linear continuity that did not exist, and it falsely implies that the Young Hegelian metaphysic had necessarily to develop into socialism. It is further misleading because it obscures areas other than socialism on which the Young Hegelians exerted profound influence. Two of these in particular need to be noted.

Theology and religious skepticism were never the same after the Young Hegelians as they had been before. For the Young Hegelians had probed the question of the origins of religion and had given to skepticism a new turn and to theology a devastating new challenge. The history of skepticism from the mid-nineteenth through the twentieth century has been in great part the story of the wide and profound influence of their ideas. Their influence primarily promoted the secular faith of humanism and denied the principle of transcendence. Its specific application was in the analysis of the historical, aesthetic, and psychological origins of religion, in the argument that man created God.[9] In this sense, modern European intellectual life is clearly the heir to the critical philosophy of the Young Hegelians.

By the same token and with the same impact, they posed all the questions that theology, if it were to survive, had to answer. Because of their influence, Schweitzer admitted that "the historical foundation of Christianity as built up by rationalistic, by liberal, and by modern theology no longer

9. For the impact of these ideas on the development of religious skepticism, see Franklin L. Baumer, *Religion and the Rise of Scepticism*, pp. 128–86.

exists . . . ." [10] Theologians quickly recognized the stern challenge that the Young Hegelians threw at them. That challenge in great part explains why theologians for the last eighty years have been seeking some basis for faith beyond the contingencies of historical and psychological inquiry.

A third area of Young Hegelian influence in addition to that on socialism and on the development of theology and religious skepticism was on the artistic and creative life of the nineteenth century. A host of artists—among them, George Eliot, Georg Herwegh, Richard Wagner, Gottfried Keller, Hoffmann von Fallersleben, Friedrich Hebbel, and Robert Prutz—declared their indebtedness to the inspiration of the Young Hegelians. The influence and inspiration stemmed from the Young Hegelian view of aesthetics, especially through the work of Vischer, Strauss, and Feuerbach. The artists and writers were much impressed by the argument of these men that, as Wagner said, an individual earned "true immortality" through his "sublime deeds and great works of art." [11] Artistic creation was the means for salvation and personal immortality, an aesthetic replacement of the old Christian idea of life after death. Works of art not only served humanity, they also helped the artist escape obliteration in a metaphysic that stressed historicism and denied a life after death in a personal and traditional sense. Art was its own principle of transcendence.

Even more, the creative figures developed from the Young Hegelians the notion of the artist as "a Christ"—it was Herwegh's choice of words[12]—who fused spirit and matter in his own person and work, created the myths for civilization, and made its ideals flesh. The artist projected his inherent spirit into the plastic material of the external world, molding that material in accord with his ideals and making it objectify freedom. They saw all human creation, in art, religion, and

10. Albert Schweitzer, *The Quest of the Historical Jesus*, p. 397.
11. Richard Wagner, *My Life*, 1:522.
12. Georg Herwegh, *Werke*, 1:xv.

philosophy, as part of an aesthetic process in which the artists served the interests of freedom and humanity by progressively uniting man and spirit and representing that union as works of art. The artists, they believed, created the ultimate metaphysical image that was the foundation for every civilization. They saw their own mission as continuing that function by developing the artistic forms which would embody the ideals for man in the new age of humanism.

The impact of the Young Hegelians on socialism, aesthetics, religious skepticism, and theology indicated that their influence was fragmentary rather than whole, diffuse rather than lineal. The members of the younger generation influenced by their ideas were both selective and critical, taking what they could use for their own purposes, and developing their own intellectual and historical contributions in the process. As Ortega y Gasset has reminded us, "life . . . for each generation is a task in two dimensions." The first is "the reception, through the agency of the previous generation, of what has had life already, e. g., ideas, values, institutions, and so on." The second is "the liberation of the creative genius inherent in the generation concerned." And, he added, "the attitude of the generation cannot be the same towards its own active agency as towards what it has received from without." [13] The younger generation accepted the Young Hegelians' work in parts rather than in its totality. They used those parts as a set of assumptions upon which to build their own efforts and insights, continuing the influence of the Young Hegelian metaphysic while transcending the specific concern that prompted its formation. Perhaps it was to be expected; the Young Hegelians had done the same with Hegel's thought.

The Young Hegelians themselves represented the continuity of Hegel's influence and its diffusion. Karl Rosenkranz, Hegel's devoted disciple and biographer, wrote in 1844—in recognition of the intellectual dependence of his generation on the great

13. José Ortega y Gasset, "The Concept of the Generation," *The Modern Theme,* tr. James Cleugh (New York, 1961), pp. 16–17.

philosophers of the early nineteenth century—that his generation had to be "the gravediggers and monument builders" for those philosophers.[14] The Young Hegelians performed this double task for Hegel. Their emphasis on history, in particular, was a monument to Hegel's influence, a monument to the debt they owed the master. Their exclusive reliance on the historical dimension was also a break from the master, indicating a major contribution to the dissolution of the Hegelian school. Hegel had intended his system as an all-embracing, all-sided grasp of reality. History was part of reality, but not all of it. His philosophy of history did not comprise his entire system, but was only a part of it, along with his philosophies of nature, law, religion, aesthetics, and logic. The Young Hegelian emphasis on the dialectic in history had the result, whatever the intention, of transforming Hegel's philosophy, for them, into historicism and dismissing the all-sided system. Once the all-inclusive quality of Hegel's system was replaced by historicism, the dichotomies bridged by that system—subject and object, spirit and matter, man and God, real and ideal, being and becoming—were separated again. The Young Hegelians, therefore, were forced to deal with these dichotomies anew, concluding in most cases with answers different from Hegel's. Indeed, their historicism became a justification for their own transcending of Hegel's thought. By continuing his philosophy of history they moved increasingly toward the diffusion of his ideas, conveying and propagating his influence, but not his philosophy. In this special way the Young Hegelians were both "the gravediggers and monument builders" for Hegel's philosophy.

Perhaps any deliberate measurement would suggest that the major influence of the Young Hegelians was in diffusing Hegel's thought, making it possible for others to accept parts of his philosophy without a commitment to its totality, and in transforming his emphasis into historicism. They thus maintained his influence while showing little concern for his own

14. Karl Rosenkranz, *Hegel's Leben*, xix.

goals and intentions. It is an interesting irony—perhaps the cunning of reason again—that those affected by their thought performed the same function for them.

A man is, of course, more than his origins, and certainly more than his influence, as the relationship of the Young Hegelians to Hegel and of Marx to the Young Hegelians suggests. It is not only in the specific lineage of their intellectual filiation and offspring that the significance of the Young Hegelians should be judged; it is surely as much in the modes of thought and comprehension that they shared with their century and strengthened for its use. They were both products and creators of the intellectual dimension of their age, and specific emphases and assumptions in their outlook showed that dual relationship.

The first characteristic of their thought was the use of criticism as a philosophical tool. "Assuredly, my work is negative and destructive," Feuerbach admitted.[15] It was an admission that all of the Young Hegelians could have made. They saw criticism as central to the progress of life, the essence of Hegel's dialectic, a relentless and demanding task imposed upon them by virtue of their position as intellectuals. It meant that they had to engage in analytical studies and careful examinations of all ideas, values, and institutions of their time, indeed, of the very foundations of their civilization. Their unyielding critical approach was the key to their own search for truth and abiding value, their own demand that what was outmoded and false had to be dismissed. It explained why their work seemed so completely destructive, why their enemies condemned them as negative critics.

It would be wrong to conclude that the aims of the Young Hegelians were destructive, although most of their productive energy centered on criticism. Criticism, they all affirmed, was the means of arriving at truth, the way to arrive at the meaning of history beneath its objective and transient forms.

15. Ludwig Feuerbach, *Das Wesen des Christentums*, p. xii.

It was the necessary path of thought to higher and more complete comprehension, the necessary agency for clearing the way for the emergence of humanism. It was the only foundation for the new revelation and the new incarnation; it was, indeed, the basis for reconstruction. Whatever method it demanded, its aim was positive. The Young Hegelians were convinced of the positive power of negative thinking, and they sought, with criticism, to duplicate in their own minds the progressive dialectical path of reason.

The second general emphasis and assumption of their thought was the reductive element. Because they had an unquestioning assurance in their own metaphysic, they were convinced that they could comprehend the basis of reality and reduce the complexity of appearances to the simplicity of that basis. The basis of reality was, of course, history, but history seen specifically as the process of man's externalizing his inherent spirit in acts of alienation and then, through awareness, progressively overcoming the alienation in stages ascending to monism. For them, history and all its forms and appearances—ideas, institutions, religions, art, philosophies, ideals—reflected this unitary process. Any stage in history could be truly understood only as a part of the process; the complexity and variety of historical experience were only appearances that should be reduced to their place in the process for understanding. Every aspect of human life, whether it be the Christianity and institutions of their own time, the art and philosophy of classical Greece, or the religious experiences of primitive man, could be reduced and explained by the one basic key to history. Their metaphysic denied historical pluralism by reducing it to monism.

The third general quality of their thought was geneticism. Here the assumption, most influential through the work of Strauss and Feuerbach, was simply that any phenomenon in history, any idea or institution, could be understood through its origins and history rather than through its intrinsic quality or worth. Renan, of course, understood the implications of this view when he admitted that it was impossible to believe in the religion whose history one wrote since faith in an object or value was incompatible with knowing its history.[16] The Young Hegelians equally understood the implications, though they happily accepted them as necessary, and concluded that the history of religion denied the possibility of faith in any of its forms as an absolute. As Strauss admitted, "the true criticism of dogma is its history." [17] It was an admission, valid for all the Young Hegelians, that to understand an object or an idea it was only necessary to know where and how it originated and by what process it became what it was. This view equated the very definition of existence with history.

To separate the three qualities of thought for summary is not to imply that they were not interrelated, for they clearly were. Even more, they were included in the fourth characteristic of the Young Hegelians' thought—their historicism. They developed it from Hegel, concluding that reality was all historical, in a vision that necessarily implied the critical, reductionist, and genetic emphases. Though they did not originate historicism, they strengthened it in their use of it and popularized it with their influence. Historicism meant replacing absolutes with relativity, permanence with movement, transcendence with immanence. It defined history as a process in which ideas and institutions were created for the time and place of their origin, only to be discarded in the further progress of history. It meant that all reality was time-bound, responsive to certain conditions that were always changing, and that nothing should be preserved when it was no longer useful. For the Young Hegelians historicism had the attraction of drawing attention away from the transient phenomena of history to the nature of the historical process itself.

Historicism is well enough known as a philosophy in the nineteenth and twentieth centuries. What was doubtless most

16. Ernest Renan, *The Life of Jesus*, ed. John Haynes Holmes (New York, 1927), p. 65.
17. *Die christliche Glaubenslehre*, 1:71.

important about it for the Young Hegelians extended even beyond their specific use of it in analysis and personal belief. It opened what was for them a central question: whether, on the basis of a philosophy of historicism, it was possible to move beyond historicism to some abiding value free from change.

Dilthey argued that the motive power for the Young Hegelians was their opposition to "the binding power of historical tradition." [18] This important insight caught the essence of their attempt to use a philosophy of history as the means of escaping historical tradition, an attempt that proved—if proof was needed—that having a philosophy of history did not necessarily lead one to revere the forms of the past and desire to continue their traditions. Rather, their historicism directed them to understand the present and to free history from the forms in which the past had momentarily embodied it. They understood that their age was one of total historical change amounting to the total transformation of civilization.

Total historical change, both transcending the past and fulfilling its meaning, was what the Young Hegelians perceived and required. Those historians are wrong who have argued that the Young Hegelians were religious critics to begin with and steadily changed into social critics, or that, even from the start, they were social critics who felt the need to conceal their real intentions beneath religious language.[19] The lives and thought of Strauss and Feuerbach stand as a sufficient refutation of this contention. Even more, such an argument actually reverses the specific concerns of the Young Hegelians, for they believed that all such concerns as society, politics, scholarship, culture, and art were themselves only derived from the spiritual basis of civilization.

It is, of course, legitimate to argue that even from the begin-

18. Dilthey, Gesammelte Schriften, 4:403.
19. See, for example, Koppel S. Pinson, Modern Germany, Its History and Civilization, p. 71; and Sidney Hook, From Hegel to Marx, pp. 81 ff.

ning the Young Hegelian religious criticism implied a total change in society and its institutions, since from the beginning it meant replacing Christianity with humanism as the foundation of society. The revolutionary implications of such a total transformation were great indeed, for the Young Hegelians believed that the ideas and institutions of any age must reflect the spiritual foundations of that age. Hence, the change from Christianity to humanism transformed the whole range of human civilization. It is, however, important to note that social and political changes followed the advent of humanism; they did not precede it, and they were certainly no substitute for it.

The priority they assigned to historical change allowed the Young Hegelians, individually, to have a wide variety of social and political views. There was no correlation between philosophical radicalism and social and political radicalism; it was possible to be philosophically radical and politically conservative like Strauss, or politically democratic like Ruge, or a proponent of political absolutism like Bauer. This range of opinion only indicated that social and political views were derivative rather than primary, and that each of the Young Hegelians conceived his derivations from the primary vision differently. The primary vision of philosophical humanism provided the basis for different results; its primacy was never in doubt.

The transition from the age of religion to the age of philosophy was the specific concern of the Young Hegelians. Possibly they never escaped from the question of religion. Most of their efforts were directed toward illuminating religious experience, explaining its origins and function, and distinguishing between its contribution to the historical process and its time-bound and now outmoded forms. Beyond their own critical contributions, they showed an awareness that the philosophy they propounded was intimately connected to religion, that humanism was the next step forward from Christianity and, in that sense, related to it. Ultimately philosophy transcended rather than negated religion; that is, it both absorbed and went beyond religion as part of the same historical process. Thus the age of philosophy broke with historical tradition precisely because it went beyond it while assimilating it, preserving its meaning and rejecting its objective form.

There was, however, a further dimension to their concern with religion, well stated by Ruge when he urged "the battle of true religion with religious illusions." [20] By religious illusions he meant, of course, Christianity, the specific external forms, now outmoded, in which the spirit was once embodied as absolute religion. By true religion he meant the very process of the immanent spirit, the process identical with and productive of a source of value that stood above the transience inherent in history. Skepticism might seem the only legitimate attitude allowed to those who accepted historicism as the description of reality, but each of the Young Hegelians avoided complete historical relativity by finding in history itself a source of value.

They had insisted that Hegel's philosophy of immanence denied the traditional notion of divine transcendence, and they rejected the efforts of the Hegelians of the right to retain the Christian God as a mainstay against the implications of constant change and relativity, against an anarchy of values. Each, in the long run, however, accepted some substitute for the transcendent principle, some area of value that would not only contribute to the new age of humanism but would also allow his own achievements to transcend mortality. Strauss found it in culture; Feuerbach in broad contributions to the well-being of humanity; Vischer in aesthetics; Ruge in politics; and Bauer, pursuing the implications of relativity almost to their limit, grasped at absolutism. Stirner saw the issue most clearly. "As long as you believe in truth," he warned the other Young Hegelians, "you do not believe in yourself; and you are a—*servant*, a—*religious man*." [21] He feared that they were

20. "Selbstkritik des Liberalismus," *Gesammelte Schriften*, 3:97.
21. *Der Einzige und sein Eigenthum*, p. 473.

setting up new absolutes to deny their own philosophy of immanence and historicism. Yet even he could not sustain his insight as skepticism; all he offered was his own ego as an absolute.

The Young Hegelians identified and set out to answer the question of their time: the meaning that men must develop from their realization that religion was no longer capable of expressing the ideal, that philosophy had transcended religion and made it obsolete. In answering the question, they probed to the depths of experience and creativity, contributing to and reflecting the intellectual life of their century. They found that accord on the question to be asked predicated sharp diversity among the answers they offered, and that their influence resulted from their disagreements rather than from their agreement.

Karl Rosenkranz, obsessed with the role of the intellectuals of the 1830s and 1840s as epigones thriving on the thought of the great philosophers of the early nineteenth century, asked the fundamental question of his generation: "Are we capable of producing for the second half of our century a brotherhood of philosophical saints?" [22] In the answer to this question lies the deeper historical significance of the Young Hegelians.

22. Rosenkranz, *Hegel's Leben,* p. xix.

Bibliographical Essay

The following essay is not intended as another listing of all the works previously cited in footnotes, nor as a catalogue of all the books consulted in the preparation of this study. It is intended, rather, as a critical appraisal of the sources and studies essential to the pursuit of the Young Hegelians. The topical distinction between sources and secondary accounts—the standard separation for bibliographies—would not be especially useful here, where the line between source and secondary interpretation is often indistinct and where the subject matter seems to divide more naturally into several integral divisions that combine sources with secondary accounts. Important English editions of the works of Hegel and the Young Hegelians that were useful in preparing the translations of passages for the text of this study are also included.

Hegel

The original edition of Hegel's complete works is in many ways the best to use in order to study his school. It was edited by some of his most eminent students—P. Marheineke, J. Schulze, E. Gans, L. von Henning, H. Hotho, C. Michelet, and F. Förster—and appeared as Hegel's *Werke* (Berlin, 1832–45) in eighteen volumes. The students supplemented Hegel's writing with their lecture notes and compiled many of the volumes in the complete edition completely from lecture notes. This edition was republished, with some changes, under the editorship of Hermann Glockner. The most useful part of this newer edition is the *Hegel-Lexikon* (Stuttgart, 1935–39), vols. 23–26 of Hegel's *Sämtliche Werke: Jubiläumsausgabe* (Stuttgart, 1927–30). Those specifically interested in distinguishing between Hegel and his students' additions and explanations—the current aim in serious Hegel scholarship—will turn to the yet unfinished *Sämtliche Werke: Kritische Ausgabe*, begun under the editorship of Georg Lasson and continued by Johannes Hoffmeister.

For the English reader several translations are available: *The Philosophy of History*, translated by J. Sibree (New York, 1899); *Lectures on the Philosophy of Religion*, translated by E. B. Speirs and J. Burdon Sanderson, 3 vols. (London, 1895); *Early Theological Writings*, translated by T. M. Knox (Chicago, 1948); *The Phenomenology of Mind*, translated by J. B. Baillie (London, 1910); *Philosophy of Right*, translated by T. M. Knox (Oxford, 1942); *The Philosophy of Fine Art*, translated by F. P. B. Osmaston, 4 vols. (London, 1920); and the edition of selections, *The Philosophy of Hegel*, edited by Carl J. Friedrich, (New York, 1953), a mixture of old, new, and revised translations.

The interpretations of Hegel's thought are legion, many of them sufficiently obscure to make the return to Hegel's prose a relief. An excellent interpretive study is J. N. Findlay, *Hegel: a Reexamination* (London, 1958), a work of perception and clarity that concentrates on Hegel's ideas. Another is Walter Kaufman, *Hegel* (Garden City, New York, 1965), at its best in seeing the development of Hegel's thought and the relationship between his philosophy and his life, at its most diverting in suggesting that everyone else has misunderstood Hegel. Hermann Glockner, *Beiträge zum Verständnis und zur Kritik Hegels* (Bonn, 1965) is a suggestive and useful work by the editor of Hegel's complete works. Glockner's *Hegel*, 2 vols. (Stuttgart, 1929–40) is also a valuable study of Hegel's thought. Two older studies are still of interest: Rudolf Haym, *Hegel und seine Zeit* (Berlin, 1857); and Kuno Fischer, *Hegels Leben, Werke, und Lehre*, 2 vols. (Heidelberg, 1901).

Specific issues in Hegel's philosophy are handled well by several works. Benedetto Croce, *What Is Living and What Is Dead of the*

Philosophy of Hegel, translated by Douglas Ainslie (London, 1915) is good on the dialectic. Karl Rosenkranz, *Hegel als deutscher Nationalphilosoph* (Leipzig, 1870) is a good contemporary study of Hegel's thought and influence. An important treatment of Hegel's political thought is Franz Rosenzweig, *Hegel und der Staat,* 2 vols. (Berlin and Munich, 1920). For Hegel's religious ideas, Iwan Iljin, *Die Philosophie Hegels als kontemplative Gotteslehre* (Bern, 1946) is a perceptive and valuable book with which to begin. A good study of what the Young Hegelians took to be Hegel's most significant book is Jean Hyppolite, *Genèse et structure de la Phénoménologie de l'esprit de Hegel* (Paris, 1946).

For biographical studies of Hegel, Karl Rosenkranz, *Hegel's Leben* (Berlin, 1844) is still the most informative. Wilhelm Dilthey, *Die Jugendgeschichte Hegels,* vol. 4 of his *Gesammelte Schriften* (Leipzig and Berlin, 1921), is a perceptive and important interpretation. Another good study of the early years of Hegel's development is Georg Lukács, *Der junge Hegel* (Zürich, 1948).

The Hegelian School

There is one collection of selected writings of the Young Hegelians: *Die Hegelsche Linke,* edited by Karl Löwith (Stuttgart, 1962). There is also one for the Hegelians of the right: *Die Hegelsche Rechte,* edited by H. Lübbe (Stuttgart, 1962).

Several available studies deal with the origin and dissolution of the Hegelian school and the appearance of the Young Hegelians. A few contemporary works stand well above the violent partisanship of the early nineteenth century. Two histories of philosophical development written by conservative Hegelians are especially enlightening and informative on the Hegelian school: Carl Ludwig Michelet, *Geschichte der letzten Systeme der Philosophie in Deutschland von Kant bis Hegel,* 2 vols. (Berlin, 1838); and Johann Eduard Erdmann, *A History of Philosophy,* 3 vols., translated by W. S. Hough (London, 1890–92). Two assaults on the Young Hegelian position that are perceptive in spite of their vindictiveness are Heinrich Leo, *Die Hegelingen* (Halle, 1838); and Hermann Marggraff, *Deutschlands jüngste Literatur- und Culturepoche* (Leipzig, 1839). Several recent works that benefit from a century's perspective are essential. The best of these is clearly Jürgen Gebhardt's *Politik und*

Eschatologie. *Studien zur Geschichte der Hegelschen Schule in den Jahren 1830–1840* (Munich, 1963); it is a solid treatment of Hegel and many of his disciples against their political background, though its treatment of the Young Hegelians is brief. The best treatment of the Hegelians of the right is in Hermann Lübbe, *Politische Philosophie in Deutschland. Studien zu ihrer Geschichte* (Basel and Stuttgart, 1963). Willy Moog, *Hegel und die Hegelsche Schule* (Munich, 1930) is a useful narrative summary, considerably briefer on the school than on Hegel, that suffers from a lack of analysis.

Karl Löwith, *Von Hegel zu Nietzsche* (Zurich, 1941) is now available in an English translation: *From Hegel to Nietzsche—the Revolution in Nineteenth-Century Thought*, translated by David Green (New York, 1964). Löwith includes some interesting treatment of some of the Young Hegelians, though he unconvincingly includes Kierkegaard in the group. His intention, however, is not to deal with the Young Hegelians as important in and of themselves, but only as they may have been involved in what Löwith claims is the major development of thought from Hegel to Nietzsche—the self-criticism of the bourgeois-Christian world. His evident distaste for this development prevents him from appreciating the actual intentions of the Young Hegelians and the positive achievements that resulted from their work.

Sidney Hook, *From Hegel to Marx: Studies in the Intellectual Development of Karl Marx* (New York, 1936) also includes some treatment of the Young Hegelians. His purpose, however, is not to understand them on their own terms, but to try to use them for the genetic purpose of explaining how Marx's thought developed from Hegel's. Consequently he has a difficult time fitting them all into this easy process: his treatment of Strauss is brief, weak, and misleading; and he does not discuss Vischer at all. He fails to see the importance of the religious issue, and he tends, unduly, to treat thinkers only in terms of their ideas and not at all in terms of their historical context.

Herbert Marcuse, *Reason and Revolution: Hegel and the Rise of Social Theory* (New York, 1941) also touches on some of the Young Hegelians, though briefly. His specific interest is in arguing that "reason" in Hegel's philosophy must be understood in a social and political context, and that, consequently, Marx must be seen as the legitimate successor to and continuer of Hegel. His concentration on society and social thought, itself an interesting commentary on the time of the book's publication, directs him to a reductionist concern with Hegel and a genetic concern with Marx. In either case, the Young Hegelians do not get their due. Several brief essays are available that deal with the Hegelian school. Useful, though limited in scope and intention, are the two essays by Hans Speier in *Social Order and the Risks of War* (New York, 1952): "From Hegel to Marx: the Left Hegelians, Feuerbach, and 'True Socialism,'" and "From Hegel to Marx: Lassalle's Philosophy of History." For the relationship of the Young Hegelians to Prussia, Gustav Mayer, "Die Junghegelianer und der preussische Staat," *Historische Zeitschrift* 121 (1920): 411–40, is essential. Two excellent and essential articles deal with the religious views of the Young Hegelians: Ernst Benz, "Hegels Religionsphilosophie und die Linkshegelianer," *Zeitschrift für Religions- und Geistesgeschichte* 7 (1955): 247–70; and Hans Rosenberg, "Theologischer Rationalismus und vormärzlicher Vulgärliberalismus," *Historische Zeitschrift* 141 (1930): 497–541, which deals with the relationship between religious and political criticism.

Strauss

The major collection of sources for Strauss is his *Gesammelte Schriften*, 12 vols. (Bonn, 1876–78), edited by Eduard Zeller. The original editions of his most significant works are also important to consult. His *Das Leben Jesu, kritisch bearbeitet*, 2 vols. (Tübingen, 1835–36) is available in the English translation by George Eliot as *The Life of Jesus, Critically Examined*, 2 vols. (New York, 1860). Strauss wrote an important defense of his work and answer to his critics that contains much useful material, *Streitschriften zur Vertheidigung meiner Schrift über das Leben Jesu und zur Charakteristik der gegenwärtigen Theologie* (Tübingen, 1841; first edition, 1837). Strauss's second great work was *Die christliche Glaubenslehre in ihrer geschichtlichen Entwicklung und im Kampfe mit der modernen Wissenschaft*, 2 vols. (Tübingen and Stuttgart, 1840–41). His second life of Jesus, *Das Leben Jesu für das deutsche Volk bearbeitet* (Leipzig, 1864), was translated into English anonymously as *A New Life of Jesus*, 2 vols. (London, 1865). His final testament, *Der alte und der neue Glaube, ein Bekenntniss* (Leipzig, 1872), also was translated into English immediately as *The Old Faith and the New, a Confession,* by Mathilde Blind (New York, 1873). An interesting forward by Strauss appears in the nineteenth edition of this work (Stuttgart, 1873).

Several collections of Strauss's correspondence are essential for a study of his life and thought: *Ausgewählte Briefe,* edited by Eduard Zeller (Bonn, 1895); *Briefwechsel zwischen Strauss und Vischer,* 2 vols., edited by Adolf Rapp (Stuttgart, 1952–53); *Briefe von David Friedrich Strauss an L. Georgii,* edited by Heinrich Maier (Tübingen, 1912); and "Zur Biographie von David Friedrich Strauss," edited by Theobald Ziegler, in *Deutsche Revue,* May–July, 1905, a collection of Strauss's early letters, important in showing his development before 1835.

Strauss wrote an important defense of his political views in "Preussen und Schwaben," in *Preussische Jahrbücher* 19 (1867): 186–99.

Several valuable biographical studies of Strauss are available. The best of these is Theobald Ziegler's *David Friedrich Strauss,* 2 vols. (Strassburg, 1908), an analytical study of Strauss and his context, always sympathetic. An indispensible critical analysis of Strauss and his thought is Adolf Hausrath's *David Friedrich Strauss und die Theologie seiner Zeit,* 2 vols. (Heidelberg, 1876–78), a work that stresses the role of Strauss as a reflector rather than a creator of his time. The uncritical, narrative account by Strauss's friend Eduard Zeller, *David Friedrich Strauss in seinem Leben und seinen Schriften* (Bonn, 1874), is available in an English translation as *David Friedrich Strauss in his Life and Writings* (London, 1874). Adolph Kohut, *David Friedrich Strauss als Denker und Erzieher* (Leipzig, 1908), is a bland and partial biography. A good summary account, though not original in any way, is Albert Lévy, *David-Frédéric Strauss, la vie et l'oeuvre* (Paris, 1910). An interesting comparative study of Strauss's life and work is Heinrich Maier, *An der Grenze der Philosophie: Melancthon, Lavater, David Friedrich Strauss* (Tübingen, 1909).

A few briefer studies on specific points in Strauss's life and work are quite valuable. Edgar Quinet's review of Strauss's scholarship, "De la Vie de Jésus par le Docteur Strauss," *Revue des deux Mondes* 16 (1838): 585–629, is singularly perceptive and incisive. Wilhelm Lang's "Ferdinand Baur und David Friedrich Strauss," *Preussische Jahrbücher* 160 (1915): 474–504; 161 (1915): 123–44, is a quite useful study of the relationship between Strauss and Baur, founder of the Tübingen School, based on their unpublished correspondence. Strauss's political activities are best treated by R. Krauss, "D. Fr. Strauss im Jahre 1848," *Württembergische Viertelsjahrhefte für Landesgeschichte* 18 (1909): 161–72. The full story, with lengthy selections from the documents, of Strauss's appointment to and dismissal from Zürich is best told in Friedrich Vogel, *Memorabilia Tigurina oder Chronik der Denkwürdigkeit der Stadt und Landschaft Zürich* (Zürich, 1841). A good contemporary collection of sober criticisms of Strauss's religious views is that edited by J. R. Beard, *Voices of the Church in Reply to Dr. D. F. Strauss, Author of "Das Leben Jesu," Comprising Essays in Defense of Christianity by Divines of Various Communions* (London, 1845), with the essay by Beard, "Strauss, Hegel, and Their Opinions," the best of the collection.

Feuerbach

The major and standard collection of Feuerbach's complete works is his *Sämmtliche Werke*, 10 vols., edited by Wilhelm Bolin and Friedrich Jodl (Stuttgart, 1903–11). Feuerbach's basic work, *Das Wesen des Christentums* (Tübingen, 1841), is available in an English translation, also by George Eliot, *The Essence of Christianity* (London, 1854).

Equally essential as a source is the standard collection of Feuerbach's correspondence, *Briefwechsel und Nachlass*, 2 vols., edited by Karl Grün (Leipzig and Heidelberg, 1874).

The standard work on Feuerbach in English is William B. Chamberlain's *Heaven Wasn't His Destination: the Philosophy of Ludwig Feuerbach* (London, 1941). Yet this work is disappointing in its lack of originality, being based almost totally on the earlier and important study by Albert Lévy, *La philosophie de Feuerbach et son influence sur la littérature allemande* (Paris, 1904). Friedrich Jodl's *Ludwig Feuerbach* (Stuttgart, 1904) is a short but useful study of Feuerbach's life and thought. A perceptive study of his ideas is S. Rawidowicz, *Ludwig Feuerbachs Philosophie: Ursprung und Schicksal* (Berlin, 1931). Two important and informative studies of Feuerbach's religious views are available: Olga Tugemann, *Ludwig Feuerbachs Religionstheorie* (Reichenberg, 1915); and Hermann

Henne, *Die religionsphilosophische Methods Feuerbachs* (Borna and Leipzig, 1918). Of course, Friedrich Engels, *Ludwig Feuerbach und der Ausgang der klassischen deutschen Philosophie* (Stuttgart, 1919) still remains a classic; it is available in an English translation, *Ludwig Feuerbach and the Outcome of Classical German Philosophy*, translated by C. P. Dutt (New York, 1941).

Vischer

Vischer's works are available in several useful editions. Most important for the study of Vischer as a Young Hegelian are the following: *Aesthetik oder Wissenschaft des Schönen*, 6 vols. (Reutlingen and Leipzig, 1846–57); *Kritische Gänge*, 6 vols. (Stuttgart, 1861–73); *Auch Einer, eine Reisebekanntschaft*, 2 vols. (Stuttgart and Leipzig, 1879); *Altes und Neues*, 3 vols. (Stuttgart, 1882); and *Das Schöne und die Kunst* (Stuttgart, 1898).

Three important collections of Vischer's correspondence have been published: *Briefwechsel zwischen Eduard Mörike und Friedrich Theodor Vischer*, edited by Robert Vischer (Munich, 1926); *Briefwechsel zwischen Strauss und Vischer*, 2 vols., edited by Adolf Rapp (Stuttgart, 1952–53), an especially significant collection of letters between the two friends; and "Eleven Unpublished Letters by Friedrich Theodor Vischer," edited by Adolph B. Benson, *Philological Quarterly* 3 (1924): 32–47, a group of letters addressed to Ruge.

The best biographical study of Vischer is Fritz Schlawe, *Friedrich Theodor Vischer* (Stuttgart, 1959). Hermann Glockner's *Friedrich Theodor Vischer und das neunzehnte Jahrhundert* (Berlin, 1931) is also an excellent and indispensable study of Vischer and his relationship to his historical context. O. Hesnard, *Fr. Th. Vischer* (Paris, 1921) is a good biographical study with heavy concentration on Vischer's aesthetics.

Three studies concentrate on significant points related to Vischer as a Young Hegelian. Friedrich Reich, *Die Kulturphilosophie Friedrich Theodor Vischers* (Leipzig, 1907) is a persuasive study of Vischer's ideas on culture and their relation to Hegel's. Willi Oelmüller, *Friedrich Theodor Vischer und das Problem der nachhegelschen Ästhetik* (Stuttgart, 1959) is an interesting and important study of the Hegelian nature of Vischer's aesthetics. An equally important work that concentrates on the relationship of Vischer to Hegel is Hermann Glockner's *Fr. Th. Vischers Ästhetik in ihrem Verhältnis zu Hegels Phänomenologie des Geistes. Ein Beitrag zur Geschichte der Hegelschen Gedankenwelt* (Leipzig, 1920).

Bauer

No modern editor has seen fit to republish Bauer's works in a complete edition. Two of Bauer's works, written before his conversion to the Young Hegelian position, are especially significant in tracing the intellectual process of his conversion. The first is his review of Strauss's *Leben Jesu* that appeared in the *Jahrbücher für wissenschaftliche Kritik* 9 (1835): 879–94, 896–911; and 10 (1836): 681–94, 696–703. The second is his *Die Religion des alten Testamentes in der geschichtlichen Entwicklung ihrer Principien,* 2 vols. (Berlin, 1838). Both of these works give hints of Bauer's future development and give some clue to the process of his thought, especially important because so little of his private life is now known.

Bauer's works after his conversion to Young Hegelianism are especially illuminating on the entire mode of thought of the school. His *Kritik der evangelischen Geschichte der Synoptiker,* 3 vols. (Leipzig, 1841–42) announced his formal conversion. His *Hegel's Lehre von der Religion und Kunst von dem Standpuncte des Glaubens aus beurtheilt* (Leipzig, 1842) defended his position in terms of Hegel's philosophy. He continued his writing in religious criticism in his *Kritik der Evangelien und Geschichte ihres Ursprungs,* 3 vols. (Berlin, 1851), and in his *Philo, Strauss und Renan und das Urchristenthum* (Berlin, 1874).

Bauer's political observations were recorded in *Die bürgerliche Revolution in Deutschland seit dem Anfang der deutsch-katholischen Bewegung bis zur Gegenwart* (Berlin, 1849), and in *Der Untergang des Frankfurter Parlaments: Geschichte der deutschen constituirenden Nationalversammlung* (Berlin, 1849). He stressed his opposition to Jewish emancipation in *Das Judenthum in der Fremde* (Berlin, 1863). His attitude toward the creation of the German Empire found expression in *Zur Orientirung über die Bismarck'sche Ära* (Chemnitz, 1880).

An important collection of documents dealing with Bauer's academic dismissal is *Gutachten der Evangelisch-theologischen Facultä-*

ten der Königlich Preussischen Universitäten über den Licentiaten Bruno Bauer in Beziehung auf dessen Kritik der evengelischen Geschichte der Synoptiker (Berlin, 1842). Bauer's own account of his dismissal is also essential, *Die gute Sache der Freiheit und meine eigene Angelegenheit* (Zürich and Winterthur, 1842). Only one collection of Bauer's correspondence is available, and it is a vital source: *Briefwechsel zwischen Bruno Bauer und Edgar Bauer während der Jahre 1839–1842 aus Bonn und Berlin* (Charlottenburg, 1844). Bauer's career has been surprisingly neglected by scholars. There is only one good biographical study, Dieter Hertz-Eichenrode's *Der Junghegelianer Bruno Bauer im Vormärz* (Berlin, 1959). Martin Kegel's *Bruno Bauer und seine Theorien über die Entstehung des Christenthums* (Leipzig, 1908) is a good analytical study of Bauer's ideas. The political implications of Bauer's religious writings are analyzed in Ernst Barnikol's excellent article, "Bruno Bauer's Kampf gegen Religion und Christentum und die Spaltung der vormärzlichen preussischen Opposition," *Zeitschrift für Kirchengeschichte* 46 (1927): 1–34. Horst Stuke, *Philosophie der Tat* (Stuttgart, 1963) contains a profitable chapter on Bauer.

Stirner

Stirner's most significant work, *Die Einzige und sein Eigenthum* (Leipzig, 1845), is available in English as *The Ego and His Own*, translated by Steven T. Byington (New York, 1919). This work is essential in assaying Stirner and his significance. Some of his further views, especially about politics, are revealed in his *Geschichte der Reaktion*, 2 vols. (Berlin, 1852). John Henry Mackay, latter-day anarchist, in his attempt to rescue Stirner from obscurity, collected all of Stirner's essays and reviews in *Kleinere Schriften* (Berlin, 1898). These three editions contain all that Stirner wrote.

Mackay has also written the standard biographical study of Stirner, *Max Stirner: sein Leben und sein Werk* (Treptow bei Berlin, 1910). Two studies handle Stirner's ideas in a convincing way: Wilhelm Cuypers, *Max Stirner als Philosoph* (Würzburg, 1937), and Matteo Lucchesi, *Die Individualitätsphilosophie Max Stirners* (Leipzig and Reudnitz, 1897). When the anarchists ceased writing on Stirner, the existentialists picked him up, as in Henry Arvon's *Aux sources de l'existentialisme: Max Stirner* (Paris, 1954), where

Stirner is seen as a precursor of twentieth-century existentialism. Two interesting and significant studies of Stirner's thought in relationship to its nineteenth-century environment are Carl August Emge, *Max Stirner, eine geistig nicht bewältigte Tendenz* (Wiesbaden, 1964), and Kurt Adolf Mautz, *Die Philosophie Max Stirners im Gegensatz zum Hegelschen Idealismus* (Berlin, 1936).

Ruge

For a study of the Young Hegelians, a basic and most important source is the journal edited by Ruge and Echtermeyer as the proposed voice of the Young Hegelian movement, the *Hallische Jahrbücher für Wissenschaft und Kunst,* published by Otto Wigand from 1838 to 1842; it changed in the latter part of its brief existence to the *Deutsche Jahrbücher für Wissenschaft und Kunst.* This journal is rich in suggestive and revealing material. Given the Young Hegelians' propensity to publish and re-publish everything they wrote, however, virtually all their essays that first appeared in this journal were collected in book form or in the individual complete works.

Ruge's collected works have been published as *Gesammelte Schriften,* 10 vols. (Mannheim, 1846–47). His *Zwei Jahre in Paris,* 2 vols. (Leipzig, 1846) is an important memoir, especially in revealing his connections with Marx. Toward the end of his life Ruge wrote his recollections, *Aus früherer Zeit,* 4 vols. (Berlin, 1862–67), an indispensable source. Ruge's religious views are presented in his *Acht Reden über die Religion "an die Gebildeten unter ihren Verehrern"* (St. Louis, Mo., 1868).

An essential source is the collection of Ruge's correspondence, *Briefwechsel und Tagebuchblätter aus den Jahren 1825–1880,* 2 vols., edited by Paul Nerrlich (Berlin, 1886). A brief additional collection of Ruge's letters on the Revolution of 1848, "Briefe von Arnold und Agnes Ruge aus den Revolutionsjahren," appeared in the *Süddeutche Monatshefte,* September, 1912.

There is only one biographical study of Ruge, Walter Neher, *Arnold Ruge als Politiker und politische Schriftsteller: ein Beitrag zur deutschen Geschichte des 19. Jahrhunderts* (Heidelberg, 1933); but it is weaker in analysis and perception than in narration. A brief but perceptive treatment of Ruge's ideas is Herbert Strauss,

"Zur Sozial- und ideengechichtlichen Einordung Arnold Ruges," *Schweizer Beiträge zur Allgemeinen Geschichte* 12 (1954): 162–73. Max Lange, "Arnold Ruge und die Entwicklung des Parteileben im Vormärz," *Einheit: theoretische Zeitschrift des wissenschaftlichen Sozialismus* 3 (1948): 636–44, is an interesting commentary on Ruge's political role. An essential article is Hans Rosenberg, "Arnold Ruge und die 'Hallischen Jahrbücher,'" *Archiv für Kulturgeschichte* 20 (1930): 281–308. For a further analysis of the Young Hegelian journal that Ruge edited, Else von Eck's *Die Literaturkritik in den Hallischen und Deutschen Jahrbüchern (1838–1842)* (Munich, 1925), is useful.

Contemporaries and Associates

Works by contemporaries of the Young Hegelians and by those influenced by their thought are frequently useful. Some of the secondary studies of these men are also pertinent.

General reading in the memoirs, recollections, and letters of the time is particularly rewarding. Many such works exist, but a few deserve special mention. Friedrich Perthes, *Leben*, edited by C. T. Perthes, 3 vols. (Hamburg and Gotha, 1848–55) gives a good insight into the intellectual and political life of Germany from 1795 to 1843, and it is especially useful on the religious concerns. Gotthart Oswald Marbach, *Der Zeitgeist und die moderne Literatur: Briefe an eine Dame* (Leipzig, 1838) is instructive and revealing. Hegel's biographer, Karl Rosenkranz, published his *Neue Studien*, 4 vols. (Leipzig, 1875–78), a collection of essays that give an inside view of intellectual development. Rudolf Haym, *Ausgewählter Briefwechsel*, edited by Hans Rosenberg (Berlin and Leipzig, 1930) offers interesting insights and personal observations. The collected works of an intimate of the Young Hegelians, Georg Herwegh, *Werke,* edited by Hermann Tardel, 3 vols. (Berlin and Leipzig, n. d.), shows the impact of their ideas on aesthetics. Richard Wagner, *My Life,* 2 vols. (New York, 1911) also reveals their influence, especially the impact of Feuerbach. The collection of essays and articles edited by Otto Wigand, the publisher of the *Hallische Jahrbücher, Die Epigonen,* 5 vols. (Leipzig, 1846–48) is especially rich; the first volume was dedicated to Ruge, the fifth to Feuerbach.

Two works by perceptive and sensitive observers are vital sources for an understanding of religious changes: Heinrich Heine, *Religion and Philosophy in Germany*, translated by John Snodgrass (London, 1882), first published in French in 1833; and Thomas Moore, *Travels of an Irish Gentleman in Search of a Religion*, 2 vols. (London, 1833).

The massive, multi-volume collection of the works of Marx and Engels, *Gesamtausgabe*, edited by D. Rjazanov and V. Adoratski (Berlin, 1927–32) is an indispensable source. The earlier volumes in particular contain much useful material on the Young Hegelians. The secondary materials on Marx and Engels is enormous, but a few works can be singled out as pertinent to the study of the Young Hegelians. Franz Mehring, *Karl Marx* (Leipzig, 1923); Gustav Meyer, *Friedrich Engels*, 2 vols. (The Hague, 1934); and Auguste Cornu, *Karl Marx und Friedrich Engels*, 2 vols. (Berlin, 1954–62) are good biographical studies. The best studies of the young Marx are Auguste Cornu, *La jeunesse de Karl Marx* (Paris, 1937); and Robert Tucker, *Philosophy and Myth in Karl Marx* (Cambridge, 1961).

The collection of essays written by Moses Hess, *Sozialistische Aufsätze, 1841–1847*, edited by Theodor Zlocisti, (Berlin, 1921), is especially useful. For Hess's relations to the Young Hegelians, the best studies are Auguste Cornu, *Moses Hess et la gauche hégélienne* (Paris, 1934); and Edmund Silberner, *Moses Hess, Geschichte seines Lebens* (Leiden, 1966).

Michael Bakunin, *Oeuvre 1*, edited by Max Nettlau (Paris, 1895) is valuable in dealing with the Young Hegelian origins of his thought. Heinz Nitzschke, *Die Geschichtsphilosophie Lorenz von Steins* (Munich and Berlin, 1932) also traces the influence of Young Hegelian ideas.

General and Special Studies.

Most books on nineteenth-century intellectual history mention the Young Hegelians, but a few of these studies are worth particular consideration for their value as background material or as solutions to particular problems.

The two standard studies of nineteenth-century Germany contain valuable material for the context of the Young Hegelians: Heinrich von Treitschke, *History of Germany in the Nineteenth Century*, translated by Eden and Cedar Paul, 6 vols. (New York, 1919);

and Franz Schnabel, *Deutsche Geschichte in neunzehnten Jahrhundert,* 4 vols. (Freiburg, 1929–37). Harald Höffding, *A History of Modern Philosophy* 2, translated by B. E. Meyer (New York, 1900) is still an excellent work, despite its age. The more recent study, Frederick Copleston, *A History of Philosophy: Volume 7, Fichte to Nietzsche* (Westminster, Maryland, 1963), is also excellent. Theobald Ziegler, *Die geistigen und socialen Strömungen des neunzenhten Jahrhunderts* (Berlin, 1901) is a singularly valuable study of German intellectual life. Karl Barth, *Die protestantische Theologie im 19. Jahrhundert, ihre Vorgeschichte und ihre Geschichte* (Zürich, 1947), now available in a shorter English version as *Protestant Thought From Rousseau to Ritschl,* translated by Brian Cozens (New York, 1959), is indispensable to the study of religious ideas. Three other works are also invaluable for the development of theological speculation: Otto Pfleiderer, *The Development of Theology in Germany Since Kant,* translated by J. F. Smith (London, 1890); F. Lichtenberger, *History of German Theology in the Nineteenth Century,* translated by W. Hastie (Edinburgh, 1889); and A. C. McGiffert, *The Rise of Modern Religious Ideas* (New York, 1915). Franklin L. Baumer, *Religion and the Rise of Scepticism* (New York, 1960) is the standard work on the development of the intellectual tradition of religious skepticism.

The study of the life of Jesus was an important religious concern in the nineteenth century, and three penetrating and invaluable works on this subject are available: Albert Schweitzer, *The Quest of the Historical Jesus,* translated by W. Montgomery (New York, 1961); Heinrich Weinel, *Jesus im neunzehnten Jahrhundert* (Tübingen, 1914), also available in an altered English version, *Jesus in the Nineteenth Century,* translated by A. G. Widgery, (Edinburgh, 1914); and H. R. Mackintosh, *The Doctrine of the Person of Jesus Christ* (New York, 1912).

The non-theological implications of the developments in religious thought are perceptively handled by the following: William O. Shanahan, *German Protestants Face the Social Question. Volume 1, The Conservative Phase, 1815–1871* (Notre Dame, Indiana, 1954), a good synthesis of the secondary literature; Alexander Dru, "The Reformation of the Nineteenth Century: Christianity in Germany from 1800 to 1848," *The Dublin Review* 226 (1952): 34–45; Fritz Fischer, "Der deutsche Protestantismus und die Politik im 19.

Jahrhundert," *Historische Zeitschrift* 171 (1951): 473–518; and Karl Löwith, "Die philosophische Kritik der christlichen Religion im 19. Jahrhundert," *Theologischer Rundschau* 5 (1933): 131–72. For the study of publishing and censorship in nineteenth-century Germany, an important issue in dealing with the Young Hegelians, G. Salomon's *Die deutsche Zeitgewesens von den ersten Anfängen bis zur Wiederaufrichtig des deutschen Reichs,* 3 vols. (Oldenburg, 1899–1905) is especially useful.

The University of Berlin was the center of activity for Hegel and for many of the Young Hegelians. The standard history of the university, Max Lenz, *Geschichte der königlichen Friedrich-Wilhelms-Universität zu Berlin,* 4 vols. (Halle, 1910–18) is essential for this subject.

Leonard Krieger's *The German Idea of Freedom* (Boston, 1957) is essential for the larger context of the political ideas of Hegel and his disciples. Some suggestive material on the literature of the period is in Ernst Kohn-Bramstedt, *Aristocracy and the Middle-Classes in Germany: Social Types in German Literature, 1830–1900* (London, 1937), and in Rudolf von Gottschall, *Die deutsche Nationalliteratur des neunzehnten Jahrhunderts,* 4 vols. (Breslau, 1891).

From the vast literature on 1848, three works may be selected that are especially pertinent for a study of the political activities of the Young Hegelians: Ludwig Bergsträsser, "Parteien von 1848," *Preussische Jahrbücher* 177 (1919): 180–211; Gustav Lüders, *Die demokratische Bewegung in Berlin im Oktober 1848* (Berlin and Leipzig, 1909); and Veit Valentin, *Geschichte der deutschen Revolution von 1848–49,* 2 vols. (Berlin, 1930–31).

Index

Young Hegelian philosophy,
69–70
Rutenberg, Adolf, 79, 82, 194

Saint-Simon, Claude Henri, 5,
270
Sand, George, 5, 207, 213
Sartre, Jean-Paul, 221–22
Sass, Friedrich, 82
Savigny, Friedrich Karl von, 48, 239
Schelling, Friedrich Wilhelm, 21,
84, 87, 100, 103, 177
Schleiermacher, Friedrich, 8, 99,
119, 183; and Bauer, 180; and
Feuerbach, 137; on miracles,
108–09; and Stirner, 208; and
Strauss, 103–04; and Vischer, 162,
169
Schmidt, Johann Kaspar. See
Stirner, Max
Schubart, Christian Friedrich
Daniel, 123
Schweitzer, Albert, 272–73
Semler, Johann, 100
Smith, Adam, 200
Stein, Lorenz von, 267–72
Stirling, J. H., 29, 32
Stirner, Max (Johann Kaspar
Schmidt), 207–225 passim;
academic career, 209, 214;
apocalyptic vision, 219, 224–25;
atheism, 211; and Bauer, 213–14,
217, 219, 220, 222, 223–25; and
Berlin Young Hegelians, 81,
209–10, 212–14; birth, 208; on
Christianity, 216; and criticism,
63, 222–23; death, 221; early
writings, 210–12; education,
208–09; and Feuerbach, 137,
212–13, 217, 219; and Hegel, 208,
211–12, 219–20, 222; humanism,
217, 223; idealism, 66–67; and

Revolution of *1848*, 221, 271; and
Rheinische Zeitung, 82, 210–11;
and Schleiermacher, 208; on the
state, 217; subjectivity, 64–65,
69; *The Unique One and His
Property*, 214–20
Strauss, David Friedrich, 97–132
passim; academic career, 106,
114–15; and Bauer, 120; birth,
102; *Christian Doctrine*, 116–18;
christology, 59, 111–13; and
criticism, 63, 106–07, 110–11, 113,
116–17, 131–32; culture, 69;
death, 131; education, 63, 102–05;
and Feuerbach, 118–19, 120, 137,
144, 145–46; and Frederick
William IV, 57, 88, 125, 127;
and German unification, 125–27;
and *Hallische Jahrbücher*, 91–92,
119–20; and Hegel, 103–04, 113,
118, 130–31, 135; on Hegelian
school, 51; humanism, 128–29,
132; and Kant, 128–29; *Life of
Jesus*, 3, 6, 73, 84, 97–101, 105–16,
178; *Life of Jesus Adapted for the
German People*, 124–25;
materialism, 66–67, 129–30; on
myth, 107–11; on objectivity, 65;
Old and New Faith, 127–31; on
Prussia, 57, 88, 125–27; and
Renan, 126; and Revolution of
1848, 120–23, 271; and Ruge,
119–20; and Schleiermacher,
103–04; and South German
Young Hegelians, 76–77; and
Vatke, 3, 104–05; and Vischer,
119, 120, 123, 159, 160–62, 164;
and Young Hegelians, 118–20

Tieck, Ludwig, 103
Treitschke, Heinrich von, 21
Tübingen School, 6, 99, 165